W9-BVL-832

LIVING THE MESSAGE

Living
the Message

Daily Reflections with

Eugene H. Peterson

Edited by Janice Stubbs Peterson

HarperSanFrancisco
An Imprint of HarperCollins*Publishers*

Permissions can be found on page 381
and constitute a continuation of this copyright page.

LIVING THE MESSAGE: *Daily Meditations with Eugene H. Peterson.* Copyright
© 1996 by Eugene H. Peterson. All rights reserved. Printed in the United States
of America. No part of this book may be used or reproduced in any manner
whatsoever without written permission except in the case of brief quotations
embodied in critical articles and reviews. For information address HarperCollins
Publishers, 10 East 53rd Street, New York, NY 10022.

HarperCollins Web Site: http://www.harpercollins.com
HarperCollins®, ≝®, and HarperSanFrancisco™ are trademarks of
HarperCollins Publishers Inc.

FIRST EDITION

Library of Congress Cataloging-in-Publication Data
Peterson, Eugene H.
Living the message : daily reflections with Eugene H. Peterson /
edited by Janice Stubbs Peterson. —1st ed.
Includes bibliographical references and index.
ISBN 0–06–066432–0 (pbk.)
1. Devotional calendars. 2. Meditations. I. Peterson, Janice
Stubbs. II. Title.
BV4811.P387 1996
242'.2—dc20
96–3413

96 97 98 99 00 ❖RRDH 10 9 8 7 6 5 4 3 2 1

CONTENTS

INTRODUCTION

Writing, for me, has nearly always been a communal act. For most of my adult life, I have worked as a pastor and written from the middle of a parish, immersed in a melange of saints and sinners as they gave voice to pain and joy, sin and holiness, prayers and curses, exclamations and mutterings, truths and lies. I have listened, listened, listened to these voices and, at what I judged to be appropriate times, added my voice to them. And, from time to time, I have written what I have heard and said. My writing is my witness.

An ordinary Christian parish is a wonderful place in which to write. Most, I think I would argue *all*, of the real action of the world comes into focus there: birth and death, salvation and damnation, sufferings and doubts, healing and reconciliation, war and peace, marriage and divorce. Every person, behavior, feeling, and event shows up in the illuminating and embracing context of holy scripture, holy days, holy Eucharist, holy baptism. In the so-called "world," virtually every thing, person, and event we come upon is out of context, obscure in a fog of function, and using words so debased by cliché and pretension that it's mighty difficult to find out what is going on, *really* going on.

A Christian congregation, on the other hand, essentially defunctionalizes every person who enters it. We come into view in the company of one another not in terms of our competence or net worth, but as saints and sinners—and nobody is able to sort out one from the other. It is the least specialized gathering of human beings on the planet. Where else can you find yourself bracketed by nursing infants on one side, nodding octogenarians on the other, and rubbing shoulders with so many people whom you acknowledge, however grudgingly, as brothers and sisters, and with whom you have nothing in common except your common humanity—and God. Especially God. A large and true context. Very large; very true.

And for a writer, this is a bonus: It is a place where words are honored as nowhere else. God, who is the Word, uses words to reveal himself to us. This Word and words are preached, read, taught, sung, believed, obeyed. Or not. But even when this Word/words is suppressed, disbelieved, or disobeyed, the negatives are still defined by the positive: The presence of the Word defines the field. But there is more, for God's Word evokes and gives dignity to our words: The names that we carry throughout our lives are conferred at baptism; invitations that bring us into the hospitality of God are issued; prayer, one of the few forms of honest speech left to us, can be offered by anyone; poetry (usually in the form of hymns) is said and sung frequently; lament is legitimized; personal stories are told. The Christian congregation is a bastion of orality. For someone interested in words, I can't think of a better place to listen to language in all its complexity and observe how it works. At least I have found it so.

Early on, I noticed that the parallel occurrence of God's Word and our words in the same place and among the same people creates a good deal of dissonance, which then forces us to pay attention to how words are used and what happens in the use. It is the very nature of words to reveal; but they are more often than not used to conceal. I soon learned that the pastor is probably the most-lied-to person in the community. As a custodian of the Word that blesses and creates, saves and heals, delights and sets free, I found myself in a sea of dissimulation; language designed to reveal our very being was being used right and left to conceal it. Not much of the lying was deliberate, or even conscious. These friends of mine were only using words the way they had been taught by their parents and teachers. But as I listened with one ear to their words, with my other ear I was listening to the Word of God. I couldn't help noticing the difference. Quite unlike God, who uses words to reveal himself fully and adequately, inviting me to enter his world of grace and love, these people weren't using words to tell me who they were, but who they wanted me to think they were, and to keep me in my place. Not totally, of course, but mostly. I don't think I would have had occasion to notice the contrast in so much astonishing detail if I had not been carrying out my daily work in a parish where the Word of God in its various forms was always there, implicitly defining what all words are in truth, namely, a means of revelation.

There are two ways to write. One is the way we are taught in our schools. This writing presupposes knowledge: Having learned something, we then write it down, passing on the information to readers. Much of what is consumed in newspaper and textbook is this kind of writing. And "consumed" is the right verb: The words are taken in, digested, and put to use.

But there is another kind of writing that is itself a way of knowing, the words taking us beyond what we already know, probing mystery, carrying us into the interior of truth where intimacies are developed and covenants formed. This is the way the Word of God works as it is written in our Scriptures—not telling us *about* reality, but leading us into it, *creating* it in us. When we are using words this way, we have the sense that we are not so much *using* words as *submitting* to them. Writing in this way is a kind of praying: "Let it be to me according to your word" (Luke 1:38). This is the kind of writing I have always wanted to do; to use words not merely to add to the already considerable accumulation of information in the world, but to its life. If only a few of the words I have written do that, I am content.

Eugene H. Peterson

For each of my grandchildren, I cross-stitched a birth sampler giving their vital statistics—full name, date and time of birth, weight, length. When I was invited to edit this book, I thought, "That's what this is—a sampler. Daily samplings through the calendar year of Eugene Peterson's writings."

What I have sought to do here is lift out samplers of themes and ideas that are some of Eugene's "vital statistics." As you use this book of daily readings, hopefully you will see themes emerge that have been so important to Eugene for all of his adult years of pastoring, teaching, writing, living.

Many times in his speaking and writing, I have thought that Eugene's words seemed like a voice crying in the wilderness, going against the current, refusing the fads. The North American church has, to use the Hosea image, "gone a-whoring." We have lost our first love and bought into the culture. Many would say that Eugene was not relevant because he stayed with scripture, told stories, and let the scripture and story sink into the marrow of the bone. There weren't any quick results to show people, nothing to excite them on the surface. During the 1960s, when many pastors turned from the Scriptures to psychology or to topical issues, he stayed with the biblical material. When I asked him why he didn't preach on fair housing (I was serving on a county fair housing committee), he said, "If people hear the Word of God, they will eventually practice fair housing." When others preached morality, he simply proclaimed the Good News of Jesus Christ. When all the programs started being offered in the churches to meet everyone's needs, he was trying to get people to worship faithfully and then go out to bear witness in the neighborhood, school, home, workplace.

Words are important. It is critical that the truth be articulated clearly and accurately. And carefully crafting the words helps them hit the target of heart and mind.

The Word was first. God pronounced words in creation: "Let there be light," and order emerged out of darkness and chaos. We need to be called "Back to Square One" (to use the title of a public lecture) to the Word.

The Word was first, which makes every word expressed thereafter carry eternal significance. God spoke his world into being. *Our* words then become co-creational.

For over thirty-seven years, especially as our marriage anniversary rolls around for yet another year, we have both been intentionally aware of serving not just each other but a third party—our marriage. It is in that spirit of being aware of *this* third party—these words—that I offer this book.

But I have had help. I did not want my own favorite passages to dominate, so I invited some friends from around the country who have been faithful readers and encouragers of these words to share some of their favorite passages. So thank you Nancy Billiat, Karen

Peterson Finch, Helen Mae (Lu) Gerard, Clare Fox Archer, Dorothy Jayne, Shirley Kuenzler, Steven F. Trotter, LaNell Sado, and Daniel R. Kern for computer assistance, and also to other supporters who have asked about the book and contributed by their interest and prayers. And to our good friend and colleague at Regent College, Lindi Lewis, who very graciously, on a spring evening walk in Vancouver, offered to read the excerpts and make comments just at the time when I needed that encouragement. And thank you to Eugene not only for speaking and writing these words, but most of all for living them.

Janice S. Peterson

LIVING THE MESSAGE

January

The Word Was First

The Word was first,
    the Word present to God,
    God present to the Word.
The Word was God,
    in readiness for God from day one.

Everything was created through him;
    nothing—not one thing!—
    came into being without him.
What came into existence was Life,
    and the Life was Light to live by.
The Life-Light blazed out of the darkness;
    the darkness couldn't put it out.

There once was a man, his name John, sent by God to point out the
way to the Life-Light. He came to show everyone where to look, who

to believe in. John was not himself the Light; he was there to show the way to the Light.

The Life-Light was the real thing:
    Every person entering Life
    he brings into Light.
He was in the world,
    the world was there through him,
    and yet the world didn't even notice.
He came to his own people,
    but they didn't want him.
But whoever did want him,
    who believed he was who he claimed
    and would do what he said,
He made to be their true selves,
    their child-of-God selves.
These are the God-begotten,
    not blood-begotten,
    not flesh-begotten,
    not sex-begotten.

The Word became flesh and blood,
    and moved into the neighborhood.
We saw the glory with our own eyes,
    the one-of-a-kind glory,
    like Father, like Son,
Generous inside and out,
    true from start to finish.

John pointed him out and called, "This is the One! The One I told you was coming after me but in fact was ahead of me. He has always been ahead of me, has always had the first word."

We all live off his generous bounty,
    gift after gift after gift.
We got the basics from Moses,
    and then this exuberant giving and receiving,
This endless knowing and understanding—
    all this came through Jesus, the Messiah.
No one has ever seen God,
    not so much as a glimpse.
This one-of-a-kind God-Expression,
    who exists at the very heart of the Father,
    has made him plain as day.

JOHN 1:1–18

Attending to Language

Anyone of us, waking up in the morning and finding ourselves included in that part of the creation called human, sooner or later finds ourselves dealing with language, with words. We are the only creatures in this incredible, vast creation doing this. Language is unique to us human beings. Turnips complete a fairly complex and useful life cycle without the use of words. Roses grace the world with an extraordinary beauty and fragrance without uttering a word. Dogs satisfy tens of thousands of us with faithful and delightful companionship without a word. Birds sing a most exquisite music to our ears, lifting our spirits, giving us happiness, all without the capability of words. It is quite impressive really, what goes on around us without words: ocean tides, mountain heights, stormy weather, turning constellations, genetic codes, bird migrations—most, in fact, of what we see and hear around us, a great deal of it incredibly complex, but without language, wordless. And we, we human beings, have words. We can use language. We are the only ones in this stunning kaleidoscopic array of geology and biology and astronomy to use words. We share a great deal with the rest of creation. We have much in common with everything around us, the dirt beneath our feet, the animals around us, the stars above us, and we recognize links in this family identity. But when it comes down to understanding our humanity, who we are in this vast scheme of things, we find ourselves attending to language, the fact that we speak words, and what happens to us when we do.

> *My heart bursts its banks,*
> *spilling beauty and goodness.*
> *I pour it out in a poem to the king,*
> *shaping the river into words . . .*

PSALM 45:1

JANUARY 3

Allies

My allies are the novelists and poets, writers who are not *telling* me something, but *making* something.

Novelists take the raw data of existence and make a world of meaning. I am in the story-making business, too. God is drawing the people around me into the plot of salvation; every word, gesture, and action has a significant place in the story. Being involved in the creation of reality like this takes endless patience and attentiveness, and I am forever taking shortcuts. Instead of assisting in the development of a character, I hurriedly categorize: active or inactive, saved or unsaved, disciple or backslider, key leader or dependable follower, leadership material or pew fodder. Instead of seeing each person in my life as unique, a splendid never-to-be duplicated story of grace, unprecedented in the particular ways grace and sin are in dramatic tension, I slap on a label so I can efficiently get through my routines. Once the label is in place I don't have to *look* at him and her any more; I know how to *use* them.

Then I read Fyodor Dostoyevsky, William Faulkner, Anne Tyler, or Walker Percy and see how an artist committed to creative work approaches the most ordinary and least promising human: the unexpected depths in the ordinary, the capacities for good and evil in the apparently conventional!

Do you know how I feel right now, and will feel until Christ's life becomes visible in your lives? Like a mother in the pain of childbirth.

GALATIANS 4:19

JANUARY 4

Poets

Poets are caretakers of language, the shepherds of words, keeping them from harm, exploitation, misuse. Words not only mean something; they *are* something, each with a sound and rhythm all its own.

Poets are not primarily trying to tell us, or get us, to do something. By attending to words with playful discipline (or disciplined playfulness), they draw us into deeper respect both for words and the reality they set before us.

I also am in the word business. I preach, I teach, I counsel using words. People often pay particular attention on the chance that God may be using my words to speak to them. I have a responsibility to use words accurately and well. But it isn't easy. I live in a world where words are used carelessly by some, cunningly by others.

Be gracious in your speech. The goal is to bring
out the best in others in a conversation, not put
them down, not cut them out.

COLOSSIANS 4:6

JANUARY 5

Artists

I am saddened when friends tell me, "I'm swamped with must reading; I don't have time for novels or poetry." What they are saying is that they choose to attend to the routines and not to the creative center.

There is no "must" reading; we choose what we read. What is not fed does not grow; what is not supported does not stand; what is not nurtured does not develop. Artists are not the only people who keep us open and involved in this essential but easily slighted center of creation, but they are too valuable to be slighted.

Cultivate these things. Immerse yourself in them. The people will see you mature right before their eyes! Keep a firm grasp on both your character and your teaching. Don't be diverted. Just keep at it. Both you and those who hear you will experience salvation.

1 TIMOTHY 4:15–16

JANUARY 6

Epiphany

Today is Epiphany. The Life-Light gets shared beyond.

After Jesus was born in Bethlehem village, Judah territory—this was during Herod's kingship—a band of scholars arrived in Jerusalem from the East. They asked around, "Where can we find and pay homage to the newborn King of the Jews? We observed a star in the eastern sky that signaled his birth. We're on pilgrimage to worship him."

When word of their inquiry got to Herod, he was terrified—and not Herod alone, but most of Jerusalem as well. Herod lost no time. He gathered all the high priests and religion scholars in the city together and asked, "Where is the Messiah supposed to be born?"

They told him, "Bethlehem, Judah territory. The prophet Micah wrote it plainly:

" 'It's you, Bethlehem, in Judah's land,
    no longer bringing up the rear.
From you will come the leader
    who will shepherd-rule my people, my Israel.' "

Herod then arranged a secret meeting with the scholars from the East. Pretending to be as devout as they were, he got them to tell him exactly when the birth-announcement star appeared. Then he told them the prophecy about Bethlehem, and said, "Go find this child. Leave no stone unturned. As soon as you find him, send word and I'll join you at once in your worship."

Instructed by the king, they set off. Then the star appeared again, the same star they had seen in the eastern skies. It led them on until it hovered over the place of the child. They could hardly contain themselves: They were in the right place! They had arrived at the right time!

They entered the house and saw the child in the arms of Mary, his mother. Overcome, they kneeled and worshiped him. Then they opened their luggage and presented gifts: gold, frankincense, myrrh.

In a dream, they were warned not to report back to Herod. So they worked out another route, left the territory without being seen, and returned to their own country.

MATTHEW 2:1–13

JANUARY 7

Communion

When my daughter, Karen, was young, I often took her with me when I visited nursing homes. She was better than a Bible. The elderly in these homes brightened immediately when she entered the room, delighted in her smile, and asked her questions. They touched her skin, stroked her hair. On one such visit we were with Mrs. Herr, who was in an advanced state of dementia. Talkative, she directed all her talk to Karen. She told her a story, an anecdote out of her own childhood that Karen's presence must have triggered, and when she completed it, she immediately repeated it word for word, and then again and again and again. After twenty minutes or so of this, I became anxious lest Karen become uncomfortable and confused about what was going on. I interrupted the flow of talk, anointed the woman with oil, laid hands on her, and prayed. In the car and driving home, I commended Karen for her patience and attentiveness. She had listened to this repeated story without showing any signs of restlessness or boredom. I said, "Karen, Mrs. Herr's mind is not working the way ours are." And Karen said, "Oh, I knew that, Daddy; she wasn't trying to tell us any *thing*. She was telling us who she *is*."

Nine years old, and she knew the difference, knew that Mrs. Herr was using words not for communication but for communion. It is a difference that our culture as a whole pays little attention to but that pastors must pay attention to. Our primary task, the pastor's primary task, is not communication but communion.

> *Words kill, words give life;*
> *they're either poison or fruit—you choose.*

PROVERBS 18:21

JANUARY 8

Communication

There is an enormous communications industry in the world that is stamping out words like buttons. Words are transmitted by television, radio, telegraph, satellite, cable, newspaper, magazine. But the words are not personal. Implicit in this enormous communications industry is an enormous lie: if we improve communications we will improve life. It has not happened and it will not happen. Often when we find out what a person "has to say," we like him or her less, not more. Better communication often worsens international relations. We know more about each other as nations and religions than we ever have before in history, and we seem to like each other less. Counselors know that when spouses learn to communicate more clearly, it leads to divorce as often as it does to reconciliation.

Stay clear of pious talk that is only talk. Words are not mere words, you know. If they're not backed by a godly life, they accumulate as poison in the soul.

2 TIMOTHY 2:16–17

Gift of Words

The gift of words is for communion. We need to learn the nature of communion. This requires the risk of revelation—letting a piece of myself be exposed, this mystery of who I am. If I stand here mute, you have no idea what is going on with me. You can look at me, measure me, weigh me, test me, but until I start to talk you do not know what is going on inside, who I really am. If you listen and I am telling the truth, something marvelous starts to take place—a new event.

Something comes into being that was not there before. God does this for us. We learn to do it because God does it. New things happen then. Salvation comes into being; love comes into being. Communion. Words used this way do not define as much as deepen mystery—entering into the ambiguities, pushing past the safely known into the risky unknown. The Christian Eucharist uses words, the simplest of words, "this is my body, this is my blood," that plunge us into an act of revelation which staggers the imagination, which we never figure out, but we enter into. These words do not describe, they point, they reach, they embrace. Every time I go to the ill, the dying, the lonely, it becomes obvious after a few moments that the only words that matter are words of communion. What is distressing is to find out how infrequently they are used. Sometimes we find we are the only ones who bother using words this way on these occasions. Not the least of the trials of the sick, the lonely and the dying is the endless stream of clichés and platitudes to which they have to listen. Doctors enter their rooms to communicate the diagnosis, family members to communicate their anxieties, friends to communicate the gossip of the day. Not all of them do this, of course, and not always, but the sad reality is that there is not a great deal of communion that goes on in these places with these ill and lonely and dying people, on street corners, in offices, in work places, in schools. That makes it urgent that the Christian becomes a specialist in words of communion.

> *The right word at the right time*
> *is like a custom-made piece of jewelry,*
> *And a wise friend's timely reprimand*
> *is like a gold ring slipped on your finger.*

PROVERBS 25:11–12

Christian Spirituality

I enjoy reading the poet-farmer Wendell Berry. He takes a small piece of land in Kentucky, respects it, cares for it, submits himself to it just as an artist submits himself to his materials. I read Berry, and every time he speaks of "farm" and "land," I insert "parish." As he talks about his farm, he talks about what I've tried to practice in my congregation, because one of the genius aspects of pastoral work is locality.

The pastor's question is, "Who are these particular people, and how can I be with them in such a way that they can become what God is making them?" My job is simply to be there, teaching, preaching Scripture as well as I can, and being honest with them, not doing anything to interfere with what the Spirit is shaping in them. Could God be doing something that I never even thought of? Am I willing to be quiet for a day, a week, a year? Like Wendell Berry, am I willing to spend fifty years reclaiming this land? With these people?

Christian spirituality means living in the mature wholeness of the gospel. It means taking all the elements of your life—children, spouse, job, weather, possessions, relationships—and experiencing them as an act of faith. God wants all the material of our lives.

Meanwhile, friends, wait patiently for the Master's Arrival. You see farmers do this all the time, waiting for their valuable crops to mature, patiently letting the rain do its slow but sure work. Be patient like that. Stay steady and strong. The Master could arrive at any time.

JAMES 5:7–8

Subversive

Jesus was a master at subversion. Until the very end, everyone, including his disciples, called him Rabbi. Rabbis were important, but they didn't make anything happen. On the occasions when suspicions were aroused that there might be more to him than that title accounted for, Jesus tried to keep it quiet—"Tell no one."

Jesus' favorite speech form, the parable, was subversive. Parables sound absolutely ordinary: casual stories about soil and seeds, meals and coins and sheep, bandits and victims, farmers and merchants. And they are wholly secular: of his forty or so parables recorded in the Gospels, only one has its setting in church, and only a couple mention the name God. As people heard Jesus tell these stories, they saw at once that they weren't about God, so there was nothing in them threatening their own sovereignty. They relaxed their defenses. They walked away perplexed, wondering what they meant, the stories lodged in their imagination. And then, like a time bomb, they would explode in their unprotected hearts. An abyss opened up at their very feet. He *was* talking about God; they had been invaded!

Jesus continually threw odd stories down alongside ordinary lives (*para*, "alongside"; *bole*, "thrown") and walked away without explanation or altar call. Then listeners started seeing connections: God connections, life connections, eternity connections. The very lack of obviousness, the unlikeness, was the stimulus to perceiving likeness: God likeness, life likeness, eternity likeness. But the parable didn't do the work—it put the listener's imagination to work. Parables aren't illustrations that make things easier; they make things harder by requiring the exercise of our imagination, which if we aren't careful becomes the exercise of our faith.

The disciples came up and asked, "Why do you tell stories?" He replied, "You've been given insight into God's kingdom. You know how it works. Not everybody has this gift, this insight; it hasn't been given to them. Whenever someone has a ready heart for this, the insights and understandings flow freely. But if there is no readiness, any trace of receptivity soon disappears. That's why I tell stories: to create readiness, to nudge the people toward receptive insight."

MATTHEW 13:10–13

JANUARY 12

Holiness

The next two weeks are reflections on the Songs of Ascent (Psalms 120–134).

There is a great market for religious experience in our world; there is little enthusiasm for the patient acquisition of virtue, little inclination to sign up for the long apprenticeship in what earlier generations of Christians called holiness.

Do you see what all this means—all these pioneers who blazed the way, all these veterans cheering us on? It means we'd better get on

with it. Strip down, start running—and never quit! No extra spiri-
tual fat, no parasitic sins. Keep your eyes on Jesus, who both began
and finished this race we're in.

HEBREWS 12:1–2A

JANUARY 13

Dissatisfaction

People submerged in a culture swarming with lies and malice feel like they are drowning in it; they can trust nothing they hear, depend on no one they meet. Such dissatisfaction with the world as it is is preparation for traveling in the way of Christian discipleship. The dissatisfaction, coupled with a longing for peace and truth, can set us on a pilgrim path of wholeness in God.

A person has to be thoroughly disgusted with the way things are to find the motivation to set out on the Christian way. As long as we think that the next election might eliminate crime and establish justice or another scientific breakthrough might save the environment or another pay raise might push us over the edge of anxiety into a life of tranquility, we are not likely to risk the arduous uncertainties of the life of faith. A person has to get fed up with the ways of the world before he, before she, acquires an appetite for the world of grace.

Psalm 120 is the song of such a person, sick with the lies and crippled with the hate, a person doubled up in pain over what is going on in the world. But it is not a mere outcry, it is pain that penetrates through despair and stimulates a new beginning—a journey to God which becomes a life of peace.

"Deliver me from the liars, GOD!
They smile so sweetly but lie through their teeth."

PSALM 120:2

JANUARY 14

Repentance

Among the more fascinating pages of American history are those that tell the stories of the immigrants to these shores in the nineteenth century. Thousands upon thousands of people, whose lives in Europe had become mean and poor, persecuted and wretched, left. They had gotten reports of a land where the environment was a challenge instead of an oppression. The stories continue to be told in many families, keeping alive the memory of the event that made an American out of what was a German or an Italian or a Scot.

My grandfather left Norway eighty years ago in the middle of a famine. His wife and ten children remained behind until he could return and get them. He came to Pittsburgh and worked in the steel mills for two years until he had enough money to go back and get his family. When he returned with them he didn't stay in Pittsburgh although it had served his purposes well enough the first time, but he traveled to Montana, plunging into new land, looking for a better place.

In all these immigrant stories there are mixed parts of escape and adventure; the escape from an unpleasant situation; the adventure of a far better way of life, free for new things, open for growth and creativity. Every Christian has some variation on this immigrant plot to tell.

"Woe is me, that I sojourn in Meshech, that I dwell among the tents of Kedar! Too long have I had my dwelling among those who hate peace." But we don't have to live there any longer. Repentance, the first word in Christian immigration, sets us on the way to traveling in the light. It is a rejection that is also an acceptance, a leaving that develops into an arriving, a no to the world that is a yes to God.

I'm doomed to live in Meshech,
cursed with a home in Kedar,
My whole life lived camping
among quarreling neighbors.

PSALM 120:5–6

J A N U A R Y   1 5

_____

Worship

Worship does not satisfy our hunger for God—it whets our appetite. Our need for God is not taken care of by engaging in worship—it deepens. It overflows the hour and permeates the week. The need is expressed in a desire for peace and security. Our everyday needs are changed by the act of worship. We are no longer living from hand to mouth, greedily scrambling through the human rat race to make the best we can out of a mean existence. Our basic needs suddenly become worthy of the dignity of creatures made in the image of God: peace and security. The words *shalom* and *shalvah* play on the sounds in Jerusalem, *jerushalom,* the place of worship.

Shalom, peace, is one of the richest words in the Bible. You can no more define it by looking up its meaning in the dictionary than you can define a person by his social security number. It gathers all aspects of wholeness that result from God's will being completed in us. It is the work of God that, when complete, releases streams of living water in us and pulsates with eternal life. Every time Jesus healed, forgave or called someone, we have a demonstration of *shalom.*

And *shalvah,* security. It has nothing to do with insurance policies or large bank accounts or stockpiles of weapons. The root meaning is leisure—the relaxed stance of one who knows that everything is all right because God is over us and for us in Jesus Christ. It is the security of being at home in a history that has a cross at its center. It is the leisure of the person who knows that every moment of our existence is at the disposal of God, lived under the mercy of God.

Worship initiates an extended, daily participation in peace and security so that we share in our daily rounds what God initiates and continues in Jesus Christ.

> *When they said, "Let's go to the house of GOD,"*
> *my heart leaped for joy.*
> *And now we're here, oh Jerusalem,*
> *inside Jerusalem's walls!*

PSALM 122:1–2

Childlike Trust

Christian faith is not neurotic dependency but childlike trust. We do not have a God who forever indulges our whims but a God whom we trust with our destinies. The Christian is not a naive, innocent infant who has no identity apart from a feeling of being comforted and protected and catered to but a person who has discovered an identity that is given by God which can be enjoyed best and fully in a voluntary trust in God. We do not cling to God desperately out of fear and the panic of insecurity; we come to him freely in faith and love.

I look to you, heaven-dwelling God,
  look up to you for help.
Like servants, alert to their master's commands,
  like a maiden attending her lady,
We're watching and waiting, holding our breath,
  awaiting your word of mercy.

PSALM 123:1–2

Expectancy

A community of faith flourishes when we view each other with this expectancy, wondering what God will do today in this one, in that one. When we are in a community with those Christ loves and redeems, we are constantly finding out new things about them. They are new persons each morning, endless in their possibilities. We explore the fascinating depths of their friendship, share the secrets of their quest. It is impossible to be bored in such a community, impossible to feel alienated among such people.

> *How wonderful, how beautiful,*
>> *when brothers and sisters get along! . . .*
> *It's like the dew on Mount Hermon*
>> *flowing down the slopes of Zion.*

PSALM 133:1, 3A

J A N U A R Y   1 8

Kneels Among Us

God gets down on his knees among us; gets on our level and shares himself with us. He does not reside afar off and send diplomatic messages, he kneels among us. That posture is characteristic of God. The discovery and realization of this is what defines what we know of God as *good* news—God shares himself generously and graciously.

> *When the time came, he [Jesus] set aside the privileges of deity and took on the status of a slave, became* human! *Having become human, he stayed human. It was an incredibly humbling process.*

PHILIPPIANS 2:7–8

Christian Joy

It is clear in Psalm 126 that the one who wrote it and those who sang it were no strangers to the dark side of things. They carried the painful memory of exile in their bones and the scars of oppression on their backs. They knew the deserts of the heart and the nights of weeping. They knew what it meant to sow in tears.

One of the most interesting and remarkable things that Christians learn is that laughter does not exclude weeping. Christian joy is not an escape from sorrow. Pain and hardship still come, but they are unable to drive out the happiness of the redeemed.

A common but futile strategy for achieving joy is trying to eliminate things that hurt: get rid of pain by numbing the nerve ends, get rid of insecurity by eliminating risks, get rid of disappointments by depersonalizing your relationships. And then try to lighten the boredom of such a life by buying joy in the form of vacations and entertainment. There isn't a hint of that in Psalm 126.

And now, GOD, do it again—
bring rains to our drought-stricken lives
So those who planted their crops in despair
will shout hurrahs at the harvest,
So those who went off with heavy hearts
will come home laughing, with armloads of blessing.

PSALM 126:4–6

The Solidity of God's Joy

The psalm [Psalm 126] does not give us this joy as a package or as a formula, but there are some things it does do. It shows up the tinniness of the world's joy and affirms the solidity of God's joy. It reminds us of the accelerating costs and diminishing returns of those who pursue pleasure as a path toward joy. It introduces us to the way of discipleship which has consequences in joy. It encourages us in the way of faith to both experience and share joy. It tells the story of God's acts which put laughter into people's mouths and shouts on their tongues. It repeats the promises of a God who accompanies his wandering, weeping children until they arrive home, exuberant, "bringing in the sheaves." It announces the existence of a people who assemble to worship God and disperse to live to God's glory, whose lives are bordered on one side by a memory of God's acts and the other by hope in God's promises, and along with whatever else is happening are able to say, at the center, "We are glad."

> *It seemed like a dream, too good to be true,*
> *when GOD returned Zion's exiles.*
> *We laughed, we sang,*
> *we couldn't believe our good fortune.*
> *We were the talk of the nations—*
> *"GOD was wonderful to them!"*
> *GOD was wonderful to us;*
> *we are one happy people.*

PSALM 126:1–3

Witness

The proper work for the Christian is witness, not apology, and Psalm 124 is an excellent model. It does not argue God's help; it does not explain God's help; it is a testimony of God's help in the form of a song. The song is so vigorous, so confident, so bursting with what can only be called reality, that it fundamentally changes our approach and our questions. No longer does it seem of the highest priority to ask, "Why did this happen to me? Why do I feel left in the lurch?" Instead we ask, "How does it happen that there are people who sing with such confidence, 'God is our help'?" The psalm is data that must be accounted for and the data are so solid, so vital, have so much more substance and are so much more interesting than the other things we hear through the day that it must be dealt with before we can go back to the whimpering complaints.

"If it had not been the LORD who was on our side, let Israel now say—if it had not be the LORD who was on our side, when men rose up against us, then they would have swallowed us up alive, when their anger was kindled against us; then over us would have gone the raging waters." The witness is vivid and contagious. One person announces the theme, and everyone joins in. God's help is not a private experience; it is a corporate reality—not an exception that occurs among isolated strangers, but the norm among the people of God.

> *If GOD hadn't been for us—*
> *all together now, Israel, sing out!—*
> *If GOD hadn't been for us*
> *when everyone went against us,*

We would have been swallowed alive
  by their violent anger . . .

PSALM 124:1–3

Faith on the Line

What is hazardous in my life is my work as a Christian. Every day I put faith on the line. I have never seen God. In a world where nearly everything can be weighed, explained, quantified, subjected to psychological analysis and scientific control I persist in making the center of my life a God whom no eye hath seen, nor ear heard, whose will no one can probe. That's a risk.

> *"If you don't go all the way with me, through thick and thin, you don't deserve me. If your first concern is to look after yourself, you'll never find yourself. But if you forget about yourself and look to me, you'll find both yourself and me."*

MATTHEW 10:38–39

Hope on the Line

Every day I put hope on the line. I don't know one thing about the future. I don't know what the next hour will hold. There may be sickness, personal or world catastrophe. Before this day is over I may have to deal with death, pain, loss, rejection. I don't know what the future holds for me, for those whom I love, for my nation, for this world. Still, despite my ignorance and surrounded by tinny optimists and cowardly pessimists, I say that God will accomplish his will and cheerfully persist in living in the hope that nothing will separate me from Christ's love.

> GOD'S *strong name is our help,*
> *the same* GOD *who made heaven and earth.*

PSALM 124:8

Love on the Line

Based on Psalm 124

Every day I put love on the line. There is nothing I am less good at than love. I am far better in competition than in love. I am far better at responding to my instincts and ambitions to get ahead and make my mark than I am at figuring out how to love another. I am schooled and trained in acquisitive skills, in getting my own way. And yet, I decide, every day, to set aside what I can do best and attempt what I do very clumsily—open myself to the frustrations and failures of loving, daring to believe that failing in love is better than succeeding in pride.

All that is hazardous work; I live on the edge of defeat all the time. I have never done any one of those things to my (or anyone else's) satisfaction. I live in the dragon's maw and at the flood's edge.

The psalm, though, is not about hazards but about help. The hazardous work of discipleship is not the subject of the psalm but only its setting. The subject is help: "Blessed be the LORD, who has not given us as prey to their teeth! We have escaped as a bird from the snare of the fowlers; the snare is broken, and we have escaped! Our help is in the name of the LORD, who made heaven and earth." Hazards or no hazards, the fundamental reality we live with is "The LORD who was on our side . . . Our help is in the name of the LORD."

We've flown free from their fangs,
free of their traps, free as a bird.
Their grip is broken;
we're free as a bird in flight.

PSALM 124:7

JANUARY 25

The Content of Our Lives

Psalm 124 is an instance of a person who digs deeply into the trouble and finds there the presence of the God who is on our side. . . . Faith develops out of the most difficult aspects of our existence, not the easiest. The person of faith is not a person who has been born, luckily, with a good digestion and sunny disposition. The assumption by outsiders that Christians are naive or protected is the opposite of the truth: Christians know more about the deep struggles of life than others, more about the ugliness of sin.

A look into the heavens can bring a breathtaking sense of wonder and majesty, and, if a person is a believer, a feeling of praise to the God who made heaven and earth. The psalm looks the other direction. It looks into the troubles of history, the anxiety of personal conflict and emotional trauma. And it sees there the God who is on our side, God can help. The close look, the microscopic insight into the dragon's terrors, the flood's waters and the imprisoning trap, sees the action of God in deliverance.

We speak our words of praise in a world that is hellish; we sing our songs of victory in a world where things get messy; we live our joy among people who neither understand nor encourage us. But the content of our lives is God, not man.

We continue to shout our praise even when we're hemmed in with troubles, because we know how troubles can develop passionate patience in us, and how that patience in turn forges the tempered steel of virtue, keeping us alert for whatever God will do next.

ROMANS 5:3–4

Prayer

Prayer is political action. Prayer is social energy. Prayer is public good. Far more of our nation's life is shaped by prayer than is formed by legislation. That we have not collapsed into anarchy is due more to prayer than to the police. Prayer is a sustained and intricate act of patriotism in the largest sense of the word—far more precise and loving and preserving than any patriotism served up in slogans. That society continues to be livable and that hope continues to be resurgent are attributable to prayer far more than to business prosperity or a flourishing of the arts. The single most important action contributing to whatever health and strength there is in our land is prayer. Not the only thing, of course, for God uses all things to effect his sovereign will, and the "all things" most certainly includes police and artists, senators and professors, therapists and steelworkers. But prayer is, all the same, the source action.

> *"The kingdom of the world is now*
> *the Kingdom of our God and his Messiah!*
> *He will rule forever and ever!"*

REVELATION 11:15

The Wise

The opposite of *foolish* in Scripture is *wise*. *Wise* refers to skill in living. It does not mean, primarily, the person who knows the right answers to things, but one who has developed the right responses (relationships) to persons, to God. The wise understand how the world works; know about patience and love, listening and grace, adoration and beauty; know that other people are awesome creatures to be respected and befriended, especially the ones that I cannot get anything out of; know that the earth is a marvelously intricate gift to be cared for and enjoyed; know that God is an ever-present center, a never-diminishing reality, an all-encompassing love; and know that there is no living being that does not reach out gladly and responsively to him and the nation/kingdom/community in which he has placed us.

The wise know that there is only one cure for the fool. Prayer that is as passionate for the salvation of others as it is for myself: "O that deliverance for Israel would come out of Zion!" Prayer that is convinced that there is no wellness until everyone is restored to a place of blessing: "When the LORD restores the fortunes of his people." And prayer that sees the community as a place not of acquisition, but of celebration: "Jacob shall rejoice, Israel shall be glad" (v. 7).

Dear friend, pay close attention to this, my wisdom;
  listen very closely to the way I see it.
Then you'll acquire a taste for good sense;
  what I tell you will keep you out of trouble.

PROVERBS 5:1–2

Our True Home

We do not begin life on our own. We do not finish it on our own. Life, especially when we experience by faith the complex interplay of creation and salvation, is not fashioned out of our own genetic lumber and cultural warehouses. It is not hammered together with the planks and nails of our thoughts and dreams, our feelings and fancies. We are not self-sufficient. We enter a world that is created by God, that already has a rich history and is crowded with committed participants—a world of animals and mountains, of politics and religion; a world where people build houses and raise children, where volcanoes erupt lava and rivers flow to the sea; a world in which, however carefully we observe and watch and study it, surprising things keep on taking place (like rocks turning into pools of water). We keep on being surprised because we are in on something beyond our management, something over our heads.

In prayer we realize and practice our part in this intricate involvement with absolutely everything that is, no matter how remote it seems to us or how indifferent we are to it. This prayer is not an emotional or aesthetic sideline that we indulge in after our real work is done; it is the connective tissue of our far-flung existence. The world of creation interpenetrates the world of redemption. The world of redemption interpenetrates the world of creation. The extravagantly orchestrated skies and the exuberantly fashioned earth are not the background to provide a little beauty on the periphery of the godlike ego; they are the large beauty in which we find our true home, room in which to live the cross and Christ expansively, openhearted in praise.

> *Tremble, Earth! You're in the Lord's presence!*
> *in the presence of Jacob's God.*
> *He turned the rock into a pool of cool water,*
> *he turned flint into fresh spring water.*

PSALM 114:7–8

A Web of Relationships

Prayer is the action that gets us in touch with and develops the most comprehensive relationships—self, God, community, creation, government, culture. We are born into a web of relationships and continue in it throughout our lifetimes. But we often don't feel like it. We feel isolated, cut off, fragmented, out of touch. We do not tolerate such isolation very well and move out to overcome it: we call up a neighbor, join a club, write a letter, get married. The disparate attempts accumulate. The self is less isolated. Society is less fragmented. The facts add up. But if we do not pray, they do not add up to enough: in prayer and only in prayer are we able to enter the complexity and depth of the dynamic and interrelated whole. A failure to pray is not a harmless omission; it is a positive violation of both self and the society.

Pray for us. We have no doubts about what we're doing or why, but it's hard going and we need your prayers. All we care about is living well before God. Pray that we may be together soon.

HEBREWS 13:18–19

A Self Problem

America is in conspicuous need of unselfing. Concerned observers using the diagnostic disciplines of psychology, sociology, economics and theology lay the blame for the deterioration of our public life and the disintegration of our personal lives at the door of the self; we have a self problem and that problem is responsible for everything else that is going wrong. . . .

In Alexander Solzhenitsyn's extensively reported and now famous sermon to America, delivered in 1978 at Harvard University, he said, "We have placed too much hope in politics and social reforms, only to find out that we were being deprived of our most precious possession; our spiritual life. It is trampled by the party mob in the East, by the commercial one in the West." . . .

What the journalists did not report—not a single pundit so much as mentioned it—is that a significant number of people are actually doing something about Solzhenitsyn's concern. . . . The work is prayer.

> *[Jesus said] "Self-help is no help at all. Self-sacrifice is the way, my way, to saving yourself, your true self. What good would it do to get everything you want and lose you . . . ?"*

MARK 8:35–36

JANUARY 31

The City of God

In contrast to the pervasive violence that constitutes the atmosphere in which we pray, the city of God is set down as a simple matter of fact. A city is a *civilized* place, a place of courtesy and trust. It is not exclusively this in our experience, but it is so characteristically (it is the exceptions that get reported). This city of God is not a blueprint for the future, not a hoped-for aspiration and not a promise that just might be enacted with the right legislation. It is here. Now. God dwells in this place, this world. God is not an occasional tourist to our shores. He has set up habitation here, not as a camper but as a citizen: there is a *city* of God. It is in the same world where the violence is, which means that we need not go off looking for God in a quiet, secluded glen.

Augustine used this image of the city to develop his exposition of the presence and action of God in the midst of human presence and action, the history of God's ways permeating the history of our ways. He wrote *The City of God* in the rough and tumble of one of the most violent times in our history, when Alaric and the barbarian hordes were streaming out of the north and ravaging Roman civilization. This is not escapist theology but something more like prayed journalism.

> *River fountains splash joy, cooling God's city,*
> *this sacred haunt of the Most High.*
> *God lives here, the streets are safe,*
> *God at your service from crack of dawn.*

PSALM 46:4–5

February

The Works of the Lord

The next four days are reflections on Psalm 46.

Two commands direct us from the small-minded world of self-help to the large world of God's help. First, "Come, behold the works of the LORD." Take a long, scrutinizing look at what God is doing. This requires patient attentiveness and energetic concentration. Everybody else is noisier than God. The headlines and neon lights and amplifying systems of the world announce human works. But what of God's works? They are unadvertised but also inescapable, if we simply look. They are everywhere. They are marvelous. But God has no public relations agency. He mounts no publicity campaign to get our attention. He simply invites us to look. Prayer is looking at the works of the Lord.

> *Reach out and experience the breadth! Test its length!*
> *Plumb the depths! Rise to the heights! Live full lives, full in*
> *the fullness of God.*

EPHESIANS 3:18–19

Creative Action

God is engaged in worldwide disarmament. All the ways in which men and women attempt to forcibly impose their wills on neighbors and enemies are thrown into the trash heap. Violence does not work. It never has worked. It never will work. Weapons are not functional.

The history of violence is a history of failures. There has never been a won war. There has never been a victorious battle. The use of force destroys the very reality that is exercised in its behalf, whether honor, truth or justice. Living in the kind of world in which we do and being the sinners we are, we sometimes cannot avoid violence. But even when it is inevitable it is not right. God does not engage in it.

A steady, sustained look at God's works sees that our frantic, foolish arms build-up (whether personal or national, whether psychological or material) is being subjected to systematic and determined disarmament. Violent action is the antithesis of creative action. When we no longer have the will or the patience to be creative, we attempt to express our will by coercion. The lazy and the immature account for most of the violence in the world. But however prevalent violence is, the person at prayer sees that that is not the way most of the world, the world of God's action, works. But it takes energy and maturity to see it and to sustain the vision.

Attention, all! See the marvels of God!
   He plants flowers and trees all over the earth,

Bans war from pole to pole,
  breaks all the weapons of war across his knee.

PSALM 46:8–9

Be Still

After the first command of Psalm 46, the second follows. . . .

The second command is "Be still, and know that I am God." *Be still.* Quit rushing through the streets long enough to become aware that there is more to life than your little self-help enterprises. When we are noisy and when we are hurried, we are incapable of intimacy—deep, complex, personal relationships. If God is the living center of redemption, it is essential that we be in touch with and responsive to that personal will. If God has a will for this world and we want to be in on it, we must be still long enough to find out what it is (for we certainly are not going to learn by watching the evening news). Baron von Hügel, who had a wise word on most subjects, always held out that "nothing was ever accomplished in a stampede."

Step out of the traffic! Take a long,
  loving look at me, your High God,
  above politics, above everything.

PSALM 46:10

Knowing and Being Known

And know. The word *know* often has sexual connotations in biblical writings. Adam knew Eve. Joseph did not know Mary. These are not, as so many suppose, timid euphemisms; they are bold metaphors. The best knowledge, the knowledge that is thorough and personal, is not information. It is shared intimacy—a knowing and being known that becomes a creative act. It is analogous to sexual relationship in which two persons are vulnerable and open to each other, the consequence of which is the creation of new life. Unamuno, a Spanish philosopher, elaborates: " 'To know' means in effect to engender, and all vital knowledge in this sense presupposes a penetration, a fusion of the innermost being of the man who knows and of the thing known" [*The Agony of Christians*]. The knowing results in a new being that is different from and more than either partner. No child is a replica of either parent; no child is a mere amalgamation of parents. There are characteristics of both, but the new life is unpredictable, full of surprises, a life of its own.

This sexual knowing that results in newly created life is the everyday experience that is used to show what happens when we pray: withdrawal from commotion, shutting the door against the outside world, insistence on leisurely privacy. This is not an antisocial act. It is not a selfish indulgence. It is no shirking of public responsibility. On the contrary, it is a fulfilling of public responsibility, a contribution to the wholeness of civilization. It is, precisely, creative: You cannot make love in traffic. For all his marvelous creativity, Michelangelo never painted or drew or sculpted anything that compares with any new-born infant. For all his wide-ranging Renaissance inventiveness, Leonardo da Vinci never faintly approximated what any peasant couple brought forth by simply going to bed together. People who pray give themselves to the creative process at this same elemental, world-enriching, self-transcending place of surprise and pleasure.

I gave up all that inferior stuff so I could know Christ personally, experience his resurrection power . . .

PHILIPPIANS 3:8

FEBRUARY 5

There Is No Private Prayer

The single most widespread American misunderstanding of prayer is that it is private. Strictly and biblically speaking, there is no private prayer. *Private* in its root meaning refers to theft. It is stealing. When we privatize prayer we embezzle the common currency that belongs to all. When we engage in prayer without any desire for or awareness of the comprehensive, inclusive life of the kingdom that is "at hand" in both space and time, we impoverish the social reality that God is bringing to completion.

Solitude in prayer is not privacy. The differences between privacy and solitude are profound. Privacy is our attempt to insulate the self from interference; solitude leaves the company of others for a time in order to listen to them more deeply, be aware of them, serve them. Privacy is getting away from others so that I don't have to be bothered with them; solitude is getting away from the crowd so that I can be instructed by the still, small voice of God, who is enthroned on the praises of the multitudes. Private prayers are selfish and thin; prayer in solitude enrolls in a multivoiced, century-layered community: with angels and archangels in all the company of heaven we sing, "Holy, Holy, Holy, Lord God Almighty."

> *While it was still night, way before dawn, he got up and went out to a secluded spot and prayed. Simon and those with him went looking for him. They found him and said, "Everybody's looking for you."*
>
> *Jesus said, "Let's go to the rest of the villages so I can preach there also. This is why I've come."*

MARK 1:35–38

FEBRUARY 6

Religion and Politics

For Christians, "political" acquires extensive biblical associations and dimensions. So rather than look for another word untainted by corruption and evil, it is important to use it just as it is so that by it we are trained to see God in the places that seem intransigent to grace. The people who warn that "religion and politics don't mix" certainly know what they are talking about. The mix has resulted in no end of ills—crusades, inquisitions, witch hunts, exploitation. All the same, God says, "Mix them." But be very careful how you mix them. The only safe way is in prayer. It is both unbiblical and unreal to divide life into the activities of religion and politics, or into the realms of sacred and profane. But how do we get them together without putting one into the unscrupulous hands of the other, politics *using* religion or religion *using* politics, when what we want is a true mixture, politics *becoming* religious and religion *becoming* political? Prayer is the only means that is adequate for the great end of getting these polarities in dynamic relation. The psalms are our most extensive source documents showing prayer in action.

So, rebel-kings, use your heads;
Upstart judges, learn your lesson:
Worship GOD in adoring embrace,
Celebrate in trembling awe. Kiss Messiah!

PSALM 2:10–12

FEBRUARY 7

Help Was There

To the objection "I prayed and cried out for help, but no help came," the answer is "But it did. The help was there; it was right at hand. You were looking for something quite different, perhaps, but God brought the help that would change your life into health, into wholeness for eternity. And not only would it change your life, but nations, society, culture." Instead of asking why the help has not come, the person at prayer learns to look carefully at what is actually going on in his or her life, in this history, its leaders, its movements, its peoples, and ask, "Could this be the help that he is providing? I never thought of *this* in terms of help, but maybe it is." Prayer gives us another, far more accurate way of reading reality than the newspapers. "Think of it!" exclaims Bernanos's country priest. "The Word was made Flesh and not one of the journalists of those days even knew it was happening" [*The Diary of a Country Priest*].

> *I call to you, God, because I'm sure of an answer.*
> *So—answer! bend your ear! listen sharp!*
> *Paint grace-graffiti on the fences;*
> *take in your frightened children who*
> *Are running from the neighborhood bullies*
> *straight to you.*

PSALM 17:6–7

FEBRUARY 8

Prayer Is Elemental

Untutored, we tend to think that prayer is what good people do when they are doing their best. It is not. Inexperienced, we suppose that there must be an "insider" language that must be acquired before God takes us seriously in our prayer. There is not. Prayer is elemental, not advanced language. It is the means by which our language becomes honest, true, and personal in response to God. It is the means by which we get everything out in the open before God.

When I call, give me answers. God, take my side!
Once, in a tight place, you gave me room;
Now I'm in trouble again: grace me! hear me!

PSALM 4:1

The Foolishness of Congregations

St. Paul talked about the foolishness of preaching; I would like to carry on about the foolishness of congregation. Of all the ways in which to engage in the enterprise of church, this has to be the most absurd—this haphazard collection of people who somehow get assembled into pews on Sundays, half-heartedly sing a few songs most of them don't like, tune in and out of a sermon according to the state of their digestion and the preacher's decibels, awkward in their commitments and jerky in their prayers.

But the people in these pews are also people who suffer deeply and find God in their suffering. These are men and women who make love commitments, are faithful to them through trial and temptation, and bear fruits of righteousness, spirit-fruits that bless the people around them. Babies, surrounded by hopeful and rejoicing parents and friends, are baptized in the name of the Father and the Son and the Holy Ghost. Adults, converted by the gospel, surprised and surprising all who have known them, are likewise baptized. The dead are offered up to God in funerals that give solemn and joyful witness to the resurrection in the midst of tears and grief. Sinners honestly repent and believingly take the body and blood of Jesus and receive new life.

But these are mixed in with the others and are, more often than not, indistinguishable from them. I can find, biblically, no other form of church.

> *Take a good look, friends, at who you were when you got called into this life. I don't see many of "the brightest and the best" among you, not many influential, not many from high-society families. Isn't it obvious that God deliberately chose men and women that the culture overlooks and exploits and abuses, chose these "nobodies" to expose the hollow pretensions of the "somebodies"?*

1 CORINTHIANS 1:26–28

FEBRUARY 10

Geographical

The gospel is emphatically geographical. Place names—Sinai, Hebron, Machpelah, Shiloh, Nazareth, Jezreel, Samaria, Bethlehem, Jerusalem, Bethsaida—are embedded in the gospel. All theology is rooted in geology. Pilgrims to biblical lands are sometimes surprised to find that the towns in which David camped and Jesus lived are no better or more beautiful than the hometowns they left behind.

If the fallout of our belief in the supernatural is a contempt for these one-horse towns and impatience with their dull-spirited citizens, we had better reexamine what we say we believe in. For supernatural in the biblical sources is not a spectacularly colored hot-air balloon floating free of awkward contingencies but a servant God with basin and towel washing dusty and callused feet.

> *Philip went and found Nathanael and told him, "We've found the One Moses wrote of in the Law, the One preached by the prophets. It's Jesus, Joseph's son, the one from Nazareth!" Nathanael said, "Nazareth? You've got to be kidding." But Philip said, "Come, see for yourself."*

JOHN 1:45–46

FEBRUARY 11

Salvation

What God has done for us far exceeds anything we have done for or against him. The summary word for this excessive, undeserved, unexpected act of God is *salvation*. Prayer explores the country of salvation, tramping the contours, smelling the flowers, touching the outcroppings. There is more to do than recognize the sheer fact of salvation and witness to it; there are unnumbered details of grace, of mercy, of blessing to be appreciated and savored. Prayer is the means by which we do this.

> *As high as heaven is over the earth,*
> *so strong is his love to those who fear him.*

And as far as sunrise is from sunset,
he has separated us from our sins.

PSALM 103:11–12

FEBRUARY 12

This New Community

In this new community, created by the Holy Spirit and called the church, much of the vocabulary used to describe relationships comes from the family as we already know it: brothers, sisters, fathers, and mothers. The message seems to be something along these lines. What you never managed in your own families naturally, you may now have in the new community supernaturally. All that was lost at Eden is regained at Gethsemane. Relationships learned at the cross of Christ, the ways of love and the techniques of forgiveness, will give you the brother and sister you longed for, the son and daughter you desired. What you learn in the community of faith you will then be able to take back into your natural families of sons and daughters, of fathers and mothers.

[Jesus said,] "Who do you think are my mother and brothers?" Looking around, taking in everyone seated around him, he said, "Right here, right in front of you—my mother and my brothers. Obedience is thicker than blood. The person who obeys God's will is my brother and sister and mother."

MARK 3:33–35

Love

This is from an exposition of Psalm 45.

If I, deeply in love with another, begin describing with passionate appreciation what has been unnoticed or ignored by everyone else for years, some people around me are sure to dismiss me, "Love is blind." They mean that love diminishes my capacity to see what is actually there so that fantasy, tailor-made to fit my desires, can be projected on another and thus make him or her acceptable as a lover. The cynical follow-up is that if this did not happen, if I saw the other truly, I would never get involved. Why? Because everyone is, in fact, quite unlovely, either visibly or invisibly, or, in some particularly unfortunate cases, both. Love doesn't see truth but creates illusions and incapacitates us for dealing with the hard-edged realities of life.

But the popular saying, as popular sayings so often are, is wrong. It is hate that is blind. It is habit, condescension, cynicism that are blind. Love opens eyes. Love enables the eyes to see what has been there all along but was overlooked in haste or indifference. Love corrects astigmatism so that what was distorted in selfishness is now perceived accurately and appreciatively. Love cures shortsightedness so that the blur of the distant other is now in wondrous focus. Love cures farsightedness so that opportunities for intimacy are no longer blurred threats but blessed invitations. Love looks at the one who had no "form or comeliness that we should look at him, and no beauty that we should desire him" and sees there the "fairest of the sons of men . . . anointed with the oil of gladness above your fellows."

If we could see the other as he is, as she is, there is no one we would not see as "fairest . . . all fragrant with myrrh and aloes and cassia." Love penetrates the defenses that have been built up to protect against rejection and scorn and belittlement, and it sees life created by God for love.

If I give everything I own to the poor and even go to the stake to be burned as a martyr, but I don't love, I've gotten nowhere. So, no matter what I say, what I believe, and what I do, I'm bankrupt without love.

1 CORINTHIANS 13:3

FEBRUARY 14

Let Not Man Put Asunder

Committed by command and habit to fidelity
I'm snug in the double bed and board of marriage:
    spontaneity's built-in
    to the covenantal dance,
    everyday routines arranged
    by the floor plan of the manse.

This unlikely fissiparous alliance
embraces and releases daily surprises.
    The ego strength we'd carefully hoarded
    in certain safe-deposit boxes
    we've now dispersed, unlamented,
    in dozens of delicate paradoxes.

A thousand domestic intimacies are straw
for making bricks resistant to erosion:
    with such uncomely stuff we've built
    our lives on ordinary sod
    and grow, finally, old. My love is
    not a goddess nor I a god.

"Asunder" is the one unpronounceable word in the world
of the wed, "one flesh" the mortal miracle.
    What started out quite tentatively
    with clumsy scrawls in a billet doux
    has now become the intricacy
    of bold marriage's pas de deux.

MARK 10:1–2

*In the original creation, God made male and female to be together.
Because of this, a man leaves father and mother, and in marriage he
becomes one flesh with a woman—no longer two individuals, but
forming a new unity. Because God created this organic union of the
two sexes, no one should desecrate his art by cutting them apart.*

MARK 10:6–9

FEBRUARY 15

To Grow Is to Love

The self cannot be itself if it does not grow, and for a creature made in
the image of God to grow is to love. No living being can be static. The

self cannot be preserved in amber. Every new act of love requires detachment from what is outgrown, what serves merely to infantilize us. Karlfried Durckheim used to insist: "You never kill the ego, you only find that it lives in a larger house than you thought." The self, if it is to become itself, must find a larger house to dwell in than the house where everyone coddles us and responds to our whims. The passage from leaving home to entering marriage is the archetypal transition from the comfortable, cared-for self to the strenuous, caring-for self.

Self-love is obsessed with keeping what it has and adding a little more of the same. That is why it is so boring. There is never anything new to say, nothing new to discover. Self-love assesses its position by what it has and is panicked at the thought of losing any of it. Forced into new relationships, into new situations, its first consideration is not of the new fields for love but of the appalling prospects of loss. So it clings. It holds. And it whines.

The detachment that is prerequisite for mature marriage prepares us for maturity in love across the board. We outlive our past over and over again. There comes a moment when I am no longer a spouse, I am no longer a parent, I am no longer employed, I am no longer healthy. There are periods of my life that are immensely valuable and enjoyable and useful but which by their very nature cannot be perpetuated. Ironically, if we try to perpetuate them in the name of love, we ruin love.

Detachment is not disloyalty; it is a requirement for the next movement of love, which is a movement into a more perfect love. Such movements almost always begin in feelings of loss, of deprivation. But detachment is not loss—it is a precondition for fresh creativity.

"Well-meaning family members can be your worst enemies. If you prefer father or mother over me, you don't deserve me. If you prefer son or daughter over me, you don't deserve me.

"If you don't go all the way with me, through thick and thin, you don't deserve me. If your first concern is to look after yourself, you'll never find yourself. But if you forget about yourself and look to me, you'll find both yourself and me."

MATTHEW 10:36–39

FEBRUARY 16

Marriage

Every marriage crosses another boundary of genealogy. Disparate histories are brought together in such a way that the other is presented for appreciation and praise, not contempt and rejection. Every marriage is proof that the other is not the enemy, not the rival, not the threat, but the friend, the ally and, at best, the lover.

All marriages are ventured into with this possibility and expectation, but they do not all confirm it. Marriages fail. Partners become rivals, jealous and threatened, rejecting and rejected. Betrayals occur. Still, the most significant recurring act of love that takes place in society is marriage. Ezra Pound was radical in his claim for it: "One humane family can humanize a whole state into courtesy; one grasping and perverse man can drive a nation to chaos."

> *. . . a man leaves father and mother and cherishes his wife. No longer two, they become "one flesh." This is a huge mystery, and I don't pretend to understand it all. What is clearest to me is the way Christ treats the church. And this provides a good picture of how each hus-*

band is to treat his wife, *loving himself in loving her, and how each wife is to honor her husband.*

EPHESIANS 5:31–33

Archetypal Act of Freedom

Marriage is an archetypal act of freedom. Marriage partners, by leaving their natural family ties, break out of networks of necessity and predictability and at that moment become prime movers in the politics of freedom. This is true even in an arranged marriage: though the free will of the partners is not consulted, the arrangement is a result of *someone's* choice and not the mere product of biological necessity. Every marriage, then, introduces into society fresh energies of love and freedom that have the power to unself not only the lovers themselves but America itself. The mere introduction of these energies is not enough, however, or we would have become Utopia long since. They need continuing and perfecting. Where can we get that but in Christ? A prayed and praying faithfulness carries us into the long life of love in which and by which the world will not perish.

Love never gives up.
Love cares more for others than for self.
Love doesn't want what it doesn't have.

1 CORINTHIANS 13:4–5

God and Love

The two most difficult things to get straight in life are love and God. More often than not, the mess people make of their lives can be traced to failure or stupidity or meanness in one or both of these areas.

The basic and biblical Christian conviction is that the two subjects are intricately related. If we want to deal with God the right way, we have to learn to love the right way. If we want to love the right way, we have to deal with God the right way. God and love can't be separated.

My beloved friends, let us continue to love each other since love comes from God. Everyone who loves is born of God and experiences a relationship with God. The person who refuses to love doesn't know the first thing about God, because God is love—so you can't know him if you don't love.

1 JOHN 4:7–8

A Greed Problem

John Calvin, preaching to his congregation in Geneva, Switzerland, pointed out to his parishioners that we must develop better and deeper concepts of happiness from those held by the world which makes a happy life to consist in "ease, honours, and great wealth."

Psalm 128 helps us do that. Too much of the world's happiness depends on taking from one to satisfy another. To increase my standard of living, someone in another part of the world must lower his. The worldwide crisis of hunger that we face today is a result of that method of pursuing happiness. Industrialized nations acquire appetites for more and more luxuries and higher and higher standards of living, and increasing numbers of people are made poor and hungry. It doesn't have to be that way. The experts on the world hunger problem say that there is enough to go around right now. We don't have a production problem. We have the agricultural capability to produce enough food. We have the transportation technology to distribute the food. But we have a greed problem: if I don't grab mine while I can, I might not be happy. The hunger problem is not going to be solved by government or by industry, but in church, among Christians who learn a different way to pursue happiness.

> . . . all the believers lived in a wonderful harmony, holding everything in common. They sold whatever they owned and pooled their resources so that each person's need was met.

ACTS 2:44–45

FEBRUARY 20

This Life of Blessing

This reading is based on Psalm 128.

Christian blessing is a realizing that "it is more blessed to give than to receive." As we learn to give and to share, our vitality increases and the people around us become "fruitful vines" and "olive shoots" around our tables.

The blessings that are promised to, pronounced upon and experienced by Christians, do not of course exclude difficulties. The Bible never indicates that. But the difficulties are not inherent in the faith: they come from the outside in the form of temptations, seductions, pressures. Not a day goes by but what we have to deal with that ancient triple threat that Christians in the Middle Ages summarized under the headings of the world, the flesh, and the devil: the world—the society of proud and arrogant mankind that defies and tries to eliminate God's rule and presence in history; the flesh—the corruption that sin has introduced into our very appetites and instincts; and the devil—the malignant will that tempts and seduces us away from the will of God. We have to contend with all of that. We are in a battle. There is a fight of faith to be waged. But the way of faith itself is in tune with what God has done and is doing. The road we travel is the well-traveled road of discipleship. It is not a way of boredom or despair or confusion. It is not a miserable groping, but a way of blessing.

There are no tricks involved in getting in on this life of blessing, and no luck required. We simply become Christians and begin the life of faith. We acknowledge God as our maker and lover, and accept Christ as the means by which we can be in living relationship with God. We accept the announced and proclaimed truth that God is at the center of our existence, find out how he has constructed this world (his creation), how he has provided for our redemption, and proceed to walk in that way. In the plain words of the psalm: "Blessed is every one who fears the LORD, who walks in his ways!"

This most generous God who gives seed to the farmer that becomes bread for your meals is more than extravagant with you. He gives

you something you can then give away, which grows into
full-formed lives, robust in God, wealthy in every way, so
that you can be generous in every way, producing with us
great praise to God.

2 CORINTHIANS 9:11–12

Reverence

"Fears the LORD." *Reverence* might be a better word. Awe. The Bible isn't interested in whether we believe in God or not. It assumes that everyone more or less does. What it is interested in is the response we have toward him: will we let God be as he is, majestic and holy, vast and wondrous, or will we always be trying to whittle him down to the size of our small minds, insist on confining him within the boundaries we are comfortable with, refuse to think of him other than in images that are convenient to our life-style? But then we are not dealing with the God of creation and the Christ of the cross, but with a dime-store reproduction of something made in our image, usually for commercial reasons. To guard against all such blasphemous chumminess with the Almighty, the Bible talks of the fear of the LORD—not to scare us but to bring us to awesome attention before the overwhelming grandeur of God, to shut up our whining and chattering and stop our running and fidgeting so that we can really see him as he is and listen to him as he speaks his merciful, life-changing words of forgiveness.

Stand in awe of God's Yes.
Oh, how he blesses the one who fears GOD!

PSALM 128:4

Wait *and* Hope

Such are the two great realities of Psalm 130: suffering is real, God is real. Suffering is a mark of our existential authenticity; God is proof of our essential and eternal humanity. We accept suffering; we believe in God. The acceptance and the belief both come from "the depths."

But there is more than a description of reality here, there is a procedure for participating in it. The program is given in two words: *wait* and *hope*. The words are at the center of the psalm. "I wait for the LORD, my soul waits, and in his word I hope; my soul waits for the LORD more than watchmen for the morning, more than watchmen for the morning. O Israel, hope in the LORD!"

The words *wait* and *hope* are connected with the image of the watchmen waiting through the night for the dawn. The connection provides important insights for the person in trouble who asks, "But surely, there is something for me to do!" The answer is yes, there is something for you to do, or more exactly there is someone you can be; be a watchman.

A watchman is an important person, but he doesn't do very much. The massive turning of the earth, the immense energies released by the sun—all that goes on apart from him. He does nothing to influence or control such things: he is a watchman. He knows the dawn is coming; there are no doubts concerning that. Meanwhile he is alert to dangers, he comforts restless children or animals until it is time to work or play again in the light of day. . . .

Nor would the psalmist have been content to be a watchman if he were not sure of God. The psalmist's and the Christian's waiting and hoping is based on the conviction that God is actively involved in his creation and vigorously at work in redemption.

Waiting does not mean doing nothing. It is not fatalistic resignation. It means going about our assigned tasks, confident that God will provide the meaning and the conclusions. It is not compelled to work away at keeping up appearances with a bogus spirituality. It is the opposite of desperate and panicky manipulations, of scurrying and worrying.

And hoping is not dreaming. It is not spinning an illusion of fantasy to protect us from our boredom or our pain. It means a confident alert expectation that God will do what he said he will do. It is imagination put in the harness of faith. It is a willingness to let him do it his way and in his time. It is the opposite of making plans that we demand that God put into effect, telling him both how and when to do it. That is not hoping in God but bullying God. "I wait for the LORD, my soul waits, and in his word I hope; my soul waits for the LORD more than watchmen for the morning, more than watchmen for the morning."

My life's on the line before God, my Lord,
waiting and watching till morning,
waiting and watching till morning.

PSALM 130:6

Grace and Gratitude

"*Charis* always demands the answer *eucharistia* (that is, grace always demands the answer of gratitude). Grace and gratitude belong together like heaven and earth. Grace evokes gratitude like the voice an echo. Gratitude follows grace as thunder follows lightning" [Karl Barth, *Church Dogmatics*]. God is personal reality to be enjoyed. We are so created and so redeemed that we are capable of enjoying him. All the movements of discipleship arrive at a place where joy is experienced. Every step of assent toward God develops the capacity to enjoy. Not only is there, increasingly, more to be enjoyed, there is steadily the acquired ability to enjoy it.

Best of all, we don't have to wait until we get to the end of the road before we enjoy what is at the end of the road. So, "Come, bless the LORD . . . The LORD bless you!"

I'm thanking you, GOD, from a full heart,
I'm writing the book on your wonders!

PSALM 9:1

Intense Imagination

Every Monday I leave the routines of my daily work and hike along the streams and through the forests of Maryland. The first hours of that walk are uneventful: I am tired, sluggish, inattentive. Then bird-song begins to penetrate my senses, and the play of light on oak leaves and asters catches my interest. In the forest of trees, one sycamore forces its solid rootedness on me, and then sends my eyes arcing across trajectories upwards and outwards. I have been walking these forest trails for years, but I am ever and again finding an insect that I have never seen before startling me with its combined aspects of ferocity and fragility. How many more are there to be found? A rock formation, absolutely new, thrusts millions of years of prehistory into my present. This creation is so complex, so intricate, so profuse with life and form and color and scent! And I walk through it deaf and dumb and blind, groping my way, stupidly absorbed in putting one foot in front of the other, seeing a mere fraction of what is there. The Monday walks wake me up, a little anyway, to what I miss in my sleepy routines. The wakefulness lasts, sometimes, through Thursday, occasionally all the way to Sunday. A friend calls these weekly rambles "Emmaus walks": "And their eyes were opened and they recognized him" (Luke 24:31).

What walking through Maryland forests does to my bodily senses, reading the Revelation does to my faith perceptions. For I am quite as dull to the marvelous word of Christ's covenant as I am to his creation. "O Lord, and shall I ever live at this poor dying rate?" Not if St. John's Revelation has its way. A few paragraphs into the Revelation, the adrenaline starts rushing through the arteries of my faith, and I am on my feet alive, tingling. It is impossible to read the Revelation and not have my imagination aroused. The Revelation both forces and enables me to look at what is spread out right before me, and to see it with fresh eyes. It forces me because, being the last book in the Bible, I cannot finish the story apart from it. It enables me because, by using the unfamiliar language of apocalyptic vision, my imagination is called into vigorous play.

In spite of these obvious benefits and necessary renewals, there are many people who stubbornly refuse to read it, or (which is just as bad) refuse to read it on its own terms. These are the same people who suppress fairy tales because they are brutal and fill children's minds with material for nightmares, and who bowdlerize Chaucer because his book is too difficult as it stands. They avoid the demands of either imagination or intellect. If they cannot read a page with a rapid skim of an eye trained under the metronome of speed reading, they abandon the effort and slump back into passivity before cartoons and commercials.

But for people who are fed up with such bland fare, the Revelation is a gift—a work of intense imagination that pulls its reader into a world of sky battles between angels and beasts, lurid punishments and glorious salvations, kaleidoscopic vision and cosmic song. It is a world in which children are instinctively at home and in which adults, by becoming as little children, recapture an elemental involvement in the basic conflicts and struggles that permeate moral existence, and then go on to discover again the soaring adoration and primal affirmations for which God made us.

"No one's ever seen or heard anything like this,
Never so much as imagined anything like it—
What God has arranged for those who love him."

But you've *seen and heard it*
because God by his Spirit has
brought it all out into the open
before you.

1 CORINTHIANS 2:9–10

A New Way to Say It

I do not read the Revelation to get additional information about the life of faith in Christ. I have read it all before in law and prophet, in gospel and epistle. Everything in the Revelation can be found in the previous sixty-five books of the Bible. The Revelation adds nothing of substance to what we already know. The truth of the gospel is already complete, revealed in Jesus Christ. There is nothing new to say on the subject. But there is a new way to say it. I read the Revelation not to get more information but to revive my imagination.

"Are your ears awake? Listen. Listen to the Wind Words, the Spirit blowing through the churches."

REVELATION 3:22

St. John

St. John is a theologian of a particularly attractive type: all his thinking about God took place under fire: "I was on the isle, called Patmos," a prison isle. He was a man thinking on his feet, running, or on his knees, praying, the postures characteristic of our best theologians. There have been times in history when the theologians were supposed to inhabit ivory towers and devote themselves to writing impenetrable and ponderous books. But the important theologians have done their thinking and writing about God in the middle of the world, in the thick of the action: Paul urgently dictating letters from his prison cell; Athanasius *contra mundum*, five times hounded into exile by three different emperors; Augustine, pastor to people experiencing the chaotic breakup of Roman order and *civitas;* Thomas, using his mind to battle errors and heresies that, unchallenged, would have turned Europe into a spiritual and mental jungle; Calvin, tireless in developing a community of God's people out of Geneva's revolutionary rabble; Barth arbitrating labor disputes and preaching to prisoners; Bonhoeffer leading a fugitive existence in Nazi Germany; and St. John, exiled on the hard rock of Patmos prison while his friends in Christ were besieged by the terrible engines of a pagan assault. . . .

The Christian community needs theologians to keep us *thinking* about God and not just making random guesses. At the deepest levels of our lives we require a God whom we can worship with our whole mind and heart and strength. The taste for eternity can never be bred out of us by a secularizing genetics. Our existence is derived from God and destined for God. St. John stands in the front ranks of the great company of theologians who convince by their disciplined and vigorous thinking that *theos* and *logos* belong together, that we live in a creation and not a madhouse.

> *I, John, with you all the way in the trial and the Kingdom and the passion of patience in Jesus, was on the island called Patmos because of God's Word, the witness of Jesus. It was Sunday and I was in the Spirit, praying.*

REVELATION 1:9–10

The Language of Imagination

A poet uses words not to explain something, and not to describe something, but to make something. Poet *(poētēs)* means "maker." Poetry is not the language of objective explanation but the language of imagination. It makes an image of reality in such a way as to invite our participation in it. We do not have more information after we read a poem, we have more experience. It is not "an examination of what happens but an immersion in what happens." (Denise Levertov, *The Poet in the World*). If the Revelation is written by a theologian who is also a poet, we must not read it as if it were an almanac in order to find out when things are going to occur, or a chronicle of what has occurred.

It is particularly appropriate that a poet has the last word in the Bible. By the time we get to this last book, we already have a complete revelation of God before us. Everything that has to do with our salvation, with accompanying instructions on how to live a life of faith, is here in full. There is no danger that we are inadequately informed. But there is danger that through familiarity and fatigue we will not pay attention to the splendors that surround us in Moses, Isaiah, Ezekiel, Zechariah, Mark, and Paul. St. John takes the familiar words and, by arranging them in unexpected rhythms, wakes us up so that we see "the revelation of Jesus Christ" entire, as if for the first time.

> *Glory and strength to Christ, who loves us,*
> *who blood-washed our sins from our lives,*

Who made us a Kingdom, Priests for his Father,
forever—and yes, he's on his way!

REVELATION 1:5B–6

FEBRUARY 28

A Goal

When we read a novel we have an analogous experience. We begin the first chapter knowing that there is a last chapter. One of the satisfying things about just picking up a book is the sure knowledge that it will end. In the course of reading we are often puzzled, sometimes in suspense, usually wrong in our expectations, frequently mistaken in our assessment of a character. But when we don't understand or agree or feel satisfied, we don't ordinarily quit. We assume meaning and connection and design even when we don't experience it. The last chapter, we are confident, will demonstrate the meaning that was continuous through the novel. We believe that the story will satisfyingly end, not arbitrarily stop.

It is St. John's pastoral vocation to reinforce this sense of connection in the chaotic first century. In the buzzing, booming confusion of good and evil, blessing and cursing, rest and conflict, St. John discerns pattern and design. He hears rhythms. He discovers arrangement and proportion. He communicates an overpowering "sense of an ending" [Frank Kermode, *The Sense of an Ending*]. We are headed towards not merely a terminus but a goal, an end that is purposed and fulfilled. He spells out this sense of an ending in such a way that the people in the middle acquire an inner conviction of being a part of something good in God.

"Yes, I'm on my way! I'll be there soon! I'm bringing my payroll with me. I'll pay all people in full for their life's work. I'm A to Z, the First and the Final, Beginning and Conclusion."

REVELATION 22:12–13

Embalming Fluid

History is full of instances of words which, after being written, lost their voice and became nouns to be etymologized, verbs to be parsed, adjectives to be admired, adverbs to be discussed. Scripture has never been exempt from that fate. Some of Jesus' sharpest disagreements were with the scribes and Pharisees, the persons in the first century who knew the words of scripture well but heard the voice of God not at all. They had an extensive and meticulous knowledge of scripture. They revered it. They memorized it. They used it to regulate every detail of life. So why did Jesus excoriate them? Because the words were studied and not heard. For them, the scriptures had become a book to use, not a means by which to listen to God. They isolated the book from the divine act of speaking covenental commands and gospel promises. They separated the book from the human act of hearing which would become believing, following, and loving. Printer's ink became embalming fluid.

> *The plan wasn't written out with ink on paper, with pages and pages of legal footnotes, killing your spirit. It's written with Spirit on spirit, his life on our lives!*

2 CORINTHIANS 3:6

March

The Prophecy of the Revelation

A common way to misunderstand prophecy, and especially the prophecy of the Revelation, is to suppose that it means prediction. But that is not the biblical use of the word. Prophets are not fortune tellers. The prophet is the person who declares, "Thus says the Lord." He speaks what God is speaking. He brings God's word into the immediate world of the present, insisting that it be heard here and now. The prophet says that God is speaking now, not yesterday; God is speaking now, not tomorrow. It is not a past word that can be analyzed and then walked away from. It is not a future word that can be fantasized into escapist diversion. It is personal address now: "for the time is near" (Rev. 1:3, 22:10). "Near" means "at hand." Not far off in the future but immediately before us; only our unbelief, or ignorance, or timid hesitancy separate us from it. Jesus also announced the immediacy of the prophetic word when he preached "the kingdom of God is at hand" (Mark 1:15). St. John's "near" and Jesus' "at hand" are the same root word (*eggus/eggzein*). The prophetic word eliminates the distance between God's speaking and our hearing. If we make the prophetic word a predictive word we are procrastinating, putting distance between ourselves and the application of the word, putting off dealing with it until some future date.

> *"Time's up! God's kingdom is here. Change your life and*
> *believe the Message."*

MARK 1:15

MARCH 2

Re-Images

This last book of the Bible takes the entire biblical revelation and re-images it in a compelling, persuading, evangelistic vision which has brought perseverance, stamina, joy, and discipline to Christians for centuries, and continues to do so. Not everything about everything is in the scriptures, but all that God intends for us to know of his love for us and his salvation for us and our responses to him is here. The law and the prophets and the writings are set under the incarnation of God in Jesus Christ and made to work for our salvation. The incarnation works retroactively on all other scripture and reshapes it in this final vision. The Revelation does not add to what is already there, but shows how all of scripture is put to work in the church and the world. The Revelation is not, as some have assumed, a change of strategy on God's part after the original plan of salvation turned out not to work; it is the original plan itself, working powerfully, gloriously, and triumphantly.

> *. . . John told everything he saw: God's Word—the witness of Jesus Christ!*
>
> > *How blessed the reader! How blessed the hearers and keepers of these oracle words, all the words written in this book!*
> >
> > *Time is just about up.*

REVELATION 1:2–3

MARCH 3

Lived Like a Vagabond

It is difficult to recapture by an act of imagination the incongruity of a person self-designated as the Son of Man, hanging pierced and bleeding on a cross. The incongruity is less dramatic but even more offensive when the Son of Man has dinner with a prostitute, stops off for lunch with a tax-collector, wastes time blessing children when there were Roman legions to be chased from the land, heals unimportant losers and ignores high-achieving Pharisees and influential Sadducees. Jesus juxtaposed the most glorious title available to him with the most menial of life-styles in the culture. He talked like a king and acted like a slave. He preached with high authority and lived like a vagabond.

The high priests, along with the religion scholars, were right there
mixing it up with the rest of them, having a great time poking fun at
him: "He saved others—but he can't save himself! Messiah, is he?
King of Israel? Then let him climb down from that cross. We'll all
become believers then!" Even the men crucified alongside him joined
in the mockery.

MARK 15:31–32

MARCH 4

Ears to Hear

St. Matthew, St. Mark, and St. Luke agree in placing Jesus' parable
about hearing, with its staccato conclusion, "He who has ears to
hear, let him hear," as the first of the parables. If the divine word is
primary, then human hearing is essential: *that* we hear is required;
the *way* we hear is significant. The parable, with its metaphor of soil
for ears, provides an ingenious tool for a self-administered hearing
test: What is the quality of my hearing? Are my ears thick with cal-
luses, impenetrable like a heavily trafficked path? Are my ears only
superficially attentive like rocky ground in which everything germi-
nates but nothing takes root? Are my ears like an indiscriminate
weed patch in which the noisy and repetitive take up all the space
without regard for truth, quality, beauty, or fruitfulness? Or are my
ears good soil which readily receives God's word, well-tilled to welcome deep roots, to discriminately choose God's word and reject
the lies of the world, to accept high responsibility for protecting

and practicing the gift of hearing in silence, reverence, and attentiveness so that God's word will be heard, understood, and believed?

"Are you listening to this?
Really listening?"

MARK 4:9

MARCH 5

Messy Family Rooms

The churches of the Revelation show us that churches are not Victorian parlors where everything is always picked up and ready for guests. They are messy family rooms. Entering a person's house unexpectedly, we are sometimes met with a barrage of apologies. St. John does not apologize. Things are out of order, to be sure, but that is what happens to churches that are lived in. They are not show rooms. They are living rooms, and if the persons living in them are sinners, there are going to be clothes scattered about, handprints on the woodwork, and mud on the carpet. For as long as Jesus insists on calling sinners and not the righteous to repentance—and there is no indication as yet that he has changed his policy in that regard—churches are going to be an embarrassment to the fastidious and an affront to the upright. St. John sees them simply as *lampstands:* they are places, locations, where the light of Christ is shown. They are not themselves the light. There is nothing particularly glamorous about churches, nor, on the other hand, is there anything particularly shameful about them. They simply are.

"Up on your feet! Take a deep breath! Maybe there's life in you yet. But I wouldn't know it by looking at your busywork; nothing of God's work has been completed."

REVELATION 3:2

MARCH 6

Failed Expectations

Much anger towards the church and most disappointments in the church are because of failed expectations. We expect a disciplined army of committed men and women who courageously lay siege to the worldly powers; instead we find some people who are more concerned with getting rid of the crabgrass in their lawns. We expect a community of saints who are mature in the virtues of love and mercy, and find ourselves working on a church supper where there is more gossip than there are casseroles. We expect to meet minds that are informed and shaped by the great truths and rhythms of scripture, and find persons whose intellectual energy is barely sufficient to get them from the comics to the sports page. At such times it is more important to examine and change our expectations than to change the church, for the church is not what we organize but what God gives, not the people we want to be with but the people God gives us to be with—a community created by the descent of the Holy Spirit in which we submit ourselves to the Spirit's affirmation, reformation, and motivation. There must be no idealization of the church.

If you only look at us, you might well miss the brightness. We carry this precious Message around in the unadorned clay pots of our ordinary lives. That's to prevent anyone from confusing God's incomparable power with us. As it is, there's not much chance of that. You know for yourselves that we're not much to look at.

2 CORINTHIANS 4:7

MARCH 7

To the Living God

Christians worship with a conviction that they are in the presence of God. Worship is an act of attention to the living God who rules, speaks and reveals, creates and redeems, orders and blesses. Outsiders, observing these acts of worship, see nothing like that. They see a few people singing unpopular songs, sometimes off-key, someone reading from an old book and making remarks that may or may not interest the listeners, and then eating and drinking small portions of bread and wine that are supposed to give nourishment to their eternal souls in the same way that beef and potatoes sustain their mortal flesh. Who is right? Is worship an actual meeting called to order at God's initiative in which persons of faith are blessed by his presence and respond to his salvation? Or is it a pathetic, and sometimes desperate, charade in which people attempt to get God to pay attention to them and do something for them (1 Kings 18)?

> *"Look at me. I stand at the door. I knock. If you hear me call and open the door, I'll come right in and sit down to supper with you. Conquerors will sit alongside me at the head table, just as I, having conquered, took the place of honor at the side of my Father."*

REVELATION 3:20–21

MARCH 8

Failure to Worship

In worship God gathers his people to himself as center: "The Lord reigns" (Ps. 93:1). Worship is a meeting at the center so that our lives are centered in God and not lived eccentrically. We worship so that we live in response to and from this center, the living God. Failure to worship consigns us to a life of spasms and jerks, at the mercy of every advertisement, every seduction, every siren. Without worship we live manipulated and manipulating lives. We move in either frightened panic or deluded lethargy as we are, in turn, alarmed by specters and soothed by placebos. If there is no center, there is no circumference. People who do not worship are swept into a vast restlessness, epidemic in the world, with no steady direction and no sustaining purpose.

*I was caught up at once in deep worship and, oh!—a Throne set in
Heaven with One Seated on the Throne. . . .*

REVELATION 4:2

M A R C H   9

People of God Sing

There are songs everywhere in scripture. The people of God sing.
They express exuberance in realizing the majesty of God and the
mercy of Christ, the wholeness of reality and their new-found ability
to participate in it. Songs proliferate. Hymns gather the voices of
men, women, and children into century-tiered choirs. Moses sings.
Miriam sings. Deborah sings. David sings. Mary sings. Angels sing.
Jesus and his disciples sing. Paul and Silas sing. When persons of
faith become aware of who God is and what he does, they sing. The
songs are irrepressible.

> *Then I heard every creature in Heaven and earth, in underworld and
> sea, join in, all voices in all places, singing:*
>
> > *"To the One on the Throne! To the Lamb!
> > The blessing, the honor, the glory, the strength,
> > For age after age after age."*
>
> REVELATION 5:13

The Church Collects Sinners

When Christian believers gather in churches, everything that can go wrong sooner or later does. Outsiders, on observing this, conclude that there is nothing to the religion business except, perhaps, business—and dishonest business at that. Insiders see it differently. Just as a hospital collects the sick under one roof and labels them as such, the church collects sinners. Many of the people outside the hospital are every bit as sick as the ones inside, but their illnesses are either undiagnosed or disguised. It's similar with sinners outside the church.

If we claim that we're free of sin, we're only fooling ourselves. A claim like that is errant nonsense. On the other hand, if we admit our sins— make a clean breast of them—he won't let us down; he'll be true to himself. He'll forgive our sins and purge us of all wrongdoing.

1 JOHN 1:8–9

A Coherent Sense of Self

For centuries it was the pastor's defined task to "prepare people for a good death." It is still not an unworthy goal for pastoral work. The true absurdity, though, is not death itself, but the appalling lives so many people lead. When pastors help people tell the stories of their lives, we contribute to a coherent sense of self. These persons become aware that their endeavors and their lives make sense and are meaningful in the actual environments in which they live at that moment. Even in Bethlehem. Pastors who have an unsatisfied hunger for the commonplace whet a similar appetite in others and enable them to find meaning where they least expect it, discover drama behind doors in their own homes and neighborhoods, and perceive a link with salvation in their own parents and children.

> *[Herod] gathered all the high priests and religion scholars in the city together and asked, "Where is the Messiah supposed to be born?" They told him, "Bethlehem, Judah territory. The prophet Micah wrote it plainly:*
>
> > *" 'It's you, Bethlehem, in Judah's land,*
> > *no longer bringing up the rear.*
> > *From you will come the leader*
> > *who will shepherd-rule my people, my Israel.' "*
>
> MATTHEW 2:4–6

Answering Speech

Language, by its very nature, is not monologue but dialogue. God does not impose his plot of salvation on the people in his story. He speaks in order to be answered. The character of each person in the story (and we are all in it) is allowed to form from the inside, in the give and take of dialogue, each with its own rhythms, at its own pace. We are in a world of salvation in which God is speaking to us. How do we answer? We are not good at this language. The Psalms instruct, train, immerse us in the answering speech which is our part in the exchange of words by which our being in the image of God and redemption by the blood of Christ is formed internally into maturity.

> *Listen, God! Please, pay attention!*
> > *Can you make sense of these ramblings,*
> > *my groans and cries?*
> > *King-God, I need your help.*
> *Every morning*
> > *you'll hear me at it again.*
> *Every morning*
> > *I lay out the pieces of my life*
> > *on your altar*
> > *and watch for fire to descend.*

PSALM 5:1–3

MARCH 13

We Find Our Voice in the Dialogue

Prayer is everywhere and always answering speech. It is never initiating speech, and to suppose that is presumptuous. *Miqra,* the Hebrew word for Bible, properly means "calling out"—the calling out of God to us. "God must become a person," but in order for us to speak in answer to him he must make us into persons. We become ourselves as we answer, sometimes angrily disputing with him about how he rules the world, sometimes humbling ourselves before him in grateful trust. Prayer is language used to respond to the most that has been said to us, with the potential for saying all that is in us. Prayer is the development of speech into maturity, the language that is adequate to answering the one who has spoken comprehensively to us. Prayer is not a narrow use of language for speciality occasions, but language catholic, embracing the totality of everything and everyone everywhere. This conversation is both bold and devout—the utterly inferior responding to the utterly superior. In this exchange we become persons. The entire life of faith is dialogue. By means of the Psalms we find our voice in the dialogue. In prayer we do not merely speak our feelings, we speak our answers. We can answer, we are permitted to answer. If we truly answer God there is nothing that we may not say to him.

> *What can I give back to God*
> *for the blessings he's poured out on me?*
> *I'll lift high the cup of salvation—a toast to GOD!*
> *I'll pray in the name of GOD;*
> *I'll complete what I promised GOD I'd do,*
> *and I'll do it together with his people.*

PSALM 116:12–14

MARCH 14

Practice the Words and Phrases

God works with words. He uses them to make a story of salvation. He pulls us into the story. When we believe, we become willing participants in the plot. We can do this reluctantly and minimally, going through the motions; or we can do it recklessly and robustly, throwing ourselves into the relationships and actions. When we do this, we pray. We practice the words and phrases that make us fluent in the conversation that is at the center of the story. We develop the free responses that answer to the creating word of God in and around us that is making a salvation story.

Every time you cross my mind, I break out in exclamations of thanks to God. Each exclamation is a trigger to prayer. I find myself praying for you with a glad heart.

PHILIPPIANS 1:3–4

MARCH 15

Nothing Merely Happened Along

. . . Everything is created. Everything carries within its form and texture the signature of its Creator. No part of this material world is unconnected with God: every cell is in the organism of salvation. Biblical religion cannot be lived apart from matter—the seen, felt, tasted, smelled, and listened to creation.

It is all, precisely, *creation.* Nothing merely happened along. Chokecherries and tundra and weasels are not random accidents. Since everything is by design, no part of creation can be bypassed if we intend to live in the fullest possible relation to our Creator in his creation. None of it is an inconvenience that we are forced to put up with. Nothing is a stumbling block introduced by the devil to trip the feet of those whose eyes are piously lifted in praise to God. Creation is our place for meeting God and conversing with him. The voice that spoke Behemoth and Leviathan into being is the same voice that says, "your sins are forgiven you," and invites us to call upon him in the day of trouble. External and internal are the same reality. Heaven and earth are formed by a single will of God.

We take box seats in this creation theater when we pray. We look around. The mountains are huge, heaving their bulk upwards. The creeks spill across the rocks, giving extravagant light shows under the hemlocks. The lakes fill up with sky, on earth as it is in heaven. A lion rips its prey. A sparrow builds its nest. Solomon and the Shulamite embrace. An eagle plummets from a cloud to a meadow and takes a rabbit in its talons; for a few moments the two genesis creatures are in a terrible and tangled harmony. An infant drinks her fill of breakfast from her mother's breast. Matter is real. Flesh is good.

> *What a wildly wonderful world, GOD!*
> *You made it all, with Wisdom at your side,*
> *made earth overflow with your wonderful creations.*

PSALM 104:24

MARCH 16

We Don't Start It

We learn to pray by being led in prayer. We commonly think of prayer as what we do out of our own needs and on our own initiative. We experience a deep longing for God, and so we pray. We feel an artesian gush of gratitude to God, and so we pray. We are crushed with a truckload of guilt before God, and so we pray. But in a liturgy we do not take the initiative; it is not our experience that precipitates prayer. Someone stands in front of us and says, "Let us pray." We don't start it; someone else starts it and we fall into step behind or alongside. Our egos are no longer front and center.

This is so important, for prayer by its very nature is answering speech. The consensus of the entire Christian community upholds the primacy of God's word in everything: in creation, in salvation, in judgment, in blessing, in mercy, and in grace.

. . . when we take our place in a worshiping congregation we are not in charge. Someone else has built the place of prayer; someone else has established the time for prayer; someone else tells us to begin to pray. All of this takes place in a context in which the word of God is primary: God's word audible in scripture and sermon, God's word visible in baptism and eucharist. This is the center in which we learn to pray.

> *Long before we first heard of Christ and got our hopes up, he had his eye on us, had designs on us for glorious living, part of the overall purpose he is working out in everything and everyone.*

EPHESIANS 1:11–12

MARCH 17

God, Give Grace!

Generous in love—God, give grace!
  Huge in mercy—wipe out my bad record.

Scrub away my guilt,
    soak out my sins in your laundry.
I know how bad I've been;
    my sins are staring me down.

You're the One I've violated, and you've seen
    it all, seen the full extent of my evil.
You have all the facts before you;
    whatever you decide about me is fair.
I've been out of step with you for a long time,
    in the wrong since before I was born.
What you're after is truth from the inside out.
    Enter me, then; conceive a new, true life.

Soak me in your laundry and I'll come out clean,
    scrub me and I'll have a snow-white life.
Tune me into foot-tapping songs,
    set these once-broken bones to dancing.
Don't look too close for blemishes,
    give me a clean bill of health.
God, make a fresh start in me,
    shape a Genesis week from the chaos of my life.

Don't throw me out with the trash,
    or fail to breathe holiness in me.
Bring me back from gray exile,
    put a fresh wind in my sails!
Give me a job teaching rebels your ways
    so the lost can find their way home.
Commute my death sentence, God, my salvation God,
    and I'll sing anthems to your life-giving ways.

Unbutton my lips, dear God;
    I'll let loose with your praise.

Going through the motions doesn't please you,
    a flawless performance is nothing to you.
I learned God-worship
    when my pride was shattered.
Heart-shattered lives ready for love
    don't for a moment escape God's notice.

Make Zion the place you delight in,
    repair Jerusalem's broken-down walls.
Then you'll get real worship from us,
    acts of worship small and large,
Including all the bulls
    they can heave onto your altar!

PSALM 51

MARCH 18

Staying True

Great crowds of people have entered into a grand conspiracy to eliminate prayer, Scripture, and spiritual direction from our lives. They are concerned with our image and standing, with what they can measure, with what produces successful church-building programs and impressive attendance charts, with sociological impact and economic viability. They do their best to fill our schedules with meetings and appointments so that there is time for neither solitude nor leisure to be before God, to ponder Scripture, to be unhurried with another person.

We get both ecclesiastical and community support in conducting a ministry that is inattentive to God and therefore without foundations. Still, that is no excuse. A professional, by some definitions, is someone who is committed to standards of integrity and performance that cannot be altered to suit people's tastes or what they are willing to pay for. Professionalism is in decline these days on all fronts—in medicine, in law, in politics, as well as among pastors—but it has not yet been repudiated. There are still a considerable number of professionals in all areas of life who do the hard work of staying true to what they were called to do, stubbornly refusing to do the easy work that the age asks of them.

> . . . we don't take God's Word, water it down, and then take it to the streets to sell cheap. We stand in Christ's presence when we speak; God looks us in the face. We get what we say straight from God and say it as honestly as we can.

2 CORINTHIANS 2:17

MARCH 19

A Good Woodworker Knows His Woods

We set out to risk our lives in a venture of faith. We committed ourselves to a life of holiness. At some point we realized the immensity of

God and of the great invisibles that socket into our arms and legs, into bread and wine, into our brains and our tools, into mountains and rivers, giving them meaning, destiny, value, joy, beauty, salvation. We responded to a call to convey these realities in word and sacrament and to give leadership to a community of faith in such a way that connected and coordinated what the men and women, children and youth in this community are doing in their work and play with what God is doing in mercy and grace. In the process we learned the difference between a profession or craft, and a job. A job is what we do to complete an assignment. Its primary requirement is that we give satisfaction to whomever makes the assignment and pays our wage. We learn what is expected and we do it. There is nothing wrong with doing jobs. To a lesser or greater extent we all have them; somebody has to wash the dishes and take out the garbage. But professions and crafts are different. In these we have an obligation beyond pleasing somebody: we are pursuing or shaping the very nature of reality, convinced that when we carry out our commitments we actually benefit people at a far deeper level than if we simply did what they asked of us. In crafts we are dealing with the visible realities, in professions with invisible. The craft of woodworker, for instance, has an obligation to the wood itself, its grain and texture. A good woodworker knows his woods and treats them with respect. Far more is involved than pleasing customers; something like integrity of material is involved. With professions the integrity has to do with the invisibles: for physicians it is health (not merely making people feel good); with lawyers, justice (not helping people get their own way); with professors, learning (not cramming cranial cavities with information on tap for examinations). And with pastors it is God (not relieving anxiety, or giving comfort, or running a religious establishment).

Teach believers with your life; by word, by demeanor, by love, by faith, by integrity. Stay at your post reading Scripture, giving counsel, teaching.

1 TIMOTHY 4:12B–13

MARCH 20

A Trained Attentiveness to God

What are the actual means by which I carry out this pastoral vocation, this ordained ministry, this professional commitment to God's word and God's grace in my life and the lives of the people to whom I preach and give the sacraments, among whom I command a life for others in the name of Jesus Christ? What connects these great realities of God and the great realities of salvation to the geography of this parish and in the chronology of this week? The answer among the masters whom I consult doesn't change: a trained attentiveness to God in prayer, in Scripture reading, in spiritual direction. This has not been tried and discarded because it didn't work, but tried and found difficult (and more than a little bit tedious) and so shelved in favor of something or other that could be fit into a busy pastor's schedule.

I deliberately kept it plain and simple: first Jesus and who he is; then Jesus and what he did—Jesus crucified.

1 CORINTHIANS 2:2

Prayer Is Dangerous

Knowing all this—that prayer is dangerous, that it moves our language into potencies we are unaccustomed to and unprepared for—it continually puzzles me that so much prayer sounds so limp, that prayer is often so utterly banal. The limpness and banality may be no more common in pastors than in laypeople, but they are more conspicuous in pastors, who are more often on public display.

Question: How does it happen that language used at the height of its powers comes out of pastoral mouths stagnant and stale?

Answer: It has been uprooted from the soil of the word of God. These so-called prayers are cut-flower words, arranged in little vases for table decorations. As long as they are artificially provided for with a container of water, they give a touch of beauty. But not for long: soon they drop and are discarded. Such flowers are often used as the centerpiece for a dinner table. They are lovely in these settings. But they are never mistaken for the real business of the table, the beef and potatoes that promise full bellies and calories for a hard day's work.

Every part of Scripture is God-breathed and useful one way or another—showing us truth, exposing our rebellion, correcting our mistakes, training us to live God's way. Through the Word we are put together and shaped for the tasks God has for us.

2 TIMOTHY 3:16–17

Prayer Enters the Lion's Den

One of the indignities to which pastors are routinely subjected is to be approached, as a group of people are gathering for a meeting or a meal with the request, "Reverend, get things started for us with a little prayer, will ya?" It would be wonderful if we would counter by bellowing William McNamara's fantasized response: "I will not! There are no *little* prayers! Prayer enters the lion's den, brings us before the holy where it is uncertain whether we will come back alive or sane, for 'it is a fearful thing to fall into the hands of a living God.'"

"Don't be flip with the sacred. Banter and silliness give no honor to God. Don't reduce holy mysteries to slogans. In trying to be relevant, you're only being cute and inviting sacrilege."

MATTHEW 7:7

Praying the Psalms

. . . St. Pius X said: "The Psalms teach mankind, especially those vowed to a life of worship, how God is to be praised." Too much is at stake here—the maturity of the word of God, the integrity of pastoral ministry, the health of worship—to permit pastors to pick and choose a curriculum of prayer as they are more or less inclined. We can as well permit a physician to concoct his medicines from the herbs and weeds in his backyard as allow a pastor to learn prayer from his or her own subjectivities. Prayer must not be fabricated out of emotional fragments or professional duties. Uninstructed and untrained, our prayers are something learned by tourists out of a foreign language phrase book: we give thanks at meals, repent of the grosser sins, bless the Rotary picnic, and ask for occasional guidance. Did we think prayer was merely a specialized and incidental language to get by on during those moments when we happened to pass through a few miles of religious country? But our entire lives are involved. We need fluency in the language of the country we live in. It is not enough merely to take notes on it for putting together the weekly report, which is a requirement of our job. We are required to be graduate students in this comprehensive grammar that provides all the parts of speech and complexities of syntax for "answering speech." Praying the Psalms, we find the fragments of soul and body, our own and all those with whom we have to do, spoken into adoration and love and faith. The Psalms, of course, are no special preserve of pastors. All who pray, Christians and Jews alike, find their praying "voice" in them—but for pastors, who are in a special place of responsibility to pray for others and to teach them to pray, it is a dereliction of duty to be ignorant or negligent in them. St. Ambrose, using a different metaphor, called the Psalms "a sort of gymnasium for the use of all souls, a sort of stadium of virtue, where different sorts of exercise are set out before him, from which he can choose the best suited to train him to win his crown."

. . . you thrill to GOD's Word,
you chew on Scripture day and night.

PSALM 1:2

MARCH 24

The Rhythms of Grace

The Hebrew evening/morning sequence conditions us to the rhythms of grace. We go to sleep, and God begins his work. As we sleep he develops his covenant. We wake and are called out to participate in God's creative action. We respond in faith, in work. But always grace is previous. Grace is primary. We wake into a world we didn't make, into a salvation we didn't earn. Evening: God begins, without our help, his creative day. Morning: God calls us to enjoy and share and develop the work he initiated. Creation and covenant are sheer grace and there to greet us every morning. George MacDonald once wrote that sleep is God's contrivance for giving us the help he cannot get into us when we are awake.

It's useless to rise early and go to bed late,
and work your worried fingers to the bone.
Don't you know he enjoys
giving rest to those he loves?

PSALM 127:2

Sabbath-Keeping

Keeping the weekly rhythm requires deliberate action. Sabbath-keeping often feels like an interruption, an interference with our routines. It challenges assumptions we gradually build up that our daily work is indispensable in making the world go. And then we find that it is not an interruption but a more spacious rhythmic measure that confirms and extends the basic beat. Every seventh day a deeper note is struck—an enormous gong whose deep sounds reverberate under and over and around the daily timpani percussions of evening/morning, evening/morning, evening/morning: creation honored and contemplated, redemption remembered and shared.

In the two biblical versions of the sabbath commandment, the commands are identical but the supporting reasons differ. The Exodus reason is that we are to keep a sabbath because God kept it (Exod. 20:8–11). God did his work in six days and then rested. If God sets apart one day to rest, we can too. There are some things that can be accomplished, even by God, only in a state of rest. The work/rest rhythm is built into the very structure of God's interpenetration of reality. The precedent to quit doing and simply *be* is divine. Sabbath-keeping is commanded so that we internalize the being that matures out of doing.

The Deuteronomy reason for Sabbath-keeping is that our ancestors in Egypt went four hundred years without a vacation (Deut. 5:15). Never a day off. The consequence: they were no longer considered persons but slaves. Hands. Work units. Not persons created in the image of God but equipment for making bricks and building pyramids. Humanity was defaced.

Lest any of us do that to our neighbor or husband or wife or child or employee, we are commanded to keep a sabbath.

The promise of "arrival" and "rest" is still there for God's people. God himself is at rest. And at the end of the journey we'll surely rest with God.

HEBREWS 4:9

MARCH 26

Hearing God Speak

The Christian's interest in Scripture has always been in hearing God speak, not in analyzing moral memos.

"The words that I speak to you [said Jesus] aren't mere words. I don't just make them up on my own. The Father who resides in me crafts each word into a divine act."

JOHN 14:10B

MARCH 27

Audio Junk

Imagine a human head with no ears. A blockhead. Eyes, nose, and mouth, but no ears. Where ears are usually found there is only a smooth, impenetrable surface, granitic bone. God speaks. No response. The metaphor occurs in the context of a bustling religious activity deaf to the voice of God: "sacrifice and offering thou dost not desire . . . burnt offering and sin offering" ([Ps.] 40:6). How did these people know about these offerings and how to make them? They had *read* the prescriptions in Exodus and Leviticus and followed instructions. They had become religious. Their eyes read the words on the Torah page and rituals were formed. They had read the Scripture words accurately and gotten the ritual right. How did it happen that they had missed the message "not required"? There must be something more involved than following directions for unblemished animals, a stone altar, and a sacrificial fire. There is: God is speaking and must be listened to. But what good is a speaking God without listening human ears? So God gets a pick and shovel and digs through the cranial granite, opening a passage that will give access to the interior depths, into the mind and heart. Or—maybe we are not to imagine a smooth expanse of skull but something like wells that have been stopped up with refuse: culture noise, throw-away gossip, garbage chatter. Our ears are so clogged that we cannot hear God speak. God, like Isaac who dug again the wells that the Philistines had filled, redigs the ears trashed with audio junk.

> *Being religious, acting pious—*
> *that's not what you're asking for.*
> *You've opened my ears*
> *so I can listen.*

PSALM 40:6

Illegal Distilleries

The great attraction for distilling Scripture into truths and morals and lessons is simply laziness. The lazy pastor no longer has to bother with the names, the cities, the odd embarrassing details and awkward miracles that refuse to fit into a modern understanding of the good life. Across this land pastors have turned their studies into "stills," illegal distilleries that extract ideas and morals from the teeming narrative of Scripture. People, of course, love it. They come to get their Mason jar lives filled with pure truth so that they won't have to deal with either the details of Scripture or the details of their own lives. Drinking this pure white lightning bypasses the laborious trouble of hoeing the garden, digging potatoes, preparing and cooking meals, eating and digesting. This distilled liquid goes directly to the bloodstream and gives a quick rush of exhilaration. But it is, in fact, poison. We are not constructed biologically or spiritually for ingestion of this 100-proof stuff. We have mental-emotional digestive systems with complicated interconnections that notice and savor an enormous variety of words and sentences, stories and songs, ruminatingly take them in and assimilate all the vitamins, enzymes, and calories that give us healthy lives.

With many stories like these, [Jesus] presented his message to them, fitting the stories to their experience and maturity. He was never without a story when he spoke.

MARK 4:33

Poured Out Like Water

I am poured out like water,
and all my bones are out of joint;
my heart is like wax;
it is melted within my breast.

PSALM 22:14

Jesus on the cross experienced just such hostility and pain. Each cruel detail was etched into the body of our Lord. Crucifixion, however, produced resurrection. The worst that men could do became the occasion for the unbelievable best that God can do.

PRAYER: On the cross, Lord Jesus, you gathered all the hostility and suffering of the world (all my hostility and suffering) and made of it a mighty act of salvation and deliverance. Praise your great name! *Amen.*

What we believe is this: If we get
included in Christ's sin-conquering
death, we also get included in his
life-saving resurrection.

ROMANS 6:8

Reading Scripture

If the Revelation is masterful in getting us involved in a living response to scripture, it is also unavoidable in its claim that scripture is God's word to us, not human words about God. Reading scripture as if it were the writings of various persons throughout history giving their ideas or experiences of God, is perhaps the commonest mistake that is made in reading scripture. And the deadliest.

God means what he says. What he says goes. His powerful Word is sharp as a surgeon's scalpel, cutting through everything, whether doubt or defense, laying us open to listen and obey.

HEBREWS 4:12

"Asking on Their Behalf"

READ John 17:9–11

"I am asking on their behalf; I am not asking on behalf of the world, but on behalf of those whom you gave me, because they are yours.

All mine are yours, and yours are mine; and I have been glorified in them" (John 17:9–10).

Jesus' ministry with us is not finished when he speaks God's word and demonstrates God's presence. He continues to guide and shape our lives by his prayers of intercession on our behalf.

How do Jesus' prayers affect you?

PRAYER: What a difference it makes as I pray, Father, to know that Jesus is praying for me; that my prayers to you are surrounded by his prayers for me. That makes me want to pray more than ever in the name of Jesus. *Amen.*

I pray for them.
I'm not praying for the God-rejecting world
But for those you gave me,
For they are yours by right.

JOHN 17:9

April

The Words of Jesus

The words of Jesus are not pious embroidery for religious pillows. The ministry of Jesus is radical and it is ultimate: it crashes the boundaries of death and summons all to a resurrection.

PRAYER: I hear thunder in your speech, O God; I see lightning in your acts. Storm through this soul of mine; wake the sleeping parts of me; raise the dead parts of me; stand me on my feet, alert and praising in your presence. *Amen.*

> *"It's urgent that you get this right: The time has arrived—I mean right now!—when dead men and women will hear the voice of the Son of God and, hearing, will come alive."*

JOHN 5:25

Spiritual Direction

Spiritual direction is no prerogative of the ordained ministry. Some of the best spiritual directors are simply friends. Some of the most famous spiritual directors have been laypersons. But the fact that anybody can do it and it can occur at any time and place must not be construed to mean that it can be done casually or indifferently. It needs to be practiced out of a life immersed in the pursuit of holiness.

What is required is that we bring the same disciplined prayer and discerning attentiveness into the commonplaces that we bring to the preparation of lectures and sermons, sharing crises of illness and death, celebrating births and marriages, launching campaigns and stirring up visions. It means putting the full spotlight of prayerful concern on the parts of life that get no other spotlights put on them. Being a spiritual director is bringing the same care and skill and intensity to the ordinary, boring, uneventful parts of our lives that we readily give to the eventful conversions and proclamations.

*Stay on good terms with each other, held together
by love. Be ready with a meal or a bed when it's needed.
Why, some have extended hospitality to angels
without ever knowing it!*

HEBREWS 13:1–2

Dissatisfaction *in* Being

The suggestion to *do* something is nearly always inappropriate, for persons who come for spiritual direction are troubled over some disorder or dissatisfaction in *being*, not *doing*. They need a friend who will pay attention to who they are, not a project manager who will order additional busywork. Precipitate actions are usually avoidances. They distract for the time being and provide temporary (and welcome) relief. The attraction for "giving a physic and letting blood" [George Fox, *Journal*] is nearly irresistible in a highly ambiguous situation. The sense of definition provided by clear-cut action provides tremendous satisfaction. But there is no growth in the spirit, no development into maturity.

Pastors are particularly imperiled in this area because of the compulsive activism, both cultural and ecclesiastical, in which we are immersed simply by being alive at this time in history. It takes wary and persistent watching to avoid falling into the activist trap.

> *[Jesus said,] "Are you tired? Worn out? Burned out on religion? Come to me. Get away with me and you'll recover your life. I'll show you how to take a real rest. Walk with me and work with me—watch how I do it. Learn the unforced rhythms of grace."*
>
> MATTHEW 11:28–29

They Want God

It is God with whom we have to do. People go for long stretches of time without being aware of that, thinking it is money, or sex, or work, or children, or parents, or a political cause, or an athletic competition, or learning with which they must deal. Any one or a combination of these subjects can absorb them and for a time give them the meaning and purpose that human beings seem to require. But then there is a slow stretch of boredom. Or a disaster. Or a sudden collapse of meaning. They want more. They want God. When a person searches for meaning and direction, asking questions and testing out statements, we must not be diverted into anything other or lesser.

> *"Steep yourself in God-reality, God-initiative, God-provisions. Don't worry about missing out. You'll find all your everyday human concerns will be met."*

MATTHEW 6:33

Light

Much of life is spent in darkness, whether literal or metaphorical. No one seems completely at home in the dark, even though most of us learn to accustom ourselves to it. We invent devices to make the dark less threatening—a candle, a fire, a flashlight, a lamp. In the darkness we are liable to lose perspective and proportion: nightmares terrorize us, fears paralyze us. In the darkness our imaginations fashion specters. Sounds are ominous. Movements are ghostly. A light that shines in the darkness shows us that the terror and the chaos have no objective reality to them. "The light shines in the darkness, and the darkness has not overcome it" (John 1:5). Light reveals order and beauty. Or, if there is something to be feared, the light shows the evil in proportionate relationship to all that is not to be feared.

We do not live in darkness, but in light. We are not cursed; we are blessed. Light, not darkness, is the fundamental reality in which we live. And God is light. Biblical writers, pondering the qualities of light, found in their meditations truth upon truth about God. It is Christ's most comprehensive work to reveal it.

Jesus once again addressed them: "I am the world's Light. No one who follows me stumbles around in the darkness. I provide plenty of light to live in."

JOHN 8:12

APRIL 6

Everyday Data

The everyday data of a typical week are assembled on the pages of the Revelation: political terrors and liturgical mysteries, painful separations and unanswered prayers, glorious hymns and unfulfilled prophecies, felt glories and brutal cruelties, heartrending deaths and unquenchable hopes. All this is the experience of persons who decide to live by faith in Christ. St. John's Revelation choreographs all this in a ballet of images. The repeated use of the number seven, a number that communicated a sense of wholeness to the ancient and biblical mind, sets up cadences of wholeness in the imagination. "Lord's Day" is the first day of resurrection in which the fallen creation enters a new week of redemption.

The pagan world assigned each day of the week to the care of a god or goddess. Each divinity made its own capricious demands and dispensed good or ill arbitrarily. The pagan deities were at odds with each other, bickering and quarreling. The week was a hodgepodge of scheming and intrigue. The Christian, in contrast, discovered all time under the lordship of Christ. Time is redeemed. God shapes creation; Christ redeems creation. The first day is the headwaters of the ever rolling stream of time. The Lord's Day is the source for the succeeding days. All the events and experiences of the week flow out of the archetypal patterns of creation and redemption.

All the best to you from THE GOD WHO IS, THE GOD WHO WAS, AND THE GOD ABOUT TO ARRIVE, and from the Seven Spirits assembled before his throne, and from Jesus Christ—Loyal Witness, Firstborn from the dead, Ruler of all earthly kings.

REVELATION 1:4–5A

God Listens

Silence in heaven for about half an hour (Rev. 8:1): God listens. Everything we say, every groan, every murmur, every stammering attempt at prayer: all this is listened to. All heaven quiets down. The loud angel voices, the piercing trumpet messages, the thundering throne songs are stilled while God listens. "Hush, hush, whisper who dares? Christopher Robin is saying his prayers." The prayers of the faithful must be heard: the spontaneous hallelujahs, the solemn amens, the desperate "Why hast thou forsaken me?" the agonized "Take this cup from me," the tempered "Nevertheless not my will but your will," the faithfully spoken "Our Father who art in heaven," the joyful "Worthy art thou, our Lord and God, to receive glory and honor and power, for thou didst create all things, and by thy will they existed and were created." All the psalms, said and sung for centuries in voices boisterous, subdued, angry, and serene are now heard—heard personally, carefully, accurately. God silences the elders and the angels. Not one of our words is lost in a wind tunnel of gossip or drowned in a cataract of the world's noise. "The distinctive feature of early Christian prayer is the certainty of being heard" [Heinrich Greeven]. We are listened to. We realize dignity. Dramatic changes take place in these moments of silence. The world rights itself. We perceive reality from the vantage point of God's saving work and not from the morass of desperate muddle. We acquire hope.

We don't have a priest who is out of touch with our reality. He's been through weakness and testing, experienced it all—all but the sin. So let's walk right up to him and get what he is so ready to give. Take the mercy, accept the help.

HEBREWS 4:15–16

APRIL 8

Immersed in God's Yes

The end result of the act of worship is that our lives are turned around. We come to God with a history of nay-saying, of rejecting and being rejected. At the throne of God we are immersed in God's yes, a yes that silences all our noes and calls forth an answering yes in us. God, not the ego, is the center. God is not someone around whom we make calculating qualifications, a little yes here, a little no there. In worship we "listen to the voice of Being" and become answers to it. The self is no longer the hub of reality, as sin seduces us into supposing. We are trained from infancy to relate to the world in an exploratory, exploitive way, refusing and grabbing, pushing and pulling, fretting and inveigling. As knower and user the ego is a predator. But in worship we cease being predators who by stealth approach everyone as prey that we can pull into our center; we respond to *the* center. We are privileged listeners and respondents who *offer* ourselves to God, who creates and redeems. Amen! Amen is recurrent and emphatic among God's people. It is robust and exuberant. There is nothing cowering, cautious, or timid in it. It is an answering word, purged of all negatives.

Whatever God has promised gets stamped with the Yes
of Jesus. In him, this is what we preach and pray,
the great Amen, God's Yes and our Yes together, gloriously
evident. God affirms us, making us a sure thing in
Christ, putting his Yes within us.

2 CORINTHIANS 1:20–21

APRIL 9

Too Much Religion

It seems odd to have to say so, but too much religion is a bad thing. We can't get too much of God, can't get too much faith and obedience, can't get too much love and worship. But *religion*—the well-intentioned efforts we make to "get it all together" for God—can very well get in the way of what God is doing for us. The main and central action is everywhere and always what God has done, is doing, and will do for us. Jesus is the revelation of that action. Our main and central task is to live in responsive obedience to God's action revealed in Jesus. Our part in the action is the act of faith.

But more often than not we become impatiently self-important along the way and decide to improve matters with our two cents worth. We add on, we supplement, we embellish. But instead of improving on the purity and simplicity of Jesus, we dilute the purity, clutter the simplicity. We become fussily religious, or anxiously religious. We get in the way.

That's when it's time to read and pray our way through the letter to the Hebrews again, written for "too religious" Christians, for "Jesus-and" Christians. In the letter, it is Jesus-and-angels, or Jesus-and-Moses, or Jesus-and-priesthood. In our time it is more likely to be Jesus-and-politics, or Jesus-and-education, or even Jesus-and-Buddha. This letter deletes the hyphens, the add-ons. The focus becomes clear and sharp again: God's action in Jesus. And we are free once more for the act of faith, the one human action in which we don't get in the way but on the Way.

"You don't make your words true by embellishing them with religious lace. In making your speech sound more religious, it becomes less true. Just say 'yes' and 'no.'"

MATTHEW 5:36–37

APRIL 10

Square One

The first few months of our lives are spent in getting things ready, getting our basic needs met so that we *can* journey. Many of you have had an analogous experience in, say, going for a backpacking trip into the mountains. You spend days getting things ready, laying out the proper clothing, measuring out quantities of food, making sure the tent is waterproofed, checking the first aid kit for essentials. And then you are at the trailhead. Up to this point nearly everything has been under your control; after this point almost nothing is under your control—most of what you are dealing with now is invisible, uncertain, unpredictable—changes in the weather, the appearance and behavior of wild animals, your own physical endurance and the mood of your hiking companions. You have arrived at Square One.

Up to Square One, you live by sight; after Square One you live by faith. Basic biology now gives way to basic spirituality. No longer confined by sense, feelings, and immediacy, we are launched into exploration and participation in the immense world of memory, anticipation, waiting, trust, belief, sacrifice, love loyalty, faithfulness— none of which can be reduced to what you can see and handle. None of these things that go into making up what is distinctively and characteristically human in us can be possessed—they all must be entered into. Most of what *is*, is not where we can touch it, put it in our mouths, be wrapped in its warm comfort. Square One is the place from which we begin learning how to live with Absence with the same ease with which we have come to live with Presence. The generic word that we use for this is Faith—in its classic and never yet improved upon definition, "the substance of things hoped for, the evidence of things not seen" (Heb. 11:1).

The fundamental fact of existence is that this trust in
God, this faith, is the firm foundation under everything
that makes life worth living. It's our handle on what
we can't see. The act of faith is what distinguished our
ancestors, set them above the crowd.

HEBREWS 11:1–2

Narcissism or Prometheanism

When we first arrive at Square One, we are breathless before the unguessed splendors of infinity, stretching out endlessly. That is wonderful. And then we begin to realize the corollary, if there is such a thing as infinity, I am not it. I am finite. If there is God then there is no room for me as god.

The virtually unanimous response to this realization is some form or other of either narcissism or Prometheanism. Narcissism is the attempt to retreat from Square One back into the spiritual sovereignty of self. Forget infinity. Forget mystery. Cultivate the wonderful self. It might be a small world, but it is my world, totally mine.

Prometheanism is the attempt to detour around Square One into the spirituality of infinity, get a handle on it, get control of it, and make something of it. All that spirituality sitting around idle, needs managing. Prometheanism is practical. Prometheanism is entrepreneurial. Prometheanism is energetic and ambitious. Prometheanism wants to put all that power and beauty to good use. Most of us, most of the time, can be found to be practicing some variation on narcissism or Prometheanism. It goes without saying then that most spirituality is a combination of narcissism and Prometheanism, with the proportions carefully customized to suit our personal temperaments and circumstances.

And that is why I use the word "return"—it's *back* to Square One, back to the place of wonder, the realization of infinity, the worship of God.

The primary way in which we counter our stubborn propensities to narcissism and Prometheanism is by cultivating humility. Learning to be just ourselves, keeping close to the ground, practicing the *human*, getting our fingers in the *humus*, the rich, loamy, garden dirt out of which we have been fashioned.

And then listen.

The only accurate way to understand ourselves is by what God is and by what he does for us, not by what we are and what we do for him.

ROMANS 12:3B

APRIL 12

Listening to God

Christian spirituality is not impressed with the supernatural. Supernatural is neither here nor there for those of us who are standing at Square One, getting ourselves oriented, coming to terms with our human finitude, getting a glimpse of God's infinitude.

We are immersed in a world of Spirit, and so why wouldn't we have spiritual experience? But such experience does not confer authority upon *our* counsel or *our* character. The return to Square One is not only a return to God, but to God *Said*. For not only is there God, there is God's Word.

Christian spirituality does not begin with us talking about our experience; it begins with listening to God call us, heal us, forgive us.

This is hard to get into our heads. We talk habitually to ourselves and about ourselves. We don't listen. If we do listen to each other it is almost always with the purpose of getting something we can use in our turn. Much of our listening is a form of politeness, courteously waiting our turn to talk about ourselves. But in relation to God especially we must break the habit and let him speak to us. God not only is; God *says*.

Christian spirituality, in addition to being an attentive spirituality, is a listening spirituality.

[Jesus said,] "I can see it now—at the Final Judgment thousands strutting up to me and saying, 'Master, we preached the Message, we bashed the demons, our God-sponsored projects had everyone talking.' And do you know what I am going to say? 'You missed the boat. All you did was use me to make yourselves important.'"

MATTHEW 7:22–23A

APRIL 13

Simplify

I want to simplify your lives. When others are telling you to read more, I want to tell you to read less; when others are telling you to do more, I want to tell you to do less. The world does not need more of you; it needs more of God. Your friends do not need more of you; they need more of God. And you don't need more of you; you need more of God. For we do not progress in the Christian life by becoming more competent, more knowledgeable, more virtuous, or more energetic. We do not advance in the Christian life by acquiring expertise. Each day, and many times each day, we need more of God. Back to Square One.

The world and all its wanting, wanting, wanting is on the way out—but whoever does what God wants is set for eternity.

1 JOHN 2:17

APRIL 14

The Christian Life

. . . The Christian Life consists in what God does for us, not what we do for God; the Christian Life consists in what God says to us, not what we say about God. We also, of course, do things and say things; but if we do not return to Square One each time we act, each time we speak, beginning from God and God's Word, we will soon be found to be practicing a spirituality that has little or nothing to do with God. And so it is necessary, if we are going to truly live a Christian life, and not just use the word Christian to disguise our narcissistic and Prometheus attempts at a spirituality without worshipping God and without being addressed by God, it is necessary to return to Square One and adore God and listen to God. Given our sin-damaged memories that render us vulnerable to every latest edition of journalistic spirituality, daily re-orientation in the truth revealed in Jesus and attested in Scripture is required. And given our ancient predisposition for reducing every scrap of divine revelation that we come across into a piece of moral/spiritual technology that we can use to get on in the world, and eventually to get on without God, a daily return to a condition of not-knowing and non-achievement is required. We have proven, time and again, that we are not to be trusted in these matters. We need to return to Square One for a fresh start as often as every morning, noon, and night.

> *Saving is all his idea, and all his work. All we do is trust him enough to let him do it. It's God's gift from start to finish! We don't play the major role. If we did, we'd probably go around bragging that we'd done the whole thing!*

EPHESIANS 2:8–9

APRIL 15

An Odd Phenomenon

The following thirteen days are meditations on the life of Jeremiah and living well.

The puzzle is why so many people live so badly. Not so wickedly, but so inanely. Not so cruelly, but so stupidly. There is little to admire and less to imitate in the people who are prominent in our culture. We have celebrities but not saints. Famous entertainers amuse a nation of bored insomniacs. Infamous criminals act out the aggressions of timid conformists. Petulant and spoiled athletes play games vicariously for lazy and apathetic spectators. People, aimless and bored, amuse themselves with trivia and trash. Neither the adventure of goodness nor the pursuit of righteousness gets headlines. . . .

This condition has produced an odd phenomenon: individuals who live trivial lives and then engage in evil acts in order to establish significance for themselves. Assassins and hijackers attempt the gigantic leap from obscurity to fame by killing a prominent person or endangering the lives of an airplane full of passengers. Often they are successful. The mass media report their words and display their actions. Writers vie with one another in analyzing their motives and providing psychological profiles on them. No other culture has been as eager to reward either nonsense or wickedness.

> *[Jesus said,] "If anyone thirsts, let him come to me*
> *and drink. Rivers of living water will brim and*
> *spill out of the depths of anyone who believes in me*
> *this way, just as the Scripture says."*

JOHN 7:37B–38

APRIL 16

Fashioned from the Same Clay

All the same, we continue to have an unquenchable thirst for wholeness, a hunger for righteousness. When we get thoroughly disgusted with the shams and cretins that are served up to us daily as celebrities, some of us turn to Scripture to satisfy our need for someone to look up to. What does it mean to be a real man, a real woman? What shape does mature, authentic humanity take in everyday life?

When we do turn to Scripture for help in this matter we are apt to be surprised. One of the first things that strikes us about the men and women in Scripture is that they were disappointingly nonheroic. We do not find splendid moral examples. We do not find impeccably virtuous models. That always comes as a shock to newcomers to Scripture: Abraham lied; Jacob cheated; Moses murdered and complained; David committed adultery; Peter blasphemed.

We read on and begin to suspect intention: a consistent strategy to demonstrate that the great, significant figures in the life of faith were fashioned from the same clay as the rest of us. We find that Scripture is sparing in the information that it gives on people while it is lavish in what it tells us about God. It refuses to feed our lust for hero worship. It will not pander to our adolescent desire to join a fan club. The reason is, I think, clear enough. Fan clubs encourage secondhand living. Through pictures and memorabilia, autographs and tourist visits, we associate with someone whose life is (we think) more exciting and glamorous than our own. We find diversion from our own humdrum existence by riding on the coattails of someone exotic.

> . . . *when I heard and saw, I fell on my face to worship*
> *at the feet of the Angel who laid it all out before me. He*
> *objected, "No you don't! I'm a servant just like you*
> *and your companions, the prophets, and all who keep*
> *the words of this book. Worship God!"*

REVELATION 22:8B–9

God's Creative Genius

Scripture, however, doesn't play that game [hero worship]. Something very different takes place in the life of faith: each person discovers all the elements of a unique and original adventure. We are prevented from following in another's footsteps and are called to an incomparable association with Christ. The Bible makes it clear that every time that there is a story of faith, it is completely original. God's creative genius is endless. He never, fatigued and unable to maintain the rigors of creativity, resorts to mass-producing copies. Each life is a fresh canvas on which he uses lines and colors, shades and lights, textures and proportions that he has never used before.

"I'll give the sacred manna to every conqueror; I'll also give a clear, smooth stone inscribed with your new name, your secret new name."

REVELATION 2:17B

Jeremiah

It is enormously difficult to portray goodness in an attractive way; it is much easier to make a scoundrel interesting. All of us have so much more experience in sin than in goodness that a writer has far more imaginative material to work with in presenting a bad character than a good person. In novels and poems and plays most of the memorable figures are either villains or victims. Good people, virtuous lives, mostly seem a bit dull. Jeremiah is a stunning exception. For most of my adult life he has attracted me. The complexity and intensity of his person caught and kept my attention. The captivating quality in the man is his goodness, his virtue, his excellence. He lived at his best. His was not a hot-house piety, for he lived through crushing storms of hostility and furies of bitter doubt. There is not a trace of smugness or complacency or naiveté in Jeremiah—every muscle in his body was stretched to the limits by fatigue, every thought in his mind subjected to rejection, every feeling in his heart put through fires of ridicule. Goodness in Jeremiah was not "being nice." It was something more like *prowess*.

[Jesus said,] "I came so they can have real and eternal life, more and better life than they ever dreamed of."

JOHN 10:10B

APRIL 19

Take Counteraction

We live in a society that tries to diminish us to the level of the ant heap so that we scurry mindlessly, getting and consuming. It is essential to take counteraction. Jeremiah is counteraction: a well-developed human being, mature and robust, living by faith.

> *[Jesus said,] "Let me tell you why you are here. You're here to be salt-seasoning that brings out the God-flavors of this earth. If you lose your saltiness, how will people taste godliness?"*

MATTHEW 5:13A

APRIL 20

Excellence

In Jeremiah it is clear that the excellence comes from a life of faith, from being more interested in God than in self, and has almost nothing to do with comfort or esteem or achievement. Here is a person who has lived life to the hilt, but there is not a hint of human pride or worldly success or personal achievement in the story. Jeremiah arouses my passion for a full life.

> *[Jesus said,] "Keep open house; be generous with your lives. By opening up to others, you'll prompt people to open up with God, this generous Father in heaven."*

MATTHEW 5:16

Personal Names

Any time that we move from personal names to abstract labels or graphs or statistics, we are less in touch with reality and diminished in our capacity to deal with what is best and at the center of life. Yet we are encouraged on every side to do just that. In many areas of life the accurate transmission of our social-security number is more important than the integrity with which we live. In many sectors of the economy the title that we hold is more important than our ability to do certain work. In many situations the public image that people have of us is more important than the personal relations that we develop with them. Every time that we go along with this movement from the personal to the impersonal, from the immediate to the remote, from the concrete to the abstract, we are diminished, we are less. Resistance is required if we will retain our humanity.

[Jesus said,] "The shepherd walks right up to the gate. The gatekeeper opens the gate to him and the sheep recognize his voice. He calls his own sheep by name and leads them out."

JOHN 10:2–3

Life in Our Times

Yoknapatawpha County, Mississippi, is the region created by novelist William Faulkner to show the spiritual and moral condition of life in our times. An examination of the men and women who live there is a powerful incentive to the imagination to realize both the comic and the tragic aspects of what is going on among us as we make it (or don't make it) through life. One of the children is named Montgomery Ward. Montgomery Ward Snopes [William Faulkner, *The Town*]. It is the perfect name for the child being trained to be a successful consumer. If you want your child to grow up getting and spending, using available leisure in the shopping malls, proving virility by getting things, that is the right name: Montgomery Ward Snopes, patron saint of the person for whom the ritual of shopping is the new worship, the department store the new cathedral, and the advertising page the infallible Scripture.

[Jesus said,] "There is far more to your life than the food you put in your stomach, more to your outer appearance than the clothes you hang on your body. Look at the birds, free and unfettered, not tied down to a job description, careless in the care of God. And you count far more to him than birds."

MATTHEW 6:25B–26

APRIL 23

The Reality of Our Lives

Before Jeremiah knew God, God knew Jeremiah: "Before I formed you in the womb I knew you." This turns everything we ever thought about God around. We think that God is an object about which we have questions. We are curious about God. We make inquiries about

God. We read books about God. We get into late night bull sessions about God. We drop into church from time to time to see what is going on with God. We indulge in an occasional sunset or symphony to cultivate a feeling of reverence for God.

But that is not the reality of our lives with God. Long before we ever got around to asking questions about God, God has been questioning us. Long before we got interested in the subject of God, God subjected us to the most intensive and searching knowledge. Before it ever crossed our minds that God might be important, God singled us out as important. Before we were formed in the womb, God knew us. We are known before we know.

> *Like an open book, you watched me grow from conception to birth;*
> *all the stages of my life were spread out before you,*
> *The days of my life all prepared*
> *before I'd even lived one day.*

PSALM 139:16

APRIL 24

What Is God Doing?

What is God doing? He is saving; he is rescuing; he is blessing; he is providing; he is judging; he is healing; he is enlightening. There is a spiritual war in progress, an all-out moral battle. There is evil and cruelty, unhappiness and illness. There is superstition and ignorance, brutality and pain. God is in continuous and energetic battle against all of it. God is for life and against death. God is for love and against hate. God is for hope and against despair. God is for heaven and against hell. There is no neutral ground in the universe. Every square foot of space is contested.

Jeremiah, before he was born, was enlisted on God's side in this war. He wasn't given a few years in which to look around and make up his mind which side he would be on, or even whether he would join a side at all. He was already chosen as a combatant on God's side. And so are we all. No one enters existence as a spectator. We either take up the life to which we have been consecrated or we traitorously defect from it. We cannot say, "Hold it! I am not quite ready. Wait until I have sorted things out" [E. F. Schumacher, *A Guide for the Perplexed*].

The world is unprincipled. It's dog-eat-dog out there! The world doesn't fight fair. But we don't live or fight our battles that way—never have and never will. The tools of our trade aren't for marketing or manipulation, but they are for demolishing that entire massively corrupt culture. We use our powerful God-tools for smashing warped philosophies, tearing down barriers erected against the truth of God. . . .

2 CORINTHIANS 10:3–5A

APRIL 25

What We Do Best

Giving is what we do best. It is the air into which we were born. It is the action that was designed into us before our birth. *Giving* is the way the world is. He makes no exceptions for any of us. We are given away to our families, to our neighbors, to our friends, to our enemies—to the nations. Our life is for others. That is the way creation works. Some of us try desperately to hold on to ourselves, to live for ourselves. We look so bedraggled and pathetic doing it, hanging on to the dead branch of a bank account for dear life, afraid to risk ourselves on the untried wings of giving. We don't think we can live generously because we have never tried. But the sooner we start the better, for we are going to have to give up our lives finally, and the longer we wait the less time we have for the soaring and swooping life of grace.

> *He gives you something you can then give away, which grows into full-formed lives, robust in God, wealthy in every way, so that you can be generous in every way, producing with us great praise to God.*

2 CORINTHIANS 9:11–12

APRIL 26

A Life of Daily Prayer

The outside is a lot easier to reform than the inside. Going to the right church and saying the right words is a lot easier than working out a life of justice and love among the people you work and live with. Showing up at church once a week and saying a hearty Amen is a lot easier than engaging in a life of daily prayer and Scripture meditation that develops into concern for poverty and injustice, hunger and war.

The first thing I want you to do is pray. Pray every way you know how, for everyone you know.

1 TIMOTHY 2:1

APRIL 27

Marriages

When I talk with people who come to me in preparation for marriage I often say, "Weddings are easy; marriages are difficult." The couple want to plan a wedding; I want to plan a marriage. They want to know where the bridesmaids will stand; I want to develop a plan for forgiveness. They want to discuss the music of the wedding; I want to talk about the emotions of the marriage. I can do a wedding in twenty minutes with my eyes shut; a marriage takes year after year of alert, wide-eyed attention.

Weddings are important. They are beautiful; they are impressive; they are emotional; sometimes they are expensive. We weep at weddings and we laugh at weddings. We take care to be at the right place at the right time and say the right words. Where people stand is important. The way people dress is significant. Every detail—this flower, that candle—is memorable. All the same, weddings are easy.

But marriages are complex and difficult. In marriage we work out in every detail of life the promises and commitments spoken at the wedding. In marriage we develop the long and rich life of faithful love that the wedding announces. The event of the wedding without the life of marriage doesn't amount to much. It hardly matters if the man and woman dress up in their wedding clothes and re-enact the ceremony every anniversary and say "I'm married, I'm married, I'm married" if there is no daily love shared, if there is no continuing tenderness, no attentive listening, no inventive giving, no creative blessing.

Make sure you don't take things for granted and go slack in working for the common good; share what you have with others. God takes particular pleasure in acts of worship—a different kind of "sacrifice"—that take place in kitchen and workplace and on the streets.

HEBREWS 13:16

APRIL 28

Forgiveness

The word *forgiveness* has been watered down by journalistic cant and careless practice. It frequently means no more than, "I'll let it go this time—I won't let it bother me—but don't do it again." It is the verbal equivalent to a shoulder shrug. So there needs to be repeated return to the New Testament to renovate the word, to discover its vitality, its strength, its power, its versatility; to realize that it is the most creative act anyone can engage in; to know that more new life springs from acts of forgiveness than anything else; and to believe that the parent who is called on to engage in an act of forgiveness is in a literally god-like position.

Be even-tempered, content with second place, quick to forgive an offense. Forgive as quickly and completely as the Master forgave you. And regardless of what else you put on, wear love. It's your basic, all-purpose garment. Never be without it.

COLOSSIANS 3:13B–14

APRIL 29

A Series of Broken Relationships

The biblical material consistently portrays the family not as a Norman Rockwell group, beaming in gratitude around a Thanksgiving turkey, but as a series of broken relationships in need of redemption, after the manner of William Faulkner's plots in Yoknapatawpha County.

At the very least, this means that no one needs to carry a burden of guilt because his or her family is deficient in the sweetness and light that Christian families are supposed to exhibit. Since models for harmonious families are missing in Scripture (and for that omission I am repeatedly grateful to the Holy Spirit), we are free to pay attention to what *is* there—a promise of new community which experiences life as the household of faith, a family in Christ. Life together consists of relationships that are created not by blood (at least not by our blood) but by grace. We get along not because we are good but because we are forgiven.

Christ came and preached peace to you outsiders and peace to us insiders. He treated us as equals, and so made us equals. Through him we both share the same Spirit and have equal access to the Father.

EPHESIANS 2:17–18

APRIL 30

Adolescence Is a Gift

Adolescents exhibit the process of growing up into adulthood in a particularly vivid form. Their parents are unavoidably involved in it. Every parent of an adolescent is thus provided with a gift—a kind of living laboratory in which to take the data of growing up, work experiments with it in personal ways, and then reexperience it in an act of faith to the glory of God. Parents don't always look at it this way. Not infrequently, they are heard to complain about it. Many stoically stick it out, assured by the experts that adolescence is self-curing and will be over in seven or eight years. They never open the gift; they never enter the laboratory.

But adolescence *is* a gift, God's gift, and it must not be squandered in complaints or stoic resistance. There is a strong Christian conviction, substantiated by centuries of devout thinking and faithful living, that everything given to us in our bodies and in our world is the raw material for holiness. Nature is brought to maturity by grace and only by grace. Nothing in nature—nothing in our muscles and emotions, nothing in our geography and our genes—is exempt from this activity of grace. And adolescence is not exempt.

No prolonged infancies among us, please. We'll not tolerate babes in the woods, small children who are an easy mark for imposters. God wants us to grow up, to know the whole truth and tell it in love—like Christ in everything.

EPHESIANS 4:14–15

May

MAY 1

You're Blessed

When Jesus saw his ministry drawing huge crowds, he climbed a hillside. Those who were apprenticed to him, the committed, climbed with him. Arriving at a quiet place, he sat down and taught his climbing companions. This is what he said:

"You're blessed when you're at the end of your rope. With less of you there is more of God and his rule.

"You're blessed when you feel you've lost what is most dear to you. Only then can you be embraced by the One most dear to you.

"You're blessed when you're content with just who you are—no more, no less. That's the moment you find yourselves proud owners of everything that can't be bought.

"You're blessed when you've worked up a good appetite for God. He's food and drink in the best meal you'll ever eat.

"You're blessed when you care. At the moment of being 'care-full,' you find yourselves cared for.

"You're blessed when you get your inside world—your mind and heart—put right. Then you can see God in the outside world.

"You're blessed when you can show people how to cooperate instead of compete or fight. That's when you discover who you really are, and your place in God's family.

"You're blessed when your commitment to God provokes persecution. The persecution drives you even deeper into God's kingdom.

"Not only that—count yourselves blessed every time people put you down or throw you out or speak lies about you to discredit me. What it means is that the truth is too close for comfort and they are uncomfortable. You can be glad when that happens—give a cheer, even!—for though they don't like it, *I* do! And all heaven applauds. And know that you are in good company. My prophets and witnesses have always gotten into this kind of trouble."

MATTHEW 5:1–11

MAY 2

Explicitly Pastoral

The book of Ruth became an explicitly pastoral document when it was assigned as a reading at the Feast of Pentecost. The kerygmatic theme of Pentecost is the covenant revelation at Sinai. The Torah reading assigned to the Feast tells the story of the revelation on Mt. Sinai in Exodus 19–20, and the liturgy of the day remembers the event. At Sinai Israel found structure and direction for the redeemed life. The past was defined, the future was established, and the everyday conduct of the people was not a random series of experiences, arbitrary, casual, and unpredictable. It was a *narrative*—there were plot, structure, purpose, and design. Each detail of each person's life is part of a larger story, and the larger story is salvation. At Sinai God revealed his ways and showed how all behavior and all relationships were included in the overall structure of redemption. The people found out who God was and where they stood in relation to him. In many congregations, still (both Jewish and Christian), the first day of Pentecost is celebrated by the confirmation of young people, confirmation being an identity rite in which who we are is confirmed on the basis of what God has shown himself to be in relation to us.

> *Point your kids in the right direction—*
> *when they're old they won't be lost.*

PROVERBS 22:6

MAY 3

Busyness Is an Illness of Spirit

Though some of the following days are directed to pastors,
any Christian vocation can be substituted for "pastor."

Busyness is an illness of spirit, a rush from one thing to another because there is no ballast of vocational integrity and no confidence in the primacy of grace. In order for there to be conversation and prayer that do the pastoral work of meeting the intimacy needs among people, there must be a wide margin of quiet leisure that defies the functional, technological, dehumanizing definitions that are imposed upon people by others in the community.

> *I've kept my feet on the ground,*
> *I've cultivated a quiet heart.*
> *Like a baby content in its mother's arms,*
> *my soul is a baby content.*

PSALM 131:2

MAY 4

God's Love

God's love is an assault on our indifference and a victory over our rebellion.

> *[Jesus said,] "This is how much God loved the world:*
> *He gave his Son, his one and only Son. And this is*
> *why: so that no one need be destroyed; by believing in*
> *him, anyone can have a whole and lasting life."*

JOHN 3:16

The Sinai Event

The Sinai event is a kind of axle for holding together two basic realities; one, everything God does involves me (election); and two, everything I do is therefore significant (covenant). Because I am chosen, I have consequence. Election creates a unique identity; covenant describes a responsible relationship. Election is the declaration that God has designs upon me; covenant is the description of how the things I do fit into those designs.

> *Long before he laid down earth's foundations, he had us in mind,*
> *had settled on us as the focus of his love, to be made whole and holy*
> *by his love.*

EPHESIANS 1:4

Where the Sufferer Is, God Is

The biblical revelation neither explains nor eliminates suffering. It shows, rather, God entering into the life of suffering humanity, accepting and sharing the suffering. Scripture is not a lecture from God, pointing the finger at unfortunate sufferers and saying, "I told you so: here and here and here is where you went wrong; now you are paying for it." Nor is it a program from God providing, step by step, for the gradual elimination of suffering in a series of five-year plans (or, on a grander scale, dispensations). There is no progress from more to less suffering from Egyptian bondage to wilderness wandering, to kingless anarchy, to Assyrian siege, to Babylonian captivity, to Roman crucifixion, to Neronian/Domitian holocaust. The suffering is *there*, and where the sufferer is, God is.

Surely he has borne our griefs
and carried our sorrows. (Isa. 53:4)

But God put his love on the line for us by offering his Son in sacrificial death while we were of no use whatever to him.

ROMANS 5:8

MAY 7

An Insistence on the Personal

Those who would bowdlerize the Bible by expurgating all references to God's anger hardly know what they are doing. They have not thought through the consequences of their "improvements." The moment anger is eliminated from God, suffering is depersonalized, for anger is an insistence on the personal—it is the antithesis of impersonal fate or abstract law.

When Jesus saw her [Mary] sobbing and the Jews with her sobbing, a deep anger welled up within him. He said, "Where did you put him?"
"Master, come and see," they said. Now Jesus wept.
The Jews said, "Look how deeply he loved him."

JOHN 11:33–36

Most Personal of Relationships

The last sentence in Lamentations is blunt and direct: ". . . hast thou utterly rejected us? Art thou exceedingly angry with us?" ([Lam.] 5:22). But this anger is addressed in the most personal of relationships, prayer. Prayer is suffering's best result. In prayer, God's anger is neither sentimentally glossed nor cynically debunked, but seized as a lever to pry open the door of redemption. The sufferer, by praying, does not ask God to think well of him or her, but asks that God will enact redemption, working "fruits meet for repentance" through Jesus Christ who suffered and died for all.

Satan's angel did his best to get me down; what he in fact did was push me to my knees.

2 CORINTHIANS 12:7B–8A

Plastic Cheerfulness

Everyone who has been ill, or in grief, or hurt, has experienced another's attempts to help—and knows how frequently the attempts are bungled. In a hospital bed, depressed, and in pain, we are not helped by the bright, plastic cheerfulness of pastor or friend who tells us to cheer up for "everything is going to be okay." We already know, in the moments when we are inclined to think about it, that everything is going to be all right (or else know that it is not), but at that moment it would help if there were someone patient and courageous enough simply to share what we are going through—give us the great honor of paying attention to us, treating us as a significant person just as we are.

Laugh with your happy friends when they're happy;
share tears when they're down.

ROMANS 12:15

MAY 10

Size Is Not a Moral Quality

There is, of course, nothing wrong with a large-membership congregation. But neither is there anything right about it. Size is not a moral quality. It is a given.

[Jesus said,] "When two of you get together on
anything at all on earth and make a prayer of it,
my Father in heaven goes into action. And when
two or three of you are together because of me,
you can be sure that I'll be there."

MATTHEW 18:19–20

Nothing to Do With Faithfulness

Statistical applause has nothing to do with faithfulness. A glowing public image has nothing to do with obedience. The prophetic oracle " 'to obey is better than sacrifice' " (1 Sam. 15:22) is a magnificent, clear proclamation of the theme which is later picked up and preached so well by Isaiah (1:11–15), Amos (5:21–27), and Hosea (6:6). It continues to divide those who manipulate the community of faith to serve themselves from those who serve the Lord of the church.

> *[Jesus said,] "You're hopeless, you religion scholars and Pharisees! Frauds! You're like manicured grave plots, grass clipped and the flowers bright, but six feet down it's all rotting bones and worm-eaten flesh. People look at you and think you're saints, but beneath the skin you're total frauds."*

MATTHEW 23:27–28

Delivered from an Immense Clutter

The image of the stones, waiting to be selected from the brook by David as he prepares for his meeting with Goliath, holds my attention. David has just discarded King Saul's armor as ill-fitting. The offer of bronze helmet and coat of mail was well intentioned. But to accept it would have been disastrous. David needed what was authentic to him. Even as I do. For even though the weaponry urged upon me by my culture in the form of science and knowledge is formidable I cannot work effectively with what is imposed from the outside. Metallic forms hung on my frame will give me, perhaps, an imposing aspect but will not help me do my proper work.

And so I kneel at the brook of scripture, selecting there what God has long been preparing for the work at hand and find smooth stones. The rough edges have been knocked off. The soft parts have been eroded away. They are bare and hard. Nothing superfluous. Nothing decorative. Clean and spare. Scripture has that quality for me—of essentiality, of the necessary. I feel that I am, again, traveling light, delivered from an immense clutter.

Every part of Scripture is God-breathed and useful one way or another—showing us truth, exposing our rebellion, correcting our mistakes, training us to live God's way. Through the Word we are put together and shaped up for the tasks God has for us.

2 TIMOTHY 3:16–17

MAY 13

A Good Woman

A good woman is hard to find,
  and worth far more than diamonds.

Her husband trusts her without reserve,
    and never has reason to regret it.
Never spiteful, she treats him generously
    all her life long.
She shops around for the best yarns and cottons,
    and enjoys knitting and sewing.
She's like a trading ship that sails to faraway places
    and brings back exotic surprises.
She's up before dawn, preparing breakfast
    for her family and organizing her day.
She looks over a field and buys it,
    then, with money she's put aside, plants a garden.
First thing in the morning, she dresses for work,
    rolls up her sleeves, eager to get started.
She senses the worth of her work,
    is in no hurry to call it quits for the day.
She's skilled in the crafts of home and hearth,
    diligent in homemaking.
She's quick to assist anyone in need,
    reaches out to help the poor.
She doesn't worry about her family when it snows;
    their winter clothes are all mended and ready to wear.
She makes her own clothing,
    and dresses in colorful linens and silks.
Her husband is greatly respected
    when he deliberates with the city fathers.
She designs gowns and sells them,
    brings the sweaters she knits to the dress shops.
Her clothes are well-made and elegant,
    and she always faces tomorrow with a smile.

When she speaks she has something worthwhile to say,
   and she always says it kindly.
She keeps an eye on everyone in her household,
   and keeps them all busy and productive.
Her children respect and bless her;
   her husband joins in with words of praise:
"Many women have done wonderful things,
   but you've outclassed them all!"
Charm can mislead and beauty soon fades.
   The woman to be admired and praised
   is the woman who lives in the Fear-of-God.
Give her everything she deserves!
   Festoon her life with praises!

PROVERBS 31:10–31

MAY 14

A Right Image

For years I have searched the scriptures for help in pursuing my life as pastor. Time after time I have come upon rich treasures, but somehow I missed Jonah. I missed, it turns out, three of the most provocative and amusing pages in the scriptures for my purpose. The Jonah story is sharply evocative of the vocational experience of pastor. Story incites story. Story-tellers swap stories. As I tell this story among my friends, listen to them tell theirs, and in turn tell a few of my own, the stories develop images and metaphors that give shape to a spirituality adequate to pastoral work. Stanley Hauerwas argues [*Vision and Virtue*], convincingly to me, that if we want to change our way of life, acquiring the right image is far more important than diligently exercising willpower. Willpower is a notoriously sputtery engine on which to rely for internal energy, but a right image silently and inexorably pulls us into its field of reality, which is also a field of energy.

The book of Jonah is a parable at the center of which is a prayer. Parable and prayer are biblical tools for bringing a sharp personal awareness of truth to people whose spiritual perceptions are dulled by living habitually in an overtly religious context.

> *Jesus asked, "Are you starting to get a handle on all this?"*
> *They answered, "Yes."*
> *He said, "Then you see how every student well-trained in God's kingdom is like the owner of a general store who can put his hands on anything you need, old or new, exactly when you need it."*

MATTHEW 13:51

MAY 15

A Lethargic Rubber Stamp

Freedom of religion, one of the four freedoms that Americans esteem, has not flowered into maturity in religion. Our constitutionally protected freedom of religion has in fact turned out to be culture-enslaved religion. Chesterton was wont to lament the mindless cultural conformism of the religious establishment in the opening decades of the twentieth century in England; the closing decades in America match them like a bookend. Far from being radical and dynamic, most religion is a lethargic rubber stamp on worldly wisdom, leading us not to freedom but, in Chesterton's words, to "the degrading slavery of being a child of [this] age."

> *Don't become so well-adjusted to your culture that you fit into it without even thinking. Instead, fix your attention on God. You'll be changed from the inside out.*

ROMANS 12:2A

MAY 16

God Constitutes Our Work

The moment we drift away from dealing with God primarily (and not merely peripherally), we are no longer living vocationally, no longer living in conscious, willing, participatory relation with the vast reality that constitutes our lives and the entire world around us. The storm either exposes the futility of our work (as in Jonah) or confirms it (as in Paul). In either case, the storm forces the awareness that God constitutes our work, and it disabuses us of any suggestion that in our work we can avoid or manipulate God. Once that is established, we are ready to learn the spirituality that is adequate to our vocation, working truly, easily, fearlessly, without ambition or anxiety, without denial or sloth.

*So let's keep focused on that goal, those of us who want everything
God has for us. If any of you have something else in mind, something
less than total commitment, God will clear your blurred vision—
you'll see it yet! Now that we're on the right track, let's stay on it.*

PHILIPPIANS 3:15–16

MAY 17

The Belly of the Fish

But Jonah didn't drown. He was swallowed by a great fish and so
saved. His first action in his newly saved condition was prayer.

This is the center of the story, a center located in the belly of the
fish. The drowning of religious careerism is followed by resurrection
into a pastoral vocation. We become what we are called to be. We become what we are called to be by praying. And we start out by praying from the belly of the fish.

The belly of the fish is a place of confinement, a tight, restricted
place. The ship to Tarshish was headed for the western horizon—
limitless expanses of sea with the lure of the mysterious and beckon-
ing unknown through the Straits of Gibraltar and beyond. The Gates
of Hercules. Atlantis. Hesperides. Ultima Thule.

Religion always plays on these sublime aspirations, these erotic
drives for completion and wholeness. Jonah, heady with this potent
elixir and cruising confidently under full sails, the sea breeze and salt
tang deepening the sensory anticipation of a thrilling life in the service of God, found himself instead in the belly of the fish.

The belly of the fish was the unattractive opposite to everything Jonah had set out for. The belly of the fish was a dark, dank, and probably stinking cell. The belly of the fish is Jonah's introduction to *askesis.*

Askesis is to spirituality what a training regimen is to an athlete. It is not the thing itself, but the means to maturity and excellence. Otherwise we are at the mercy of glands and weather. It is a spiritual equivalent to the old artistic idea that talent grows by its very confinement, that the genie's strength comes from his confinement in the bottle.

> *[Jesus said,] "Anyone who intends to come with me has to let me lead. You're not in the driver's seat; I am. Don't run from suffering; embrace it. Follow me and I'll show you how. Self-help is no help at all."*

MARK 8:34B

MAY 18

Organically Grown

Spirituality requires context. Always. Boundaries, borders, limits. "The Word became flesh and dwelt among us." No one becomes more spiritual by becoming less material. No one becomes exalted by ascending in a gloriously colored hot-air balloon. Mature spirituality requires *askesis,* a training program custom-designed for each individual-in-community, and then continuously monitored and adapted as development takes place and conditions vary. It can never be mechanically imposed from without; it must be organically grown in locale. *Askesis* must be context sensitive.

> *You have bedded me down in lush meadows,*
> * you find me quiet pools to drink from.*
> *True to your word,*
> * you let me catch my breath*
> * and send me in the right direction.*

PSALM 23:2–3

MAY 19

Golden Calf Country

The people in our congregations are, in fact, out shopping for idols. They enter our churches with the same mind-set in which they go to the shopping mall, to get something that will please them or satisfy an appetite or need. John Calvin saw the human heart as a relentlessly efficient factory for producing idols. Congregations commonly see the pastor as the quality-control engineer in the factory. The moment we accept the position, though, we defect from our vocation. The people who gather in our congregations want help through a difficult time; they want meaning and significance in their ventures. They want God, in a way, but certainly not a "jealous God," not the "God and Father of our Lord Jesus Christ." Mostly they want to be their own god and stay in control but have ancillary idol assistance for the hard parts, which the pastor can show them how to get. With the development of assembly-line mass production, we are putting these idols out in great quantities and in a variety of colors and shapes to suit every taste. John Calvin's insight plus Henry Ford's technology equals North American Religion. Living in golden calf country as we do, it is both easy and attractive to become a successful pastor like Aaron [Exod. 32].

> *[Jesus said,] "Be wary of false preachers who smile a lot, dripping with practiced sincerity. Chances are they are out to rip you off some way or other. Don't be impressed with charisma; look for character."*

MATTHEW 7:15–16

MAY 20

Serious Apostasy

There are a thousand ways of being religious without submitting to Christ's lordship, and people are practiced in most of them. We live in golden calf country. Religious feeling runs high but in ways far removed from what was said on Sinai and done on Calvary. While everyone has a hunger for God, deep and insatiable, none of us has any great *desire* for him. What we really want is to be our own gods and to have whatever other gods that are around to help us in this work. We are trained from an early age to be discriminating consumers on our way to higher standards of living. It should be no great surprise to pastors when congregations expect us to collaborate in this enterprise. But it is serious apostasy when we go along. "And

Moses said to Aaron, 'What did this people do to you that you have brought a great sin upon them?' " (Exod. 32:21). Aaron's excuse is embarrassingly lame but more than matched by the justifications pastors make for abandoning worship in our enthusiasm to make the congregation flourishingly successful.

> *[Jesus said,] "When people realize it is the living God you are presenting and not some idol that makes them feel good, they are going to turn on you, even people in your own family. There is a great irony here: proclaiming so much love, experiencing so much hate!"*

MATTHEW 10:21–22A

MAY 21

Hunger for God

All men and women hunger for God. The hunger is masked and misinterpreted in many ways, but it is always there. Everyone is on the verge of crying out "My Lord and my God!" but the cry is drowned out by doubts or defiance, muffled by the dull ache of their routines, masked by their cozy accommodations with mediocrity. Then something happens—a word, an event, a dream—and there is a push toward awareness of an incredible Grace, a dazzling Desire, a defiant Hope, a courageous Faithfulness. But awareness, as such, is not enough. Untended, it trickles into religious sentimentalism or romantic blubbering. Or, worse, it hardens into patriotic hubris or pharisaic snobbery. The pastor is there to nudge the awareness past subjectivities and ideologies into the open and say "God."

You're going to find that there will be times when people will have no stomach for solid teaching, but will fill up on spiritual junk food—catchy opinions that tickle their fancy. They'll turn their backs on truth and chase mirages. But you*—keep your eye on what you're doing; accept the hard times along with the good; keep the Message alive; do a thorough job as God's servant.*

2 TIMOTHY 4:3–5

MAY 22

At the Mercy of God

Anything formulaic or technological contributes to a consumer approach to the spiritual life, and we must be on guard against it. So easily "spirituality" becomes a cafeteria through which we walk making selections according to our taste and appetite. This consumer mentality is distressingly common, and we must do everything possible to combat it. We begin by insisting that *askesis* is not a spiritual technology at our beck and call but is rather immersion in an environment in which our capacities are reduced to nothing or nearly nothing and we are at the mercy of God to shape his will in us.

On the road someone asked if he could go along. "I'll go with you, wherever," he said.

Jesus was curt: "Are you ready to rough it? We're not staying in the best inns, you know."

LUKE 9:57–58

MAY 23

The Future

The way we conceive the future sculpts the present, gives contour and tone to nearly every action and thought through the day. If our sense of future is weak, we live listlessly. Much emotional and mental illness and most suicides occur among men and women who feel that they "have no future."

The Christian faith has always been characterized by a strong and focused sense of future, with belief in the Second Coming of Jesus as the most distinctive detail. From the day Jesus ascended into heaven, his followers lived in expectancy of his return. He told them he was coming back. They believed he was coming back. They continue to believe it. For Christians, it is the most important thing to know and believe about the future.

The practical effect of this belief is to charge each moment of the present with hope. For if the future is dominated by the coming again of Jesus, there is little room left on the screen for projecting our anxieties and fantasies. It takes the clutter out of our lives. We're far more free to respond spontaneously to the freedom of God.

He who testifies to all these things says it again: "I'm on my way! I'll be there soon!"
    Yes! Come, Master Jesus!

REVELATION 22:20

MAY 24

Christian Hope Alerts Us

Hope is a response to the future which has its foundations in the promises of God. It looks at the future as time for the completion of God's promise. It refuses to extrapolate either desire or anxiety into the future, but instead believes that God's promise gives the proper content to it. But hope is not a doctrine *about* the future: it is a grace cultivated in the present, it is a stance in the present which deals with the future. As such it is misunderstood if it is valued only for the comfort it brings; as if it should say, "Everything is going to be all right in the future because God is in control of it, therefore relax and be comforted." Hope operates differently. Christian hope alerts us to the possibilities of the future as a field of action, and as a consequence fills the present with energy.

So roll up your sleeves, put your mind in gear, be totally ready to receive the gift that's coming when Jesus arrives.

1 PETER 1:13

His School Was the Psalms

So Jonah prayed. *That* Jonah prayed is not remarkable; we commonly pray when we are in desperate circumstances. But there is something very remarkable about the *way* Jonah prayed. He prayed a "set" prayer. Jonah's prayer is not spontaneously original self-expression. It is totally derivative. Jonah had been to school to learn to pray, and he prayed as he had been taught. His school was the Psalms. . . .

If we want to pray our true condition, our total selves in response to the living God, expressing our feelings is not enough—we need a long apprenticeship in prayer. And then we need graduate school. The Psalms are the school. Jonah in his prayer shows himself to have been a diligent student in the school of Psalms. His prayer is kicked off by his plight, but it is not reduced to it. His prayer took him into a world far larger than his immediate experience. He was capable of prayer that was adequate to the largeness of the God with whom he was dealing.

[Jesus said,] "The person who trusts in me will not only do what I'm doing but even greater things, because I, on my way to the Father, am giving you the same work to do that I've been doing. You can count on it. From now on whatever you request along the lines of who I am and what I am doing, I'll do it."

JOHN 14:12B–14

The Impulse to Pray

For there is no lack in us of the impulse to pray. And there is no scarcity of requests to pray. Desire and demand keep the matter of prayer before us constantly. So why are so many lives prayerless? Simply because "the well is deep and you have nothing to draw with." We need a bucket. We need a container that holds water. Desires and demands are a sieve. We need a vessel suited to lowering desires and demands into the deep Jacob's Well of God's presence and word and bringing them to the surface again. The Psalms are such a bucket.

> *[Jesus said,] "This is what I want you to do: Ask the Father for whatever is in keeping with the things I've revealed to you. Ask in my name, according to my will, and he'll most certainly give it to you. Your joy will be a river overflowing its banks!"*

JOHN 16:26

The Virus of Gnosticism

The reason we get restless with where we are and want, as we say, "more of a challenge" or "a larger field of opportunity" has nothing to do with prophetic zeal or priestly devotion; it is the product of spiritual sin. The sin is generated by the virus of gnosticism.

Gnosticism is the ancient but persistently contemporary perversion of the gospel that is contemptuous of place and matter. It holds forth that salvation consists in having the right ideas, and the fancier the better. It is impatient with restrictions of place and time and embarrassed by the garbage and disorder of everyday living. It constructs a gospel that majors in fine feelings embellished by sayings of Jesus. Gnosticism is also impatient with slow-witted people and plodding companions and so always ends up being highly selective, appealing to an elite group of people who are "spiritually deep," attuned to each other, and quoting a cabal of experts.

The gospel, on the other hand, is local intelligence, locally applied, and plunges with a great deal of zest into the flesh, into matter, into place—and accepts whoever happens to be on the premises as the people of God. One of the pastor's continuous tasks is to make sure that these conditions are honored: *this* place just as it is, *these* people in their everyday clothes, "a particularizing love for local things, rising out of local knowledge and local allegiance" [Wendell Berry, *Home Economics*].

Bring the winter coat I left in Troas with Carpus; also the books and parchment notebooks.

2 TIMOTHY 4.13

MAY 28

Work in the Particulars

When I work in the particulars, I develop a reverence for what is actually there instead of a contempt for what is not, inadequacies that seduce me into a covetousness for someplace else. A farm, Wendell Berry contends, is a kind of small-scale ecosystem, everything working with everything else in certain rhythms and proportions. The farmer's task is to understand the rhythms and the proportions and then to nurture their health, not bullyingly to invade the place and decide that it is going to function on his rhythms and according to the size of his ego. If all a farmer is after is profit, he will not be reverential of what is actually there but only greedy for what he can get out of it.

The parallel with my parish could not be more exact. I substitute my pastoral vocabulary for Berry's agricultural and find Berry urging me to be mindful of my congregation, in reverence before it. These are souls, divinely worked-on souls, whom the Spirit is shaping for eternal habitations. Long before I arrive on the scene, the Spirit is at work. I must fit into what is going on. I have no idea yet what is taking place here; I must study the contours, understand the weather, know what kind of crops grow in this climate, be in awe of the complex intricacies between past and present, between the people in the parish and those outside.

Be quick to give a meal to the hungry, a bed to the homeless—cheerfully. Be generous with the different things God gave you, passing them around so all get in on it. . . .

1 PETER 4:9–10A

MAY 29

Quarreling with God

Quarreling with God is a time-honored biblical practice: Moses, Job, David, and St. Peter were all masters at it. It is a practice in which men and women in ministry have much practice. We get a lot of practice in this because we are dealing with God in some way or other most of the time, and God doesn't behave the way we expect.

Jonah is quarreling because he has been surprised by grace. He is so taken aback that he is disagreeable about it. His idea of what God is supposed to do and what God in fact does differs radically. Jonah sulks. Jonah is angry. The word *anger* occurs six times in this final chapter.

> *Has God forgotten his manners?*
> *Has he angrily stalked off and left us?*
> *"Just my luck," I said. "The High God goes out of business*
> *just the moment I need him."*

PSALM 77:9–10

MAY 30

Anger Is Our Sixth Sense

Anger is most useful as a diagnostic tool. When anger erupts in us, it is a signal that something is wrong. Something isn't working right. There is evil or incompetence or stupidity lurking about. Anger is our sixth sense for sniffing out wrong in the neighborhood. Diagnostically it is virtually infallible, and we learn to trust it. Anger is infused by a moral/spiritual intensity that carries conviction: when we are angry, we know we are on to something that matters, that really counts. When God said to Jonah, "Do you do well to be angry?" Jonah shot back, "I do well to be angry, angry enough to die" [Jonah 4:9].

What anger fails to do, though, is tell us whether the wrong is outside or inside us. We usually begin by assuming that the wrong is outside us—our spouse or our child or our God has done something wrong, and we are angry. That is what Jonah did, and he quarreled with God. But when we track the anger carefully, we often find it leads to a wrong within us—wrong information, inadequate understanding, underdeveloped heart. If we admit and face that, we are pulled out of our quarrel with God into something large and vocational in God.

> Go ahead and be angry. You do well to be angry—but don't use your anger as fuel for revenge. And don't stay angry. Don't go to bed angry. Don't give the Devil that kind of foothold in your life.
>
> EPHESIANS 4:26–27

MAY 31

Into the Risky Unknown

Communion is not as much interested in using words to define meaning as to deepen mystery, to enter into the ambiguities, push past the safely known into the risky unknown. The Christian Eucharist uses the simplest of words—this is my body, this is my blood—to plunge us into the depths of love, to venture into what is not tied down, into love, into faith. These words do not describe; they reveal, they point, they reach.

> *I am the Bread—living Bread!—who came down out of heaven. Anyone who eats this Bread will live—and forever! The Bread that I present to the world so that it can eat and live is myself, this flesh-and-blood self.*

JOHN 6:51

June

The Praying Community

The praying people, whose prayers are the Psalms, prayed as a worshiping community. All the psalms are prayers in community: people assembled, attentive before God, participating in a common posture, movement and speech, offering themselves and each other to their Lord. Prayer is not a private exercise, but a family convocation.

In the presence of God, "alone" is not good. Summon Eve. Call a friend. "Where two or three are gathered together in my name, there I am in the midst of them." By ourselves, we are not ourselves. Solitary confinement is extreme punishment; private prayer is extreme selfishness. Prayer, in itself, is not an automatic good. It is possible to practice prayer in such a way that it drives us deep into a conniving, calculating egotism. And it is possible to practice prayer in such a way that it bloats us into a prideful ostentation. Jesus was not indiscriminate in his praise of prayer; some people who prayed got a severe tongue-lashing from him.

Prayer often originates when we are alone. Deep within us are "sighs too deep for words." We pray our guilt, our hurt, our gaiety on the spot, not waiting until we can meet with a congregation or get into a church. All the same, for these prayers to develop into full maturity, they must be integrated into the praying community.

And prayer continues into places of solitude. We pray on our beds at night, silently and secretly when surrounded by unbelievers, deliberately withdrawn from society in order to cleanse the "doors of perception" [William Blake]. We neither can or should be with others continuously; and we are with God continuously.

But the believing community at worship, at regular times in assigned places, is the *base* of prayer. All the psalms were prayed in such communities. This is not obvious on the surface—we are apt to think of a shepherd on a grassy slope, or a traveler on a dangerous road—nevertheless, it is one of the assured results of devout research, confirmed in the practice of Israel and church. We are most congruent with the conditions in which the Psalms were produced and prayed when we pray in a praying congregation.

> *Here in this great gathering for worship*
> *I have discovered this praise-life.*
> *And I'll do what I promised right here*
> *in front of the God-worshipers.*

PSALM 22:25

JUNE 2

Meditation Is Mastication

As we prepare to pray, to answer the words God addresses to us, we learn that all of God's words have this characteristic: they are *torah* and we are the target. God's word is not a reference book in a library that we pull off the shelf when we want information. There is nothing inert or bookish in these words. God's words, creating and saving words every one, hit us where we live.

The moment we know this, that God speaks to us, delight is spontaneous. "The psalms are the liturgy for those whose concern and delight is the torah of the Lord" [James Luther May]. These are not words that we laboriously but impersonally study, as if for an exam. These are not words that we anxiously scan lest we inadvertently transgress a boundary or break a protocol. These are words we *take* in—words designed for shaping new life in us, feeding the energies of salvation. This delight develops into meditation, torah-meditation. Meditate (*hagah*) is a bodily action; it involves murmuring and mumbling words, taking a kind of physical pleasure in making the sounds of the words, getting the *feel* of the meaning as the syllables are shaped by larynx and tongue and lips. Isaiah used this word "meditate" for the sounds that a lion makes over its prey (Isa. 31:4). A lion over its catch and a person over the torah act similarly. They purr and growl in pleasurable anticipation of taking in what will make them more themselves, strong, lithe, swift: "I will run in the way of thy commandments when thou enlargest my understanding!" (Ps. 119:32).

This is quite different from merely reading God's word, or thinking about it. This is not so much an intellectual process, figuring our meanings, as it is a physical process, hearing and rehearing these words as we sound them again, letting the sounds sink into our muscles and bones. Meditation is mastication.

> *These are the words in my mouth;*
> *these are what I chew on and pray.*
> *Accept them when I place them*
> *on the morning altar,*

O God, my Altar-Rock,
    God, Priest-of-My-Altar.

PSALM 19:14

JUNE 3

Better Vision

When we find ourselves deficient in wisdom, it is not because the Word of God has pages missing, but because we have not seen all there is on the pages we already have. It is not another book we need, but better attention to the book we have; it is not more knowledge we require, but better vision to see what has already been revealed in Jesus Christ.

No doubt about it! God is good—
    good to good people, good to the good-hearted.
But I nearly missed it,
    missed seeing his goodness.
I was looking the other way . . .

PSALM 73:1–3A

JUNE 4

The Unfolding of Your Words

READ
Psalm 119:129–134

When we first look at the word of God, it is like a bud—a small concentration of beauty. As we hold it before us in meditation, it unfolds, layer by layer, until the full flower is in blossom, ready to be viewed in all its intricately related parts.

PRAYER: O Father, there is so much that I am eager to learn from your word. I have seen so little, but that little has whetted my appetite for more. As I hunger and thirst for your righteousness, fill me with your Holy Spirit. *Amen.*

Every word you give me is a miracle word—
   how could I help but obey?
Break open your words, let the light shine out,
   let ordinary people see the meaning.

PSALM 119:129–130

JUNE 5

Quiet Rhythms

Daily we give up consciousness, submitting ourselves to that which is deeper than consciousness in order to grow and be healed, be created and saved. Going to sleep is biological necessity; it can also be an act of faith. People who live by faith have always welcomed the evening prayer, disengaging themselves from the discordant, arhythmic confusion of tongues, and sinking into the quiet rhythms of God's creating and covenanting words.

At day's end I'm ready for sound sleep,
For you, GOD, have put my life back together.

PSALM 4:8

JUNE 6

Sacrifice

Psalm 5 is the Hebrew morning prayer.

The work of God begins while we are asleep and without our help. He continues to work through the day in our worship and obedience. A sacrifice is the material means of assembling a life before God in order to let God work with it. Sacrifice isn't something we do for God, but simply setting out the stuff of life for him to do something with. On the altar the sacrificial offering is changed into what is pleasing and acceptable to God. In the act of offering we give up ownership and control, and watch to see what God will do with it. With a deep awareness that the God who speaks life into us also listens when we speak, we put into words the difficulties and delights that we foresee in the hours ahead. We assemble fears and hopes, apprehensions and anticipations, and place them on the altar as an offering: "I prepare a sacrifice, and watch."

Every morning
I lay out the pieces of my life

on your altar
and watch for fire to descend.

PSALM 5:3B

JUNE 7
_____

Morning Prayer

Watch is the pivotal word in morning prayer. A biblically trained ear hears a story in the word. Jacob, fleeing from his father-in-law Laban, was caught in Gilead. Laban thought he had been defrauded by Jacob; Jacob was sure he had been gypped by Laban. In Gilead, through argument and prayer, they came to an agreement. They set up an altar pillar and ate a covenantal meal before it. They named the pillar, "Watching Place" (*Mizpah*). They had spent twenty years watching each other suspiciously, watching for opportunities to take advantage of each other. Here they agreed to quit watching each other and let God watch them. Early in the morning the two old antagonists parted—Laban returning to Haran and Jacob entering Canaan where he still had to face the enmity of his brother Esau—with their morning prayer echoing across the Gilead hills: "The Lord watch between you and me, while we are absent one from the other." Leaving the place of morning prayer and watching, the first things Jacob saw were the angels of God. He exclaimed: "This is God's army!" (Gen. 31).

Mizpah is a borderline experience repeated as often as every morning. We watch to see what God will do with the assemblage of hopes and fears we set before him. Morning prayer places us before the watchful God and readies us to enter the day watchful, watching our dangerous past recede, watching the dangerous day fill with God's angels. High tide.

> *"Wake up from your sleep,*
> *Climb out of your coffins;*
> *Christ will show you the light!"*

EPHESIANS 5:14

J U N E 8

Against All Spiritual Elitism

The Psalms that teach us to pray by metaphor, using the experience of the senses to develop within us the experience of faith, come to fulfillment in Christ who was actual flesh and blood ("which we have seen with our eyes, which we have looked upon and touched with our hands," 1 John 1:1) thereby vindicating the goodness of the entire material creation. Jesus consistent with the diction of metaphor was also embarrassingly ordinary—"Is this not Joseph's son?" (Luke 4:22); "Why does your teacher eat with tax collectors and sinners?" (Matt. 9:11)—thereby slamming the door hard against all spiritual elitism. Jesus, in continuity with the Psalms, also taught us to pray in metaphor: "When you pray say, Father" (Luke 11:2).

> *But they also said, "Isn't this Joseph's son, the one we've known since he was a youngster?"*

LUKE 4:22

The Master Sacramentalist

The metaphors of the Psalms via the incarnation of Christ become a sacramental life, a life in which everything, every thing and person mediates God. Jesus was the master sacramentalist. He used anything at hand to bring us into an awareness of God and then into a response to God. The moment Jesus picked up something it was clear that it was not alien but belonging, a piece of God's creation that was a means for meeting God. Jugs of water at Cana, the sound of the wind in Jerusalem, Galilean sea waves, a paralytic's pallet at the Bethzathan pool, the corpse of Lazarus. Things. "There is no good trying to be more spiritual than God. God never meant man to be a purely spiritual creature. That is why He used material things like bread and wine to put new life into us. We may think this rather crude and unspiritual. God does not: He invented eating. He liked matter. He invented it" [C. S. Lewis, *Mere Christianity*].

They still couldn't believe what
they were seeing. It was too much;
it seemed too good to be true.
 He asked, "Do you have any
food here?" They gave him a piece of
leftover fish they had cooked. He took
it and ate it right before their eyes.

LUKE 24:41–42

Liturgy

Liturgy is not, as some suppose, aesthetics. It is courtesy. And theology. It is being mindful that there are others to whom God speaks and who risk their lives in an answer. It is the gracious acknowledgment that others in the family also have needs and rights, and that I am neither the only nor the favorite child.

Liturgy clears a space for meeting, appoints a time, and provides an order. Prayer takes place in space and time; we are not angels. Prayer takes place with people; we are not nomads. Liturgy can be elaborate or simple, baroque or bare, but it always provides for these three things: space, time, order. We know next to nothing about the liturgy of Israel, and not much more about the early church, but that does not matter; we do not pray by archeology. The important thing is that *there was* a liturgy, and we know that beyond cavil. People came together at appointed times in agreed upon places and used psalms to pray—this most personal and individual of all acts!—as a community. Jesus confirmed the basic liturgical character of prayer when he said, "Where two or three are gathered in my name there am I in the midst of them" (Matt. 18:20).

So here's what I want you to do. When you gather for worship, each of you be prepared with something that will be useful for all: Sing a hymn, teach a lesson, tell a story, lead a prayer, provide an insight.

1 CORINTHIANS 14:26

"Let Us Pray"

We commonly think of prayer as what we do out of our own needs and on our own initiative. We experience a deep longing for God, and so we pray. We feel an artesian gush of gratitude to God, and so we pray. We are crushed with a truckload of guilt before God, and so we pray. But in a liturgy we do not take the initiative; it is not our experience that precipitates prayer. Someone stands in front of us and says, "Let us pray." We don't start it; someone else starts it, and we fall into step behind or alongside. Our egos are no longer front and center.

> *So come, let us worship: bow before him,*
> *on your knees before GOD, who made us!*
> *Oh yes, he's our God,*
> *and we're the people he pastures, the flock he feeds.*

PSALM 95:6–7

Primacy of God's Word

This is so important, for prayer by its very nature is answering speech. The consensus of the entire Christian community upholds the primacy of God's word in everything: in creation, in salvation, in judgment, in blessing, in mercy, and in grace. But in the practice of prayer, inebriated as we often are by our own heady subjectivity, we boozily set aside the primacy of God's word and substitute the primacy of our words. We are so sure that here, at least, we get the first word!

But when we take our place in a worshiping congregation we are not in charge. Someone else has built the place of prayer; someone else has established the time for prayer; someone else tells us to begin to pray. All of this takes place in a context in which the word of God is primary: God's word audible in scripture and sermon, God's word visible in baptism and eucharist. This is the center in which we learn to pray. We do not, of course, remain in this center: lines of praying radiate and lead us outward. From this center we go to our closets or the mountains, into the streets and the markets, and continue our praying. But it is essential to understand that the prayer goes from the center *outwards;* if we suppose that it proceeds inwards from the convergence of praying individuals we are at cross-purposes with the praying experience of Israel and the church.

> *"Yes, I see it all now [said Mary]:*
> *I'm the Lord's maid, ready to serve.*
> *Let it be with me*
> *just as you say."*

LUKE 1:38

JUNE 13

The Cruelest Verb

The last book of the Bible, the Revelation to St. John, is frequently indicted for its violent language and vindictive spirit against the wicked. But St. John learned it all in the school of the Psalms and from Jesus who was also, as the mountain people say, a good cusser. Jesus called Peter the very devil, the Pharisees vipers on their way to hell, and shouted down woes on the heads of those who used religion as a way to make themselves comfortable at the terrible cost of oppressing the weak and exploiting the poor (Matt. 16:23, Matt. 23). As the end approached Jesus took the cruelest verb in Psalm 137 and used it against Babylon, alias Jerusalem, as the enemies of God prepared to murder the messiah of God.

> *Jerusalem! Jerusalem! Murderer of prophets! Killer of the ones who brought you God's news!*

MATTHEW 23:37A

JUNE 14

Praying for Our Enemies

The last word on the enemies is with Jesus, who captured the Psalms: "Love your enemies and pray for them that persecute you." But loving enemies presupposes that we know that they are there, whether many or few, and have begun to identify them. Enemies, especially for those who live by faith, are a fact of life. If we don't know we have them or who they are, we live in a dangerous naiveté, unguarded from the "pestilence that stalks in darkness" and "the destruction that wastes at noonday," witless when we pray "deliver us from evil."

Our hate is used by God to bring the enemies of life and salvation to notice, and then involve us in active compassion for the victims.

Once involved we find that while hate provides the necessary spark for ignition, it is the wrong fuel for the engines of judgment; only love is adequate to sustain these passions.

But we must not imagine that loving and praying for our enemies in love is a strategy that will turn them into good friends. Love is the last thing that our enemies want from us and often acts as a goad to redoubled fury. Love requires vulnerability, forgiveness, and response; the enemies want power and control and dominion. The enemies that Jesus loved and prayed for killed him.

> *If you see your enemy hungry, go buy him lunch;*
> *if he's thirsty, bring him a drink.*
> *Your generosity will surprise him with goodness,*
> *and GOD will look after you.*

PROVERBS 25:21–22

JUNE 15

At Odds with God

Sin is not what is wrong with our minds; it is the catastrophic disorder in which we find ourselves at odds with God. This is the human condition. The facts of this disorder are all around and within us, but we would prefer to forget them. To remember them is also to remember God, and to remember God is to have to live strenuously, vigorously, and in love. We have moments when we desire to do this, but the moments don't last long. We would rather play golf. We would rather take another battery of tests at the hospital. We would rather take another course at the university. We keep looking for ways to improve our lives without dealing with God. But we can't do it.

When we pray, we immerse ourselves in the living presence of God. When we pray the Psalms we pray through all the parts of our lives and our history and cover the ground of our intricate implication in sin. We acquire a colorful lexicon of words by which we recognize our detailed involvement in the race's catastrophic separation from God: rebel, wanderer, lawless, evil-doer, guilty, liar, fool, corrupt, wicked. The seven "penitential psalms" (6, 32, 38, 51, 102, 130, 143) are the most famous for bringing us to this awareness but hardly a psalm goes by that does not bring another detail of our sin out of the shadows of our practiced forgetfulness.

> *I'm tired of all this—so tired. My bed*
> *has been floating forty days and nights*
> *On the flood of my tears.*
> *My mattress is soaked, soggy with tears.*

PSALM 6:6

JUNE 16

Your Promise Is Well Tried

READ Psalm 119:137–144.

No one is asked to believe the word of God on the evidence of a slick brochure or the sales pitch of a smooth-talking witness. There are centuries of evidence to show its consistent truth and working power. No human words are so well tried and thoroughly tested as the words of God.

PRAYER: I have spent far too much time, Lord, in wondering if your promises work. I ought to be spending my time testing them out. By your grace I will do that today. Reveal to me the word you would have me test in this day's belief and behavior. *Amen.*

Let your love dictate how you deal with me;
teach me from your textbook on life.

PSALM 119:124

JUNE 17

Why You Are Here

This is part of the Sermon on the Mount. Jesus is speaking.

"Let me tell you why you are here. You're here to be salt-seasoning that brings out the God-flavors of this earth. If you lose your saltiness, how will people taste godliness? You've lost your usefulness and will end up in the garbage.

"Here's another way to put it: You're here to be light, bringing out the God-colors in the world. God is not a secret to be kept. We're going public with this, as public as a city on a hill. If I make you light-bearers, you don't think I'm going to hide you under a bucket, do you? I'm putting you on a light stand. Now that I've put you there on a hilltop, on a light stand—shine! Keep open house; be generous with your lives. By opening up to others, you'll prompt people to open up with God, this generous Father in heaven."

MATTHEW 5:13–16

JUNE 18

Happiness

But happiness is not a word we can understand by looking it up in the dictionary. In fact, none of the qualities of the Christian life can be learned out of a book. Something more like apprenticeship is required, being around someone who out of years of devoted discipline shows us, by his or her entire behavior, what it is. Moments of verbal instruction will certainly occur, but mostly an apprentice acquires skill by daily and intimate association with a "master," picking up subtle but absolutely essential things, such as timing and rhythm and "touch."

When we read what Paul wrote to the Christian believers in the city of Philippi, we find ourselves in the company of just such a master. Paul doesn't tell us that we can be happy, or how to be happy. He simply and unmistakably is happy. None of his circumstances contribute to his joy: He wrote from a jail cell, his work was under attack by competitors, and after twenty years or so of hard traveling in the service of Jesus, he was tired and would have welcomed some relief.

And I'm going to keep that celebration going because I know how it's going to turn out. Through your faithful prayers and the generous response of the Spirit of Jesus Christ, everything he wants to do in and through me will be done.

PHILIPPIANS 1:19

JUNE 19

The Choice Is Free

Christians are not determinists. We do not believe that environment makes a person a Christian, and we do not believe that heredity makes a person righteous; we do not believe that training can make a person moral, and we do not believe that baptism can create a person of faith. Christian theology maintains that every person makes his or her own decisions for or against God. Every life is an accumulation of such decisions. No one can choose right for another. The choice is free. The decision is open. Anyone, regardless of background and upbringing, can choose either way. "Multitudes, multitudes, in the valley of decision!" (Joel 3:14). As a matter of fact, we know that people do make both kinds of choices, and that there is no neat correlation between upbringing and right choices—as if all who are reared in Christian homes make Christian choices, and all who are not reared in Christian homes do not make Christian choices.

Better yet, redouble your efforts. Be energetic in your life of salvation, reverent and sensitive before God.

PHILIPPIANS 2:12A

Spiritual Poverty

Spiritual hunger in a culture of spiritual poverty makes men and women vulnerable to drugs. This spiritual poverty crosses social/economic lines as well as adult/adolescent lines. Drug use is as common among the educated as among the illiterate, as common among the rich as among the poor, as common in the suburbs as in the slums, as common among the respectable as among the disreputable—and as common among adolescents as among adults.

> *Open your mouth and taste, open your eyes and see—*
> *how good GOD is.*
> *Blessed are you who run to him.*

PSALMS 34:8

An Offer of Godlike Independence

Emerging into adolescence, children become capable of realizing the spirituality of sin. Sin is not merely something that they are forbidden to do because God says they must not under penalty of hellfire. They gradually (or suddenly!) realize that sin is an offer of godlike independence, it is an offer to "be like God, knowing good and evil"

(Gen. 3:5). It not only promises sensual gratification ("good for food . . . a delight to the eyes"), but it promises spiritual deepening (". . . to make one wise," v. 6). Until they become adolescents, with their growth spurt in spiritual capacity and their huge hunger for transcendence, children are not capable of being tempted in this way. As long as they are children, mostly dependent on others for their welfare, it never occurs to them that they might make it "on their own." But at adolescence, with adulthood in sight, they are impatient to throw off the restrictions of childhood and reach for adulthood, and the devil promises a shortcut by promising godhead. Prohibitions are no longer accepted as "for their own good," but resented as restrictive, denying them access to a spirituality which is theirs by right.

Here is one place that the adolescent insight is absolutely right. Sin is, in fact, mostly spiritual. There are moral dimensions to it, of course, matters of behavior that put them in danger and/or make them hard to live with, but mostly what sin involves is spirituality, the quest for meaning and purpose and significance. It is the moral dimensions of sin that are prominent in childhood; it is the spiritual dimensions of sin that surface in adolescence. The first sin, to aspire to "be like God," is nothing if not spiritual. Most, if not all, sins ever since are attempts, primarily, at spirituality—attempts to become something other or better than we are, attempts at experiencing something that takes us beyond our humdrum mortality, if only momentarily.

> *If we claim we've never sinned, we out and out contradict God—make a liar out of him. A claim like that only shows off our ignorance of God.*

1 JOHN 1:10

Growing Up

We are only capable of renouncing a false life when we are familiar with a real life. Those years of association with Jesus for the disciples, years of "growing up," were years of realizing in sharp and precise detail that life is what God gives us in Jesus: grace, healing, forgiveness, deliverance from evil, a miraculous meal, the personal presence and word of God. And now that they know what it is, they know it is *not* self-preservation, self-help, self-aggrandizement, self-importance. Life is the Jesus-revealed life that becomes plain as day on the cross— the sacrificial life, the life that loves generously and extravagantly, the life that through voluntary and sacrificial death to self becomes resurrection for the world. So—"deny yourself and take up your cross."

Then he [Jesus] told them what they could expect for themselves: "Anyone who intends to come with me has to let me lead. You're not in the driver's seat—I am."

LUKE 9:23

Renunciation

Renunciation clears out the clutter of self, of false spiritualities, of pseudo-life so that there is room in us for God and true spirituality and eternal life.

[Jesus said,] "If your hand or your foot gets in the way of God, chop it off and throw it away. You're better off maimed or lame and alive than the proud owners of two hands and two feet, godless in a furnace of eternal fire."

MATTHEW 18:8

JUNE 24

Pseudo-Spiritualities

Not infrequently in dealing with these matters of intense and precious and endangered spirituality in our youth, we parents in a shock of recognition see that *our* spirituality is in question: we have let a busy life substitute for a spiritual life, and a responsible life replace a responsive life. Sometimes, to our surprise, we realize that pseudo-spiritualities have turned into addictions that are destroying our inner life, robbing us of freedom, leaving us flatfooted and tuneless in our midlife. When that happens the adolescent in our home very often is in a position to do John the Baptist work for us as a "prophet of the Most High" (Luke 1:76) and make us aware of the presence and glory of Jesus. We're given a second chance to cultivate the resonant depths of soul that make it possible to both "glorify God and enjoy him forever" [Westminster Shorter Catechism].

"And you, my child, 'Prophet of the Highest,'
will go ahead of the Master to prepare his ways."

LUKE 1:76

A Means of Grace

A Kierkegaardian insight helps here, namely, that catastrophe can be a means of grace. It can be an instrument used by God by which we can cease floating passively on all manner of external attractions. It is by the grace of catastrophe that people sometimes come to themselves and see what is before them as if for the first time. Catastrophe can, like a mighty wind, blow away the abstracting veils of theory and ideology and enable our own sovereign seeing.

Now I'm glad—not that you were upset, but that you were jarred into turning things around. You let the distress bring you to God, not drive you from him. The result was all gain, no loss.

2 CORINTHIANS 7:9

Condoning and Condemning

Condoning is the way of the sentimental humanist, the person who cannot bear to see others suffer the consequences of his own actions and wants to make everything all right with Mercurochrome and Band-Aids. Condemning is the way of revengeful barbarians, people who cannot bear to face themselves and who want to make everything all right by getting rid of the offense. Condoning and condemning are both wrong for the same reasons: they refuse to take seriously the integrity of the other person, and to accept the fact that personal choice has personal consequences; they refuse to accept children as persons in their own right and not just extensions of the parent; and they refuse to take seriously the promises of God, to believe that God is capable of bringing good out of evil, healing out of suffering, peace out of disorder, resurrection out of crucifixion. They refuse to believe in Jesus Christ.

> *Jesus stood up and spoke to her. "Woman, where are they? Does no one condemn you?"*
> *"No one, Master."*
> *"Neither do I," said Jesus. "Go on your way. From now on, don't sin."*

JOHN 8:10–11

JUNE 27

Religious Manipulation

When men and women get their hands on religion, one of the first things they often do is turn it into an instrument for controlling others, either putting or keeping them "in their place." The history of such religious manipulation and coercion is long and tedious. It is little wonder that people who have only known religion on such terms experience release or escape from it as freedom. The problem is that the freedom turns out to be short-lived.

You were running superbly! Who cut in on you, deflecting you from the true course of obedience?

GALATIANS 5:13A

JUNE 28

A Destiny to Freedom

No one is born free. Our common human experience prepares us to receive this revealed truth; for when we leave the warm security of the womb, we are immediately embraced in protecting and nurturing arms. If we were set free then, we would merely die. Hunger and thirst, weather and disease, accidents and animals would make short work of us if we were set free. An infant is not born into freedom, but into a network of security and care. If the infant is care*free* it is because of the constant attendance of many who are care*ful*. We begin our lives in an intricate arrangement of constraints, limits, boundaries and restrictions. No one counts that bad. Everyone, in fact, agrees that it is good. But it is not free. If we have nostalgic longings for those years of golden innocence, they are longings not for freedom but for security. We are, if we are fortunate, born secure; we are not born free. We are, however, born with a destiny to freedom and a capacity for freedom which are realized in a life of faith.

Until the time when we were mature enough to respond freely in faith to the living God, we were carefully surrounded and protected by the Mosaic law. The law was like those Greek tutors, with which you are familiar, who escort children to school and protect them from danger or distraction, making sure the children will really get to the place they set out for.

GALATIANS 3:23–24

The Experience of Freedom

There are moments when a single truth seems to cry out for focused proclamation. For me one of these moments came in the early 1980s; freedom in Christ seemed the truth in need of focus. The end of a millennium was in sight. It would soon be two thousand years since Christ lived and died and rose again. The world had seen a succession of political and social revolutions that had featured the word *freedom*. Especially in the Western world, but hardly confined there, aspirations to freedom were very strong. But when I looked at the people I was living with as pastor—fairly affluent, well educated, somewhat knowledgeable about the Christian faith—I realized how unfree they were. They were buying expensive security systems to protect their possessions from burglary. They were overcome with anxieties in the face of rising inflation. They were pessimistic about the prospects for justice and peace in a world bristling with sophisticated weapons systems and nuclear devices. They were living huddled, worried, defensive lives. I wanted to shout in objection: Don't live that way! You are Christians! Our lives can be a growth into freedom instead of a withdrawal into anxious wariness.

Instead of shouting I returned to my regular round of work—preaching and teaching, visiting and counseling, praying and writing, encouraging and directing—but I was determined to seek ways in which I could awaken a hunger and thirst for the free life among people who had lost an appetite for it, and then, having awakened the appetite, to find the food and drink that would satisfy it. The more I did this, the more I became convinced that the experience of freedom in the life of faith is at the very heart of what it means to be human.

Christ has set us free to live a free life. So take your stand! Never again let anyone put a harness of slavery on you.

GALATIANS 5:1

J U N E   3 0

The Specialist in Matters of Freedom

Freedom is not an abstraction, and it is not a thing. It is a gift and a skill. It is a gift that another provides; it is a skill that must be exercised by each person within the learned limits of reality. If we would understand freedom, we must be taught; if we would acquire freedom, we must be trained.

I found my best help in doing this in St. Paul's letter to the Galatians. Among the writers of Scripture, Paul is the specialist in matters of freedom.

My counsel is this: Live freely, animated and motivated by God's Spirit. Then you won't feed the compulsions of selfishness. For there is a root of sinful self-interest in us that is at odds with a free spirit, just as the free spirit is incompatible with selfishness.

GALATIANS 5:16–17

July

Grace . . . Peace

The next fourteen days explore the theme of freedom.

It takes a certain bold courage to receive freedom. The free life is a strenuous life. Living in freedom is demanding and sometimes painful. If security is our highest priority, we will not want to live free. Erich Fromm's book *Escape from Freedom* traces the elaborate attempts by which people avoid the freedom that is given to them, preferring to exist in the secure slaveries provided by totalitarian governments, or totalitarian habits, or totalitarian emotions, or totalitarian addictions.

In every generation great crowds of people mindlessly shuffle along with the herd and do nothing beyond providing statistics for sociological surveys. But also in every generation a few persons live intelligently and courageously in freedom. For these persons, the letter to the Galatians has often been the catalyst to the free life. At several critical times in history this letter, listened to by small groups of Christians, has shifted the direction of the age just enough to make the difference between a surge of new life and a drifting into decline. When people have felt victimized by fear and oppression, it has been a means of setting them free. When many have been paralyzed by anxiety and apprehension, it has stimulated them to an energetic hope. When there has been widespread confusion and bickering and uncertainty about what life was, it has clarified and convinced people of exactly what it means to live openly and well, convinced them to the point of participation in the rescue by which God sets us free to live.

Paul's greeting anticipates what we can expect: "grace . . . and peace." Grace! Life is a gift. Peace! Life is whole. The two words declare that we are, fundamentally and finally, free to live. Life is what we are given, not what we salvage out of the ruins of home and culture. Life is an entirety into which we grow, not a fragment that we snatch on the run.

> *So I greet you with the great words, grace and peace! We know the meaning of those words because Jesus Christ rescued us from this evil world we're in by offering himself as a sacrifice for our sins. God's plan is that we all experience that rescue.*

GALATIANS 1:3–4

JULY 2

Lie About God

Nothing counts more in the way we live than what we believe about God. A failure to get it right in our minds becomes a failure to get it right in our lives. A wrong idea of God translates into sloppiness and cowardice, fearful minds and sickly emotions.

One of the wickedest things one person can do to others is to lie to them about God, to represent God as other or less than he is.

Jesus said, ". . . here you are trying to kill me, a man who has spoken to you the truth he got straight from God!"

JOHN 8:40A

JULY 3

Wicked

It is wicked to tell a person that God is an angry tyrant storming through the heavens, out to get every trespasser and throw him into the lake of fire. It is wicked to tell a person that God is a senile grandfather dozing in a celestial rocking chair with only the shortest of attention spans for what is going on in the world. It is wicked to tell a person that God is a compulsively efficient and utterly humorless manager of a tightly run cosmos, obsessed with getting the highest productivity possible out of history and with absolutely no concern for persons apart from their usefulness.

If we believe that God is an angry tyrant, we are going to defensively avoid him if we can. If we believe that God is a senile grandfather, we are going to live carelessly and trivially with no sense of transcendent purpose. If we believe that God is an efficiency expert, we are going to live angry at being reduced to a function and never appreciated as a person.

It is wicked to tell a person a lie about God because, if we come to believe the wrong things about God, we will think the wrong things about ourselves, and we will live meanly or badly. Telling a person a lie about God distorts reality, perverts life and damages all the processes of living.

While we were in conference we were infiltrated by spies pretending to be Christians, who slipped in to find out just how free true Christians are. Their ulterior motive was to reduce us to their brand of servitude.

GALATIANS 2:4

JULY 4

Recalled to Freedom

God is cosmic and sovereign. God has the first word and the last. "The kingdom of God is at hand." "Do not fear." History shows that people who believe and live in response to the good news are not naive innocents, but the most clearsighted realists. We are recalled to freedom. We will not abandon the free life of the gospel. Let the people who tell us those lies about God be cursed!

Let me be blunt: If one of us—even if an angel from heaven!—were to preach something other than what we preached originally, let him be cursed.

GALATIANS 1:8

Good News About Ourselves

The personal dimension of the gospel is good news about ourselves. The reality of what is within us is every bit as important as the news from the political, industrial and scientific centers of the world. Even if world peace were an accomplished fact and the domestic economy stabilized to everyone's satisfaction, we still must deal with ourselves.

No matter how nice a house we live in, no matter how well educated we become, no matter how secure we feel in job or family, no matter how well we manage to provide an appearance of competence and happiness, if we are filled with anxieties and guilt and hopelessness, we cannot make it. If we cannot escape the conviction that we are no good or have no meaning, that is bad news. We need a sense of integrity and purpose. We need to count, to mean something, to be important to somebody, to make a difference.

*It is no longer important that I appear
righteous before you or have your
good opinion, and I am no longer driven
to impress God. Christ lives in me. The
life you see me living is not "mine,"
but it is lived by faith in the Son of God,
who loved me and gave himself for me.
I am not going to go back on that.*

GALATIANS 2:20B

He Sets Things Right

Someone says, "Listen, God doesn't have time for your little problems. He is busy in the Middle East right now. He has bigger fish to fry. If you want something for yourself, you better get it the best way you can: buy this product and you will be important; wear these clothes and everyone will realize how distinguished you are; read this book and the knowledge will set you a cut above the crowd. Take care of yourself."

That sounds good; we begin to respond. And then we hear Paul's indignant, "I am astonished that you are so quickly deserting him who called you in the grace of Christ." Instinctively, immediately, we know that he is right. The only good news that will make a difference is that the living God personally addresses and mercifully forgives us. He sets things right at the center. That is what we need, what we want. We determine that we will not abandon the free life of the gospel and live in the fantasy dreams that others paint for us and then sell to us for a fee. We will live forgiven and in faith, not as a parasite on others, but creatively for others. We will not mope or cringe or whine. We will praise and venture and make. Let the people who tell us those lies about God be cursed!

I can't believe your fickleness—how easily you have turned traitor to him who called you by the grace of Christ by embracing a variant message!

GALATIANS 1:6

In Praise of God

Any time we look into the newspapers, or into our own hearts, and despair, we do well to remember that God's people have faced similar prospects, similar reversals, similar headlines, similar assaults on faith, and have recovered from the doubt, been rescued from the pessimism and foreboding, and gone on to live in praise of God.

> *[Jesus said,] "Give your entire attention to what God is doing right now, and don't get worked up about what may or may not happen tomorrow. God will help you deal with whatever hard things come up when the time comes."*

MATTHEW 6:34

By His Grace

Life is not an aimless groping. We are called. "By his grace" means that God does not look around to see who will best suit his purposes and then single them out because he is pretty sure that they will do a good job. It means that God has a capacity so large in love and purpose that he calls us in order to do something for us—to give us something. Grace.

Is it not clear to you that to go back to that old rule-keeping peer-pleasing religion would be an abandonment of everything personal and free in my relationship with God? I refuse to do that, to repudiate God's grace.

GALATIANS 2:21A

JULY 9

Overflow

No life of faith can be lived privately. There must be overflow into the lives of others.

Stoop down and reach out to those who are oppressed. Share their burdens, and so complete Christ's law. If you think you are too good for that, you are badly deceived.

GALATIANS 6:3–4

JULY 10

The Poor

Our attitude toward the poor is still one of the surest tests of the health of our freedom. The moment freedom is used to avoid acts of mercy or help or compassion, it is exposed as a fraud. A free person who finds ways to enhance the lives of the poor demonstrates the truest and most mature freedom. A free person who diminishes the lives of the poor by dealing out ridicule or withholding gifts is himself diminished, is herself diminished.

We are free to resist the pressures to conform to an established formula for being rightly related to God; we are free to resist established precedents for working in God's name; we are not free to dismiss poor people from our awareness, to turn a deaf ear to voices that ask for help, to harbor even the slightest contempt for the failures and rejects in our society.

The only additional thing they asked
was that we remember the poor, and I was
already eager to do that.

GALATIANS 2:10

JULY 11

The Least Religious People

In some ways Christians are the least religious people in town—there is so much that we don't believe! We don't believe in good-luck charms, in horoscopes, in fate. We don't believe the world's promises or the world's curses. And we don't believe—this comes to some as a surprise!—in good works.

Paul repeats the phrase "not by works of the law" three times in two verses. He means something quite specific by it. He means the acts that we perform in order to get God's approval. He means religious or moral activity that is designed to save our own skin. It is good behavior or religious behavior that is performed because someone else is looking, or because God is looking. It is life by performance, by show, by achievement. And, of course, it imprisons us because someone is always looking. We never have the pleasure of doing something just for the pleasure that it brings to someone or for the sense of rightness it has in our own lives.

> *Let me put this question to you: How did*
> *your new life begin? Was it by working your*
> *heads off to please God? Or was it by*
> *responding to God's Message to you?*

GALATIANS 3:2

JULY 12

Sinners

All of us are sinners. And we are not going to cease being sinners by redoubling our efforts at being good.

Living in the open means that we don't have to hide who we really are, whitewash our reputations or disguise our hearts. We can be open about who we are, about what we have thought and felt and done. We don't have to exhaust ourselves to project the blame for who we are on God or on our parents or on society. We don't have to make up fancy excuses.

How refreshing that is!

Since we've compiled this long and sorry record as sinners (both us and them) and proved that we are utterly incapable of living the glorious lives God wills for us, God did it for us. Out of sheer generosity he put us in right standing with himself. A pure gift.

ROMANS 3:23–24A

JULY 13

All Is Gift

Where all is gift, I do not own things or persons and thus don't have to protect them. Therefore I don't have to be anxious. In a world of grace I do not live in laborious struggle trying to fashion a world that suits my needs and desires, hammering together a life out of the bits and pieces of scrap lumber that come my way. I do not live in anxious suspicion, nervous about what others might do to me, what others might think of me. I simply discover and receive.

All the great stories of exploration and discovery are parables of Christian venture. Columbus didn't sail across the ocean, decide to create a new continent, go back to Spain and organize a flotilla of ships to bring loads of dirt in order to make the Americas. It was already there. He discovered it and explored it. There is a world to enjoy, a salvation in which to rejoice. God gives. "Grace is everywhere" [George Bernanos]. We receive and explore. We do not nullify the grace of God.

Answer this question: Does the God who lavishly provides you with his own presence, his Holy Spirit, working things in your lives you

could never do for yourselves, does he do these things because of your
strenuous moral striving or because you trust him to do them in you?

GALATIANS 3:5

A Vast Reservoir

There is plenitude in God. That great fact must never be lost or obscured. We must not exchange this immense graciousness for a few
scraps of human morality or a few shopworn proverbs. God is a vast
reservoir of blessing who supplies us abundantly. If we lose touch
with the reality of God, we will live clumsily and badly.

> *Everything comes from him;*
> *Everything happens through him;*
> *Everything ends up in him.*
> *Always glory! Always praise!*
> *Yes. Yes. Yes.*

ROMANS 11:36

Hypocrites

The Christian has more to fear from hypocrisy than anything else.
Nothing stirred Jesus to hotter indignation. Jesus unfailingly ap-

proached the everyday sort of sinners who robbed, broke the sabbath, engaged in prostitution, and even murdered, with inviting compassion. Hypocrites got nothing but His denunciation. The fiery passage in Matthew 23 seethes with anger as Jesus lets loose a string of "woes" against those who practice none of it, who spend enormous amounts of time tidying up the externals and ignore all the internal realities that count with God.

[Jesus said,] "I've had it with you! You're hopeless,
you religion scholars, you Pharisees! Frauds!
Your lives are roadblocks to God's kingdom. You
refuse to enter, and won't let anyone else in either."

MATTHEW 23:13

JULY 16

A Healthy Noun

While the following days speak of "pastor,"
each of us can substitute our name or title.

A healthy noun doesn't need adjectives. Adjectives clutter a noun that is robust. But if the noun is culture-damaged or culture-diseased, adjectives are necessary.

"Pastor" used to be that kind of noun—energetic and virile. I have always loved the sound of the word. From an early age, the word called to mind a person who was passionate for God and compassionate with people. And even though the pastors I knew did not embody those characteristics, the word itself held its own against its exemplars. Today still, when people ask me what I want to be called, I always say, "Pastor."

But when I observe the way the vocation of pastor is lived out in America and listen to the tone and context in which the word *pastor* is spoken, I realize that what I hear in the word and what others hear is very different. In general usage, the noun is weak, defined by parody and diluted by opportunism. The need for strengthening adjectives is critical.

I find I have to exercise this adjectival rehabilitation constantly, redefining by refusing the definitions of *pastor* that the culture hands me, and reformulating my life with the insights and images of Scripture. The culture treats me so amiably! It encourages me to maintain my orthodox creed; it commends me for my evangelical practice; it praises me for my singular devotion. All it asks is that I accept its definition of my work as an encourager of the culture's good will, as the priest who will sprinkle holy water on the culture's good intentions. Many of these people are my friends. None, that I am aware of, is consciously malign.

But if I, even for a moment, accept my culture's definition of me, I am rendered harmless. I can denounce evil and stupidity all I wish and will be tolerated in my denunciations as a court jester is tolerated. I can organize their splendid goodwill and they will let me do it, since it is only for weekends.

The essence of being a pastor begs for redefinition.

You've been raised on the Message of the faith and have followed sound teaching. Now pass on this counsel to the Christians there, and you'll be a good servant of Jesus. Stay clear of silly stories that get dressed up as religion.

1 TIMOTHY 4:6–7A

The Intense Work of Listening

Listening is in short supply in the world today; people aren't used to being listened to. I know how easy it is to avoid the tough, intense work of listening by being busy—as when I let a hospital patient know there are ten more people I have to see. (Have to? I'm not indispensable to any of them, and I am here with this one.) Too much of pastoral visitation is punching the clock, assuring people we're on the job, being busy, earning our pay.

Answering before listening
is both stupid and rude.

PROVERBS 18:13

Ambiance of Leisure

Pastoral listening requires unhurried leisure, even if it's only for five minutes. Leisure is a quality of spirit, not a quantity of time. Only in that ambiance of leisure do persons know they are listened to with absolute seriousness, treated with dignity and importance. Speaking to people does not have the same personal intensity as listening to them. The question I put to myself is not "How many people have you spoken to about Christ this week?" but "How many people have you listened to in Christ this week?" The number of persons listened to must necessarily be less than the number spoken to. Listening to a story always takes more time than delivering a message, so I must discard my compulsion to count, to compile the statistics that will justify my existence.

I can't listen if I'm busy. When my schedule is crowded, I'm not free to listen: I have to keep my next appointment; I have to get to the next meeting. But if I provide margins to my day, there is ample time to listen.

Jesus said, "Come off by yourselves; let's take a break and get a little rest." For there was constant coming and going. They didn't even have time to eat.

So they got in the boat and went off to a remote place by themselves.

MARK 6:31–32

JULY 19

Quiet and Poised, Waiting

In Herman Melville's *Moby Dick,* there is a turbulent scene in which a whaleboat scuds across a frothing ocean in pursuit of the great, white whale, Moby Dick. The sailors are laboring fiercely, every muscle taut, all attention and energy concentrated on the task. The cosmic conflict between good and evil is joined; chaotic sea and demonic sea monster versus the morally outraged man, Captain Ahab. In this boat, however, there is one man who does nothing. He doesn't hold an oar; he doesn't perspire; he doesn't shout. He is languid in the crash and the cursing. This man is the harpooner, quiet and poised, waiting. And then this sentence: "To insure the greatest efficiency in the dart, the harpooners of this world must start to their feet out of idleness, and not out of toil."

Melville's sentence is a text to set alongside the psalmist's "Be still, and know that I am God" (Ps. 46:10), and alongside Isaiah's "In returning and rest you shall be saved; in quietness and in trust shall be your strength" (Isa. 30:15).

> *God, the one and only—*
> > *I'll wait as long as he says.*
> *Everything I need comes from him,*
> > *so why not?*
> *He's solid rock under my feet,*
> > *breathing room for my soul . . .*

PSALM 62:1–2A

A State of Catatonic Disbelief

But America and suburbia and the ego compose my parish. Most of the individuals in this amalgam suppose that the goals they have for themselves and the goals God has for them are the same. It is the oldest religious mistake: refusing to countenance any real difference between God and us, imagining God to be a vague extrapolation of our own desires, and then hiring a priest to manage the affairs between self and the extrapolation. And I, one of the priests they hired, am having none of it.

But if I'm not willing to help them become what they want to be, what am I doing taking their pay? I am being subversive. I am undermining the kingdom of self and establishing the kingdom of God. I am helping them to become what God wants them to be, using the methods of subversion.

But isn't that dishonest? Not exactly, for I'm not misrepresenting myself. I'm simply taking my words and acts at a level of seriousness that would throw them into a state of catatonic disbelief if they ever knew.

Repeat these basic essentials over and over to God's people. Warn them before God against pious nitpicking, which chips away at the faith. It just wears everyone out. Concentrate on doing your best for God, work you won't be ashamed of, laying out the truth plain and simple.

2 TIMOTHY 2:14–15

JULY 21

A Master at Subversion

The kingdom of self is heavily defended territory. Post-Eden Adams and Eves are willing to pay their respects to God, but they don't want him invading their turf. Most sin, far from being a mere lapse of morals or a weak will, is an energetically and expensively erected defense against God. Direct assault in an openly declared war on the god-self is extraordinarily ineffective. Hitting sin head-on is like hitting a nail with a hammer; it only drives it in deeper. There are occasional exceptions, strategically dictated confrontations, but indirection is the biblically preferred method.

Jesus was a master at subversion. Until the very end, everyone, including his disciples, called him Rabbi. Rabbis were important, but they didn't make anything happen. On the occasions when suspicions were aroused that there might be more to him than that title accounted for, Jesus tried to keep it quiet—"Tell no one."

[Jesus said,] "God's kingdom is like yeast that a woman works into the dough for dozens of loaves of barley bread—and waits while the dough rises."

MATTHEW 13:33

JULY 22

The Parable

Jesus' favorite speech form, the parable, was subversive. Parables sound absolutely ordinary: casual stories about soil and seeds, meals and coins and sheep, bandits and victims, farmers and merchants. And they are wholly secular: of his forty or so parables recorded in the Gospels, only one has its setting in church, and only a couple mention the name God. As people heard Jesus tell these stories, they saw at once that they weren't about God, so there was nothing in them threatening their own sovereignty. They relaxed their defenses. They walked away perplexed, wondering what they meant, the stories lodged in their imagination. And then, like a time bomb, they would explode in their unprotected hearts. An abyss opened up at their very feet. He *was* talking about God; they had been invaded!

All Jesus did that day was tell stories—a long storytelling afternoon. His storytelling fulfilled the prophecy:

> *"I will open my mouth and tell stories;*
> *I will bring out into the open*
>   *things hidden since the world's first day."*

MATTHEW 13:34–35

JULY 23

Slip Past Our Defenses

Parables subversively slip past our defenses. Once they're inside the citadel of self, we might expect a change of method, a sudden brandishing of bayonets resulting in a palace coup. But it doesn't happen. Our integrity is honored and preserved. God does not impose his reality from without; he grows flowers and fruit from within. God's truth is not an alien invasion but a loving courtship in which the details of our common lives are treated as seeds in our conception, growth, and maturity in the kingdom. Parables trust our imaginations, which is to say, our faith. They don't herd us paternalistically into a classroom where we get things explained and diagrammed. They don't bully us into regiments where we find ourselves marching in a moral goose step.

[Jesus said,] "God's kingdom is like a pine nut that a farmer plants. It is quite small as seeds go, but in the course of years it grows into a huge pine tree, and eagles build nests in it."

MATTHEW 13:31–32

JULY 24

Poetry Is Essential

Isn't it odd that pastors, who are responsible for interpreting the Scriptures, so much of which come in the form of poetry, have so little interest in poetry? It is a crippling defect and must be remedied. The Christian communities as a whole must rediscover poetry, and the pastors must lead them. Poetry is essential to the pastoral vocation because poetry is original speech. The word is creative: it brings into being what was not there before—perception, relationship, belief. Out of the silent abyss a sound is formed: people hear what was not heard before and are changed by the sound from loneliness into love. Out of the blank abyss a picture is formed by means of metaphor: people see what they did not see before and are changed by the image from anonymity into love. Words create. God's word creates; our words can participate in the creation.

> [*Jesus said,*] *"We're not keeping secrets, we're telling them; we're not hiding things, we're bringing them out into the open.*
> *"Are you listening to this?*
> *"Really listening?"*

MARK 4:22–23

JULY 25

Blessed Are the Poor in Spirit

A beech tree in winter, white
Intricacies unconcealed
Against sky blue and billowed
Clouds, carries in his emptiness
Ripeness: sap ready to rise
On signal, buds alert to burst
To leaf. And then after a season
Of summer a lean ring to remember
The lush fulfilled promises.
Empty again in wise poverty
That lets the reaching branches stretch
A millimeter more towards heaven,

The bole expands ever so slightly
And push roots into the firm
Foundation, lucky to be leafless:
Deciduous reminder to let it go.

[Jesus said,] "You're blessed when you're at the end of your rope.
With less of you there is more of God and his rule."

MATTHEW 5:3

Blessed Are Those Who Mourn

Flash floods of tears, torrents of them,
Erode cruel canyons, exposing
Long forgotten strata of life
Laid down in the peaceful decades:
A badlands beauty. The same sun
That decorates each day with colors
From arroyos and mesas, also shows
Every old scar and cut of lament.
Weeping washes the wounds clean
And leaves them to heal, which always
Takes an age or two. No pain
Is ugly in past tense. Under
The Mercy every hurt is a fossil
Link in the great chain of becoming.

Pick and shovel prayers often
Turn them up in valleys of death.

*[Jesus said,] "You're blessed when you feel you've lost what is most dear
to you. Only then can you be embraced by the One most dear to you."*

MATTHEW 5:4

J U L Y   2 7

Blessed Are Those Who Hunger and Thirst

Unfeathered unbelief would fall
Through the layered fullness of thermal
Updrafts like a rock; this red-tailed
Hawk drifts and slides, unhurried
Though hungry, lazily scornful
Of easy meals off carrion junk,
Expertly waiting elusive provisioned
Prey: a visible emptiness
Above an invisible plenitude.
The sun paints the Japanese
Fantail copper, etching
Feathers against the big sky
To my eye's delight, and blesses
The better-sighted bird with a shaft
Of light that targets a rattler
In a Genesis-destined death.

[Jesus said,] "You're blessed when you've worked up a good appetite for God. He's food and drink in the best meal you'll ever eat."

MATTHEW 5:6

JULY 28

Blessed Are the Merciful

A billion years of pummeling surf,
Shipwrecking seachanges and Jonah storms
Made ungiving, unforgiving granite
Into this analgesic beach:
Washed by sea-swell rhythms of mercy,
Merciful relief from city
Concrete. Uncondemned, discalceate,
I'm ankle deep in Assateague sands,
Awake to rich designs of compassion
Patterned in the pillowing dunes.
Sandpipers and gulls in skittering,
Precise formation devoutly attend
My salt and holy solitude,
Then feed and fly along the moving,
Imprecise ebb- and rip-tide
Border dividing care from death.

> *[Jesus said,] "You're blessed when you care. At the moment of being 'care-full,' you find yourselves cared for."*
>
> MATTHEW 5:7

Religiopath

The marathon is one of the most strenuous athletic events in sport. The Boston Marathon attracts the best runners in the world. The winner is automatically placed among the great athletes of our time. In the spring of 1980, Rosie Ruiz was the first woman to cross the finish line. She had the laurel wreath placed on her head in a blaze of lights and cheering.

She was completely unknown in the world of running. An incredible feat! Her first race a victory in the prestigious Boston Marathon! Then someone noticed her legs—loose flesh, cellulite. Questions were asked. No one had seen her along the 26.2 mile course. The truth came out: she had jumped into the race during the last mile.

There was immediate and widespread interest in Rosie. Why would she do that when it was certain that she would be found out? Athletic performance cannot be faked. But she never admitted her fraud. She repeatedly said that she would run another marathon to validate her ability. Somehow she never did. People interviewed her, searching for a clue to her personality. One interviewer concluded that she really believed that she had run the complete Boston Marathon and won. She was analyzed as a sociopath. She lied convincingly and naturally with no sense of conscience, no sense of reality in terms of right and wrong, acceptable and unacceptable behavior. She appeared bright, normal and intelligent. But there was no moral sense to give coherence to her social actions.

In reading about Rosie I thought of all the people I know who want to get in on the finish but who cleverly arrange not to run the race. They appear in church on Sunday wreathed in smiles, entering into the celebration, but there is no personal life that leads up to it or out from it. Occasionally they engage in spectacular acts of love and compassion in public. We are impressed, but surprised, for they were never known to do that before. Yet, you never know. Better give them the benefit of the doubt. Then it turns out to be a stunt: no personal involvement either precedes or follows the act. They are plausible and convincing. But in the end they do not run the race, believing through the tough times, praying through the lonely, angry, hurt hours. They have no sense for what is *real* in religion. The proper label for such a person is *religiopath*.

> *I don't know about you, but I'm running hard for the finish line. I'm giving it everything I've got. No sloppy living for me! I'm staying alert and in top condition. I'm not going to get caught napping, telling everyone else all about it and then missing out myself.*

1 CORINTHIANS 9:26–27

JULY 30

In the Midst of Alienation

The essential meaning of exile is that we are where we don't want to be. We are separated from home. We are not permitted to reside in the place where we comprehend and appreciate our surroundings. We are forced to be away from that which is most congenial to us. It is an experience of dislocation—everything is out of joint; nothing fits together. The thousand details that have been built up through the years that give a sense of at-homeness—gestures, customs, rituals, phrases—are all gone. Life is ripped out of the familiar soil of generations of language, habit, weather, story-telling, and rudely and unceremoniously dropped into some unfamiliar spot of earth. The place of exile may boast a higher standard of living. It may be more pleasant in its weather. That doesn't matter. It isn't home.

But this very strangeness can open up new reality to us. An accident, a tragedy, a disaster of any kind can force the realization that the world is not predictable, that reality is far more extensive than our habitual perception of it. With the pain and in the midst of alienation a sense of freedom can occur.

Friends, this world is not your home, so don't make yourselves cozy in it. Don't indulge your ego at the expense of your soul. Live an exemplary life among the natives so that your actions will refute their prejudices. They'll be won over to God's side and be there to join in the celebration when he arrives.

1 PETER 2:11–12

JULY 31

Coherent

Cultivate your own relationship with God, but don't impose it on others. You're fortunate if your behavior and your belief are coherent. But if you're not sure, if you notice that you are acting in ways inconsistent with what you believe—some days trying to impose your opinions on others, other days just trying to please them—then you know that you're out of line. If the way you live isn't consistent with what you believe, then it's wrong.

ROMANS 14:19–23

August

Quite Free to Resist

There are always some in the church who say that the best way to express the Christian faith is as a pastor, or missionary, or monk, or nun—or in medicine, or social work, or educational enterprises. There are always some who know exactly what another is best suited for. But no one knows us well enough for that. Each of us has unique gifts, for which there are no precedents, yet which will be used in ministry. And we are quite free to resist anyone who tells us differently.

> *Each person is given something to do*
> *that shows who God is: Everyone gets in*
> *on it, everyone benefits. All kinds of*
> *things are handed out by the Spirit, and to*
> *all kinds of people!*

1 CORINTHIANS 12:7

A Helper Fit for Him

READ Genesis 2:19–23

God does not provide a bare biological minimum in creation but a glorious personal richness. We are not created to be self-sufficient. We are made for personal relationships, and until we engage in them we are not complete.

What are your most important personal relationships?

PRAYER: I thank you, O God, not only for creating me, but for creating others, for placing me in a world where I can recognize and explore the meaning of your purposes in the gift of another human face. *Amen.*

So since we find ourselves fashioned into all these excellently formed and marvelously functioning parts in Christ's body, let's just go ahead and be what we were made to be, without enviously or pridefully comparing ourselves with each other, or trying to be something we aren't.

ROMANS 12:5–6A

Not Stuck in a Rut

We all know people who spend a lifetime at the same job, or the same marriage, or the same profession, who are slowly, inexorably diminished in the process. They are persistent in the sense that they keep doing the same thing for many years, but we don't particularly admire them for it. If anything, we feel sorry for them for having got stuck in such an uninteresting rut with neither the energy nor imagination to get out.

But we don't feel sorry for Jeremiah. He was not stuck in a rut; he was committed to a purpose. The one thing that Jeremiah shows no evidence of is bored drudgery. Everything we know of him shows that after the twenty-three years his imagination is even more alive and his spirit even more resilient than it was in his youth. He wasn't putting in his time. Every day was a new episode in the adventure of living the prophetic life. The days added up to a life of incredible tenacity, of amazing stamina.

> *So we're not giving up. How could we! Even though on the outside it often looks like things are falling apart on us, on the inside, where God is making new life, not a day goes by without his unfolding grace.*

2 CORINTHIANS 4:16

AUGUST 4

Never Give Up

The mark of a certain kind of genius is the ability and energy to keep returning to the same task relentlessly, imaginatively, curiously, for a lifetime. Never give up and go on to something else; never get distracted and be diverted to something else. Augustine wrote fifteen commentaries on the book of Genesis. He began at the beginning. He never felt that he had got to the depths of the first book of the Bible, down to the very origins of life, the first principles of God's ways with us. He kept returning to those first questions. Beethoven composed sixteen string quartets because he was never satisfied with what he had done. The quartet form intrigued and challenged him. Perfection eluded him—he kept coming back to it over and over in an attempt at mastery. We think he did pretty well with them, but he didn't think so. So he persisted, bringing fresh, creative energy to each day's attempt. The same thing over and over, and yet it is never the same thing, for each venture is resplendent with dazzling creativity.

Not one of these people, even though their lives of faith were exemplary, got their hands on what was promised. God had a better plan for us: that their faith and our faith would come together to make one completed whole, their lives of faith not complete apart from ours.

HEBREWS 11:39–40

AUGUST 5

Our Words

For, somewhere along the line things went wrong (Genesis tells that story, too) and are in desperate need of fixing. The fixing is all accomplished by speaking—God speaking salvation into being in the person of Jesus. Jesus, in this account, not only speaks the word of God; he is the Word of God.

Keeping company with these words, we begin to realize that our words are more important than we ever supposed. Saying "I believe," for instance, marks the difference between life and death. Our words accrue dignity and gravity in conversations with Jesus. For Jesus doesn't impose salvation as a solution; he narrates salvation into being through leisurely conversation, intimate personal relationships, compassionate responses, passionate prayer, and—putting it all together—a sacrificial death. We don't casually walk away from words like that.

This Son perfectly mirrors God, and is stamped with God's nature. He holds everything together by what he says—powerful words!

HEBREWS 1:3

AUGUST 6

The Waters of the Flood

READ Genesis 7:6–10

Chaos was commanded into order in creation (Genesis 1:2, 6–7). Now, by God's command, the chaos returns. It is evident now that sin was not a minor dislocation of creation, a bothersome disturbance in history. Sin is catastrophic.

What are your emotional responses to the word "flood"?

PRAYER: As I attempt, O God, to comprehend the totality of your judgment, help me to realize that all my life, and everything I know about life, is deeply disturbed by sin and must be included in your salvation. *Amen.*

Neither did he let the ancient ungodly world off. He wiped it out with a flood, rescuing only eight people—Noah, the sole voice of righteousness, was one of them.

2 PETER 2:5

AUGUST 7

Embarrassingly Banal

The pastoral vocation in America is embarrassingly banal. It is banal because it is pursued under the canons of job efficiency and career management. It is banal because it is reduced to the dimensions of a job description. It is banal because it is an idol—a call from God exchanged for an offer by the devil for work that can be measured and manipulated at the convenience of the worker. Holiness is not banal. Holiness is blazing.

"But why do you let that Jezebel who calls herself a prophet mislead my dear servants into Cross-denying, self-indulging religion? I gave her a chance to change her ways, but she has no intention of giving up a career in the god-business."

REVELATION 2:20–21

Lip Service

Pastors commonly give lip service to the vocabulary of a holy vocation, but in our working lives we more commonly pursue careers. Our actual work takes shape under the pressure of the marketplace, not the truth of theology or the wisdom of spirituality. I would like to see as much attention given to the holiness of our vocations as to the piety of our lives.

> *And oh, my dear Timothy, guard the treasure you were given! Guard it with your life. Avoid the talk-show religion and the practiced confusion of the so-called experts.*

1 TIMOTHY 6:20

Pestilence that Stalks at Noonday

It is no more difficult to pursue the pastoral vocation than any other. Vocations in homemaking, science, agriculture, education, and business when embraced with biblically informed commitments are likewise demanding and require an equivalent spirituality. But each requires its own specific attention. What is essential for pastors is that we focus on our particular "pestilence that stalks at noonday." In our eagerness to be sympathetic to others and meet their needs, to equip

them with a spirituality adequate to their discipleship, we must not
fail to take with full seriousness *our* straits, lest when we have saved
others we ourselves should be castaways.

There are some, you know, who by relaxing their grip and thinking
anything goes have made a thorough mess of their faith. Hymenaeus
and Alexander are two of them.

1 TIMOTHY 1:19–20A

AUGUST 10

A Taste of God

A curious thing happens to us when we get a taste of God. It happened first in Eden and it keeps happening. The experience *of*
God—the ecstasy, the wholeness of it—is accompanied by a temptation to reproduce the experience *as* God. The taste *for* God is debased into a greed to *be* God. Being loved by God is twisted into a
lust to God-performance. I get a glimpse of a world in which God is
in charge and think maybe I have a chance at it. I abandon the personal presence of God and take up with the depersonalized and
canny serpent. I flee the shining face of God for a slithery world of
religion that gives me license to manipulate people and acquire god-
like attributes to myself. The moment I begin cultivating the possibility of acquiring that kind of power and glory for myself, I most
certainly will want to blot out the face, flee from the presence of the
Lord, and seek a place where I can develop pride and acquire
power.

When Simon saw that the apostles by merely laying on hands conferred the Spirit, he pulled out his money, excited, and said, "Sell me your secret! Show me how you did that! How much do you want? Name your price!"

Peter said, "To hell with your money! And you along with it. Why, that's unthinkable—trying to buy God's gift!"

ACTS 8:18–20

AUGUST 11

In the Form of a Virtue

There is a long and well-documented tradition of wisdom in the Christian faith that any venture into leadership, whether by laity or clergy, is hazardous. It is necessary that there be leaders, but woe to those who become leaders. On the assumption of leadership—even modest forays into leadership—possibilities for sin that were previously inaccessible immediately present themselves. And these new possibilities are exceedingly difficult to recognize as sins, for each comes in the form of a virtue. The unwary embrace these new "opportunities" to do service for the Lord, innocent of the reality that they are swallowing bait—a promise that turns, whether soon or late, into curse. "Let not many become teachers" warned St. James, who knew the perils firsthand.

Don't be in any rush to become a teacher, my friends. Teaching is highly responsible work. Teachers are held to the strictest standards. And none of us are perfectly qualified.

JAMES 3:1–2A

AUGUST 12

Suffering

We live in a culture that doesn't know how to suffer. We grow up thinking that if we are good we won't suffer; or that if we raise our standard of living sufficiently we won't suffer; or that if we acquire an education we will be smart enough not to suffer. If suffering rudely intrudes anyway, we call for anesthesia. Anesthesia, which is most useful on occasions of surgery, is most harmful in matters of soul.

This is the kind of life you've been invited into, the kind of life Christ lived. He suffered everything that came his way so you would know that it could be done, and also know how to do it, step by step.

1 PETER 2:21

AUGUST 13

Careers of Anesthesiology

Despite (could it be because of?) our vaunted affluence and learning, we men and women of North America seem for the most part to be scandalously ignorant with regard to human suffering. More scandalous still, a great many Christians are currently complicitous in this ignorance. Christians right and left, Christians whose identifying symbol is the cross of Jesus and whose vocation is determined by that same cross, are abandoning it for careers in anesthesiology.

This is a scandal because Christians are the world's experts on suffering. The world deserves to know what we know about suffering, it *needs* to know what we have learned from Jesus at the cross of Jesus. The people in our neighborhoods need to know that suffering is not the worst thing that can happen to them, that oblivion is not preferable to suffering.

> *Since Jesus went through everything you're going through and more, learn to think like him. Think of your sufferings as a weaning from that old sinful habit of always expecting to get your own way. Then you'll be able to live out your days free to pursue what God wants instead of being tyrannized by what you want.*

1 PETER 4:1–2

AUGUST 14

Dismissing Your Servant in Peace

READ *Luke 2:27–32*

The song of Simeon displays the wise contentment of a long life lived in devotion to God. Simeon is prepared to die peacefully, not because of the great things he has accomplished that he can view with pride, but because he has seen God accomplish *his* purpose.

What would you like to see before you die?

PRAYER: Help me so to live, O God, that when I approach the time of my death I may look back with neither regret nor panic, but rather with quiet gratitude for all I have seen and experienced of your grace through Jesus Christ. *Amen.*

> *God, you can now release your servant;*
> *release me in peace as you promised.*
> *With my own eyes I've seen your salvation;*
> *it's now out in the open for everyone to see.*

LUKE 2:29–31

AUGUST 15

Enslaving

All of us grow up with an inferiority complex. Some of us are able to disguise it better than others, but the feelings of inferiority are there all the same. One reason is that during the most formative years of our lives, we were small, less knowledgeable, weaker and less experienced than the important people in our lives (parents, teachers, older children in the neighborhood). There was always someone around who was better than we were in some way or other. We lose some of those feelings as we mature, but never entirely. We are always vulnerable to self-doubt. Am I worth anything at all? Does anyone care if I really exist? If I disappeared tomorrow, how long would it take before everything was normal? A week, a month, a year? We try in various ways to become indispensable to people around us so that we can have our significance verified, but our efforts are not convincing.

We cannot experience freedom when we live that way. A feeling of inadequacy is enslaving. No matter how free we are told that we are, if we don't think we are worth anything, we will not be motivated to express our strengths, will not be confident in developing our gifts, will not feel up to enjoying the blessings of the day.

That means that we will not compare ourselves with each other as if one of us were better and another worse. We have far more interesting things to do with our lives. Each of us is an original.

GALATIANS 5:26

AUGUST 16

Redemption

The gospel counters that enslaving experience by telling the story of our redemption: "We were slaves to the elemental spirits of the universe. But when the time had fully come, God sent forth his Son, born of woman, born under the law, to redeem those who were under the law, so that we might receive adoption as sons." That action-packed sentence is a powerful description of Christ's great work on behalf of all of us. One word in it tells us what we are worth: *redeem.*

All Paul's readers would have been familiar with the first century Greek process for freeing slaves. The word *redeem* describes this process. Sometimes a slave caught the attention of a wealthy free person and for some reason or other—compassion, affection, justice— the free person decided to free the slave. The free person would then go to the temple or shrine and deposit with the priests the sum of money required for manumission. The priests would then deliver an oracle: The god Apollo has purchased this slave so-and-so from owners such-and-such and is now free. The priests then passed the redemption price on to the recent owner. The ex-slave who all his or her life had been treated as an inferior, useful only for purposes of running someone else's errands, doing someone else's work, was no longer subject to such evaluation. The person was free. No price could be put on that head again. The person was valuable not to *do* something but to *be* someone.

That, says Paul, is what has happened to each and everyone of us: we have been singled out for redemption.

> *But when the time arrived that was set by God the Father, God sent his Son, born among us of a woman, born under the conditions of the law so that he might redeem those of us who have been kidnapped by the law. Thus we have been set free to experience our rightful heritage.*

GALATIANS 4:4–5

AUGUST 17

An Extension . . . *Not as an* Exemption

Paul will not permit us to compensate for neglecting those nearest us by advertising our compassion for those on another continent. Jesus, it must be remembered, restricted nine-tenths of his ministry to twelve Jews because it was the only way to redeem all Americans. He

couldn't be bothered, says Martin Thornton, with the foreign Ca-
naanites because his work was to save the whole world. The check for
the starving child must still be written and the missionary sent, but as
an *extension* of what we are doing at home, not as an *exemption* from it.

> *For everything we know about God's Word is summed up in*
> *a single sentence: Love others as you love yourself. That's an act*
> *of true freedom.*

GALATIANS 5:14

AUGUST 18

A Living Presence

Spirit is the scriptural word for God sharing his life in our lives. It
means that God is not an anonymous somebody "out there" or an
idea explained in a book, but a living presence whom I experience in
the life I live day by day. God gives himself to me. I receive God into
myself. Spirit is God's gift of himself in my experience.

> *When God lives and breathes in you (and he*
> *does, as surely as he did in Jesus), you are delivered*
> *from that dead life. With his Spirit living in you,*
> *your body will be as alive as Christ's!*

ROMANS 8:11B

Use Your Heads

The gospel introduces us to a life that begins by receiving the life of God. God pours out his love for us. He mercifully provides access to forgiveness. All that is very exhilarating. It is a clear and vast improvement over living on the basis of appetites and impulses, getting and grabbing. We embark on the way of faith. We become free. We are filled with hope. We live more intensely and more amply than ever before.

Now, having begun there, what is the next step? What is the next step after love? Cautious mistrust? That is silly. What is the next step after faith? Anxious attempts to avoid anything that might displease God? That is silly. What is the next step after grace? Cannily bargaining with God so that we can manipulate him for our benefit? That is silly. That is like saying, "Having learned algebra, I will now go back to counting on my fingers."

"Use your heads," says Paul. Common sense ought to keep you from abandoning the gospel of grace. Only as we remain rooted in the gospel can we apply the great truths of love and forgiveness and grace to everyday affairs.

Are you going to continue this craziness? For only crazy people would think they could complete by their own efforts what was begun by God. If you weren't smart enough or strong enough to begin it, how do you suppose you could perfect it? Did you go through this whole painful learning process for nothing? It is not yet a total loss, but it certainly will be if you keep this up!

GALATIANS 3:3

A Healthy Value System

What are our values? In the Christian way we acquire a healthy value system. We find that persons are more important than property. We learn that forgiveness is preferable to revenge. We realize that worshiping God is more central than impressing our neighbors. . . .

Values infuse life with a steady sense of direction and purpose. They free us from the petty dictatorships of fashion and fad and free us to pour ourselves into large goals for high purposes. The gospel keeps us in touch with sane and healthy values.

Summing it all up, friends, I'd say you'll do best by filling your minds and meditating on things true, noble, reputable, authentic, compelling, gracious—the best, not the worst; the beautiful, not the ugly; things to praise, not things to curse. Put into practice what you learned from me, what you heard and saw and realized. Do that, and God, who makes everything work together, will work you into his most excellent harmonies.

PHILIPPIANS 4:8–9

The Claim of the Gospel

The claim of the gospel is that it puts us in touch with reality—all of it, not just a part. It puts us in touch with a God who creates and with the people and world he created. It puts us in touch with a Christ who redeems and the people whom he loves. It puts us in touch with our feelings of hope and despair, with our thoughts of doubt and faith, with our acts of virtue and vice. It puts us in touch with everything, visible and invisible, right and wrong, good and evil. It puts us in touch and then trains us in mature ways of living.

We live in a world where people are going crazy. We have a gospel that sets us free to think, and in so doing it develops us in a rich and robust sanity. The sanity of the gospel is one of its most attractive features. Persons who truly live by faith are in touch with reality and become conspicuously sane.

Then Jesus turned to the Jews who had claimed to believe in him. "If you stick with this, living out what I tell you, you are my disciples for sure. Then you will experience for yourselves the truth, and the truth will free you."

JOHN 8:31–32

AUGUST 22

Life . . . Death

On the first page of the Bible we read that God creates life; two pages later man and woman choose death. History narrates the antiphony between God's will to life and the human will to death.

The word *life,* in the Bible and in all deeply imagined literature, means far more than biological existence. The word *death,* likewise, means far more than the termination of biological function. Each word is rich in both literal and metaphorical nuance. Using the words in these deep and penetrating ways, the Bible tells the story of the life of God and of the death of persons.

> *Here it is in a nutshell: Just as one person did it wrong and got us in all this trouble with sin and death, another person did it right and got us out of it. But more than just getting us out of trouble, he got us into life! One man said no to God and put many people in the wrong; one man said yes to God and put many in the right.*

ROMANS 5:18–19

AUGUST 23

Sing to God

Hallelujah!
Sing to GOD a brand-new song,
　　praise him in the company of all who love him.
Let all Israel celebrate their Sovereign Creator,
　　Zion's children exult in their King.
Let them praise his name in dance;
　　strike up the band and make great music!
And why? Because GOD delights in his people,
　　festoons plain folk with salvation garlands!

Let true lovers break out in praise,
　　sing out from wherever they're sitting,

Shout the high praises of God,
    brandish their swords in the wild sword-dance—
A portent of vengeance on the God-defying nations,
    a signal that punishment's coming,
Their kings chained and hauled off to jail,
    their leaders behind bars for good,
The judgment on them carried out to the letter—
    and all who love God in the seat of honor!
Hallelujah!

PSALM 149

Knelt Down on the Beach

READ Acts 21:1–6

Any place is the proper place to pray; wherever Christians kneel in the vast cathedral of creation, altars appear unbidden. There can be few places left on earth that have not been consecrated by someone's prayers, whether formal or spontaneous.

Where are some of the significant places you have prayed?

PRAYER: Wherever I am today, O God—in car, kitchen, school, office, workroom—I will make it a place of prayer. As I bend or bow my head, meet me in the power of your Spirit and lead me in the way of your salvation. In Jesus' name. *Amen.*

Then Paul went down on his knees, all of them kneeling with him,
and prayed.

ACTS 20:36

AUGUST 25

Supernatural Excitement

The visions come to an end. St. John, dazed in adoration, falls at the feet of the revealing angel, prostrate in worship. The angel rebukes the misplaced devotion: "You must not do that! I am a fellow servant with you and your brethren the prophets, and with those who keep the words of this book. Worship God" (Rev. 22:9). This is the second time that St. John has tried to worship the revealing angel instead of the revealed God (Rev. 19:10). Why is he having such a hard time getting it right? Why do we? Because it is easier. It is easier to indulge in ecstasies than to engage in obedience. It is easier to pursue a fascination with the supernatural than to enter into the service of God. And because it is easier, it happens more often. We have recurrent epidemics of infatuation with religion. People love being entertained by miracles. A religion of angels is a religion of supernatural excitement, of miraculous ecstasy. It is heady stuff. Around it for very long, any of us are apt to get swept off our feet and carried along in the general delirium. Revealing angels have always proved more popular than the revealed God.

When the crowd saw what Paul had done, they went wild,
calling out in their Lyconian dialect, "The gods have come down!

*These men are gods!"... When Barnabas and Paul finally
realized what was going on, they stopped them ...
"What do you think you're doing! We're not gods! We
are men just like you, and we're here to bring you the
Message, to persuade you to abandon these silly
god-superstitions and embrace God himself, the living God."*

ACTS 14:11, 14–15A

AUGUST 26

It Is About God

The way St. John's Book of Revelation has been treated by many of
his readers is similar to the way he himself treated the revealing
angel, but without the promptly heeded angelic rebuke. It is difficult
to worship God instead of his messengers. And so people get interested in everything in this book except God, losing themselves in
symbol hunting, intrigue with numbers, speculating with frenzied
imaginations on times and seasons, despite Jesus' severe stricture
against it (Acts 1:7). The number of intelligent and devout people
prostrate before the angel, deaf to his rebuke, is depressing and inex-
cusable. For nothing is more explicit in this book than that it is about
God. It is the revelation of Jesus Christ, not the end of the world, not
the identity of antichrist, not the timetable of history. The use of the
"I" throughout the text makes this unmistakable: Jesus Christ as
Lord, and the God of Jesus Christ, speak in the first person to tell us
who Jesus is ("I am the Alpha and the Omega," in the opening

proclamation). Nothing in the book is comprehensible except through faith in Christ. Nothing has meaning apart from his lordship. There is not a line here that is not rigorously theological.

> *He [Jesus] told them, "You don't get to know*
> *the time. Timing is the Father's business. What*
> *you'll get is the Holy Spirit."*

ACTS 1:7–8A

AUGUST 27

What God Is Up To

What God is up to in the world and what goes on in the world because of it has now been revealed to us in a succession of stunning images. God creates in ways past finding out, with energy and in beauty exceeding anything that we have eyes and ears for. Nothing that we encounter from birth to burial merely *is*. It is the marvelous result of God's making. There is a verb behind every noun, the first verb in cosmos and scripture: create. God saves in ways past finding out, with a persistence and wisdom exceeding anything we can will or understand. No person we meet from the moment we open our eyes in the morning till we shut them in sleep at night is *finished*.

> *I saw Heaven and earth new-created. Gone the first Heaven, gone the*
> *first earth, gone the sea.*

I saw Holy Jerusalem, new-created, descending resplendent out of
Heaven, as ready for God as a bride for her husband.

REVELATION 21:1–2

AUGUST 28

The Moment of Jesus Christ

But this creating is taking place in a world that is visibly in decay; this saving is taking place in persons who are visibly damned, which is to say that the creation and the salvation are not obvious. St. John is showing us what is not obvious but is nevertheless deeply true. These are not the big stories that editors arrange in print and film to tell us what is going on in the world and what we are up against. There was one moment, though, when the creating and saving were perfectly obvious, the moment of Jesus Christ. The actions weren't obvious for very long, or to very many people, but for the few hours that spanned the crucifixion and resurrection of Jesus, for the few men and women who were his disciples—for those few hours among those few believers—everything was in focus: God creating, God saving, in and through Jesus Christ.

At that moment, open-eyed, wide-eyed, they recognized him. And then he disappeared.

Back and forth they talked. "Didn't we feel on fire as he conversed with us on the road, as he opened up the Scriptures for us?"

LUKE 24:31–32

At Risk

The effort to keep the focus is always at risk. The command requires repetition, again and again. St. John repeated it: worship God. He is one of the world's masters in calling Christians to worship.

> *The Twenty-four Elders and the Four Animals fell to their knees and worshiped God on his Throne, praising,*
>   *"Amen! Yes! Hallelujah!"*

REVELATION 19:4

The Work of Worship

The work of worship gathers everything in our common lives that has been dispersed by sin and brings it to attention before God; at the same time it gathers everything in God's revelation that has been forgotten in our distracted hurrying and puts it before us so that we can offer it up in praise and obedience. All of this does not take place merely in a single hour of worship. But, faithfully repeated, week after week, year after year, there is an accumulation to wholeness.

The Throne of God and of the Lamb is at the center. His servants will offer God service—worshiping, they'll look on his face, their foreheads mirroring God. Never again will there be any night.

REVELATION 22:3B–5A

Vigilance

Spirituality is always in danger of self-absorption, of becoming so intrigued with matters of soul that God is treated as a mere accessory to my experience. This requires much vigilance. Spiritual theology is, among other things, the exercise of this vigilance. Spiritual theology is the discipline and art of training us into full and mature participation in Jesus' story while at the same time preventing us from taking over the story.

You could fall flat on your face as easily as anyone else. Forget about self-confidence; it's useless. Cultivate God-confidence.

1 CORINTHIANS 10:12

September

Evidence of Pathology

If all your friends were suddenly to begin talking about the state of their digestion—comparing symptoms, calling up for advice, swapping remedies—you would not consider it a hopeful sign. Nor does the widespread interest in spirituality today lead me to think that the North American soul is in a flourishing condition.

A person who has a healthy digestion does not talk about it. Neither does a person who has a healthy soul. When our bodies and souls are working well, we are, for the most part, unaware of them. The frequency with which the word *spirituality* occurs these days is more likely to be evidence of pathology than health.

By taking this stance, I am not dismissing current interest in spirituality as sick. The interest itself is not sick, but sickness has provoked the interest. There is considerable confusion regarding the appropriate treatment, but virtual unanimity in the diagnosis: Our culture is sick with secularism.

But deeper and stronger than our illness is our cure. The Spirit of God that hovered over the primordial chaos (Gen. 1:2) hovers over our murderous and chaotic cities. The Spirit that descended on Jesus like a dove (Matt. 3:16) descends on the followers of Jesus. The Holy Spirit that filled men and women with God at nine o'clock in the morning in Jerusalem during Pentecost (Acts 2:1–4) fills men and women still in Chicago and Calcutta, Moscow and Montreal, around the clock, 365 days a year.

> *The moment Jesus came up out of the baptismal waters, the skies opened up and he [John] saw God's Spirit—it looked like a dove—descending and landing on him. And along with the Spirit, a voice: "This is my Son, chosen and marked by my love, delight of my life."*

MATTHEW 3:16–17

SEPTEMBER 2

A Secular Culture

Our culture has failed precisely because it is a *secular* culture. A secular culture is a culture reduced to *thing* and *function*. Typically, at the outset, people are delighted to find themselves living in such a culture. It is wonderful to have all these *things* coming our way, without having to worry about their nature or purpose. And it is wonderful to have this incredible freedom to *do* so much, without bothering about relationships or meaning. But after a few years of this, our delight diminishes as we find ourselves lonely among the things and bored with our freedom.

Our first response is to get more of what brought us delight in the first place: acquire more things, generate more activity. Get more.

Do more. After a few years of this, we are genuinely puzzled that we are not any better.

We North Americans have been doing this for well over a century now, and we have succeeded in producing a culture that is reduced to thing and function. And we all seem to be surprised that this magnificent achievement of secularism—all these things! all these activities!—has produced an epidemic of loneliness and boredom. We are surprised to find ourselves lonely behind the wheel of a BMW or bored nearly to death as we advance from one prestigious job to another.

And then, one by one, a few people begin to realize that getting more and doing more only makes the sickness worse. They realize that if it gets much worse, the culture will be dead—a thoroughly secularized culture is a corpse.

> *Still, when I tried to figure it out,*
> *all I got was a splitting headache . . .*
> *Until I entered the sanctuary of God.*
> *Then I saw the whole picture:*
> *The slippery road you've put them on,*
> *with a final crash in a ditch of delusions.*

PSALM 73:16–18

SEPTEMBER 3

Intimacy and Transcendence

People begin to see that secularism marginalizes and eventually obliterates the two essentials of human fullness: intimacy and transcendence. *Intimacy:* we want to experience human love and trust and joy. *Transcendence:* we want to experience divine love and trust and joy. We are not ourselves by ourselves. We do not become more human, more *ourselves,* when we are behind the wheel of a BMW, or, when capped and gowned we acquire another academic degree so we can get a better job and do more and better things. Instead, we long for a human touch, for someone who knows our name. We hunger for divine meaning, someone who will bless us.

And so spirituality, a fusion of intimacy and transcendence, overnight becomes a passion for millions of North Americans. It should be no surprise that a people so badly trained in intimacy and transcendence might not do too well in their quest. Most anything at hand that gives a feeling of closeness—whether genitals or cocaine—will do for intimacy. And most anything exotic that induces a sense of mystery—from mantras to river rafting—will do for transcendence.

It is commendable that we have a nation of men and women who, fed up with things as such and distraught with activity as such, should dignify their hearts with something more than a yearly valentine card. It is heartening that our continent is experiencing a recovery of desire to embrace intimacies and respond to transcendence. But it is regrettable that these most human and essential desires are so ignorantly and badly served.

I will not leave you orphaned. I'm coming back. In just a little while the world will no longer see me, but you're going to see me because I am alive and you're about to come alive. At that moment you will know absolutely that I'm in my Father, and you're in me, and I'm in you.

JOHN 14:18–20

Internalizing the World's Ways

Historically, evangelical Christians have served the church by bringing sharpness and ardor to matters of belief and behavior, insisting on personal involvement, injecting energy and passion, returning daily to the Scriptures for command and guidance, and providing communities of commitment. But presently there is not an equivalent in matters of spirituality. It turns out that we have been affected by our secularizing culture far more than we had realized. Evangelicals have been uncritically internalizing the world's ways and bringing them into churches without anyone noticing. In particular, we have internalized the world's fascination with technology and its enthusiasm for activities.

> *Don't love the world's ways. Don't love the world's goods. Love of the world squeezes out love for the Father. Practically everything that goes on in the world—wanting your own way, wanting everything for yourself, wanting to appear important—has nothing to do with the Father.*

1 JOHN 2:15–16

Instead of . . .

Instead of being brought before God ("O come, let us worship and bow down") and led to acquire a taste for the holy mysteries of tran-

scendence in worship, we are talked to and promoted endlessly, to try
this and attend that. We are recruited for church roles and positions in
which we can shine, validating our usefulness by our function.

> *The Master said, "Martha, dear Martha, you're fussing far too much
> and getting yourself worked up over nothing. One thing only is essen-
> tial, and Mary has chosen it—it's the main course, and won't be
> taken from her."*

LUKE 10:41–42

Our Leaders

We go to our leaders for help, and they don't seem to know what we
are talking about. They sign us up for a program in stress management. They recruit us for a tour of the Holy Land. They enroll us in a
course in family dynamics. They give us a Myers-Briggs personality-
type indicator so they can fit us into the slot where we can function efficiently. When we don't seem interested, they talk faster and louder.
When we drift somewhere else, they hire a public-relations consultant
to devise a campaign designed to attract us and our friends. Sometimes the advertising campaign is successful in enlisting people who
want something to do without the inconvenience of community and
want to know how to be on good terms with God without having to
give up the final say-so on their own lives. But they don't attract *us*. We
are after what we came for in the first place: intimacy and transcendence, personal friends and a personal God, love and worship.

[Jesus said,] "If your little boy asks for a serving of fish, do you scare him with a live snake on his plate? If your little girl asks for an egg, do you trick her with a spider? As bad as you are, you wouldn't think of such a thing—you're at least decent to your own children. And don't you think the Father who conceived you in love will give the Holy Spirit when you ask him?"

LUKE 11:11–13

SEPTEMBER 7

Among the Laity

Spirituality is mostly of concern among the laity, the men and women who are running markets, raising children, driving trucks, cooking meals, selling cars, believing in God while changing a flat tire in the rain, and praying for an enemy while studying for an exam.

Contemporary spirituality desperately needs focus, precision, and roots: focus on Christ, precision in the Scriptures, and roots in a healthy tradition. In these times of drift and dilettantism, evangelical Christians must once again serve the church by providing just such focus and precision and rootage. That it is primarily lay Christians who are left to provide this service to the church is not at all crippling. The strength and impact of evangelicalism has often been in its laity—transcending denominational divisions, subverting established structures, working behind the scenes, beginning at the bottom.

Stick with me, friends. Keep track of those you see running this same course, headed for this same goal. There are many out there taking

other paths, choosing other goals, and trying to get you to go along
with them. I've warned you of them many times; sadly, I'm having to
do it again. All they want is easy street. They hate Christ's Cross. But
easy street is a dead-end street.

PHILIPPIANS 3:17–19A

SEPTEMBER 8

Five Items of Counsel

I have five items of counsel in matters of spirituality for all who
hunger and thirst after intimacy and transcendence. Each item provides evangelical focus, precision, and rootage to spirituality. As we
get it straight ourselves, we will be equipped to provide leadership to
others, an *evangelical* leadership that is so conspicuously lacking at
present.

1. Discover what Scripture says about spirituality and immerse
   yourself in it. . . .
2. Shun spirituality that does not require commitment. . . .
3. Embrace friends in the faith wherever you find them. . . .
4. But then return home and explore your own tradition. . . .
5. Look for mature guides; honor wise leaders. . . .

Spirituality is not the latest fad but the oldest truth. Spirituality,
the alert attention we give to a living God and the faithful response we
make to him in community, is at the heart of our Scriptures and is on

display throughout the centuries of Israel and the church. We have been at this a long time. We have nearly four millennia of experience to draw upon. When someone hands you a new book, reach for an old one. Isaiah has far more to teach us about spirituality than Carl Jung.

> *Take the old prophets as your mentors. They put up with anything, went through everything, and never once quit, all the time honoring God. What a gift life is to those who stay the course!*

JAMES 5:10–11A

SEPTEMBER 9

Into a Consumer Activity

Because an appetite for God is easily manipulated into a consumer activity, we need these wise, sane friends as guides and companions. There are entrepreneurs among us who see the wide-spread hunger for spirituality as a marketplace and are out there selling junk food. The gullibility of the unwary who bought relics from itinerant monks in the Middle Ages—splinters of wood from the true cross, finger bones from the saints, a few pieces of thread from Jesus' seamless robe—is more than matched by North Americans in matters of spirituality.

We are trained from the cradle to be good consumers. It is understandable that we seek to satisfy our hunger for God along the lines in which we have been brought up. But it is not excusable, for we have clear counsel in the Gospels to steer us away from this consumer world: "Blessed are the poor . . . Deny yourself, take up your cross, and follow me . . . Love not the world nor the things that are in the world." And our Lord's counsel is confirmed and expanded in numerous ways by our wise evangelical ancestors in the faith.

The world with all its wanting, wanting, wanting is on the way out— but whoever does what God wants is set for eternity.

1 JOHN 2:17

No Outsiders

Most of us, most of the time, feel left out—misfits. We don't belong. Others seem to be so confident, so sure of themselves, "insiders" who know the ropes, old hands in a club from which we are excluded.

One of the ways we have of responding to this is to form our own club, or join one that will have us. Here is at least one place where we are "in" and the others "out." The clubs range from informal to formal in gatherings that are variously political, social, cultural, and economic. But the one thing they have in common is the principle of exclusion. Identity or worth is achieved by excluding all but the chosen. The terrible price we pay for keeping all those other people out so that we can savor the sweetness of being insiders is a reduction of reality, a shrinkage of life.

Nowhere is this price more terrible than when it is paid in the cause of religion. But religion has a long history of doing just that, of reducing the huge mysteries of God to the respectability of club rules, of shrinking the vast human community to a "membership." But with God there are no outsiders.

> *God is the God of outsider non-Jews as well as insider Jews. How could it be otherwise since there is only one God? God sets right all who welcome his action and enter into it, both those who follow our religious system and those who have never heard of our religion.*

ROMANS 3:29B–30

SEPTEMBER 11

A Theologian at Our Side

The reason that we who pray need a theologian at our side is that most of the difficulties of prayer are of our own making, the making of well-meaning friends, or the lies of the devil who always seems to be looking after our best self-interests. We get more interested in ourselves than in God. We get absorbed in what is or is not happening in us. We get bewildered by the huge discrepancies between our feelings and our intentions; we get unsettled by moralistic accusations that call into question our worthiness to even engage in prayer; we get attracted by advertisements of secrets that will give us access to a privileged, spiritual elite.

But prayer has primarily to do with God, not us. . . . And the theologian's task is to train our thinking, our imagination, our understanding to begin with God not ourselves.

Start with GOD—the first step in learning is bowing down to GOD;
only fools thumb their noses at such wisdom and learning.

PROVERBS 1:7

Re-Attending to God

The plain fact is that we cannot be trusted in prayer. Left to ourselves we become selfish—preoccupied with our pious feelings, our
religious progress, our spiritual standing. We need guides and masters to refocus our attention on God, to keep us ever mindful of the
priority of God's word to us.

In the process of re-attending to God, all the intervening doubts
and cynicisms and seductions in which we have become entangled
by our self-attentiveness have to be attended to. We require an alert
theologian at our right hand. A good theologian brings the requisite
skill, single-mindedness, and patience that can help us re-establish
the primacy of God in our prayers.

Peter Taylor Forsyth is just such a theologian. A British Congre-
gationalist, he was dead (in 1921) before I was born, but I have kept
him at my side for thirty-five years as a friend and ally in my own life
of prayer and the lives of my friends. I find him utterly trustworthy
and immensely energizing.

Good friend, take to heart what I'm telling you;
collect my counsels and guard them with your life.

Tune your ears to the world of Wisdom;
set your heart on a life of Understanding.

PROVERBS 2:1–2

A Theologian Who Stays a Theologian

Maybe the thing that I like best about Forsyth is that he is a theologian who stays a theologian. He cannot be distracted, will not be diverted. Here is a no-nonsense theologian who goes for the jugular. In Forsyth's company we are aware of both the glory and the gravity of what we are doing when we go to our knees in prayer.

> *. . . every time I prayed, I'd think of you and give thanks. But I do more than thank. I ask—ask the God of our Master, Jesus Christ, the God of glory—to make you intelligent and discerning in knowing him personally.*

EPHESIANS 1:16–17

Lady Wisdom

Do you hear Lady Wisdom calling?
Can you hear Madame Insight raising her voice?

She's taken her stand at First and Main,
    at the busiest intersection.
Right in the city square
    where the traffic is thickest, she shouts,
"You—I'm talking to all of you,
    everyone out here on the streets!
Listen, you idiots—learn good sense!
    You blockheads—shape up!
Don't miss a word of this—I'm telling you how to live well,
    I'm telling you how to live at your best.
My mouth chews and savors and relishes truth—
    I can't stand the taste of evil!
You'll only hear true and right words from my mouth;
    not one syllable will be twisted or skewed.
You'll recognize this as true—you with open minds;
    truth-ready minds will see it at once.
Prefer my life-disciplines over chasing after money,
    and God-knowledge over a lucrative career.
For Wisdom is better than all the trappings of wealth;
    nothing you could wish for holds a candle to her. . . .

"So, my dear friends, listen carefully;
    those who embrace these my ways are most blessed.
Mark a life of discipline and live wisely;
    don't squander your precious life.
Blessed the man, blessed the woman, who listens to me,
    awake and ready for me each morning,
    alert and responsive as I start my day's work.
When you find me, you find life, real life,
    to say nothing of God's good pleasure.

But if you wrong me, you damage your very soul;
when you reject me, you're flirting with death."

PROVERBS 8:1–11; 32–36

SEPTEMBER 15

The Central Reality

The main difference between Christians and others is that we take God seriously and they do not. We really do believe that he is the central reality of all existence. We really do pay attention to what he is and to what he does. We really do order our lives in response to that reality and not to some other. Paying attention to God involves a realization that he works. . . .

God works. The work of God is defined and described in the pages of Scripture. We have models of creation, acts of redemption, examples of help and compassion, paradigms of comfort and salvation. . . .

In every letter St. Paul wrote he demonstrated that a Christian's work is a natural, inevitable and faithful development out of God's work. Each of his letters concludes with a series of directives which guide us into the kind of work that participates in God's work. The curse of some people's lives is not work, as such, but senseless work, vain work, futile work, work that takes place apart from God . . .

*Be prepared. You're up against far more than you can
handle on your own. Take all the help you can get,*

every weapon God has issued, so that when it's
all over but the shouting you'll still be on your feet.

EPHESIANS 6:10–11

SEPTEMBER 16

Being a Writer and Being a Pastor

Being a writer and being a pastor are virtually the same thing for me—an entrance into chaos, the *mess* of things, and then the slow mysterious work of making something out of it, something good, something blessed: poem, prayer, conversation, sermon, a sighting of grace, a recognition of love, a shaping of virtue. This is the *yeshua'* of the Hebrew faithful, the *sotêria* of the Greek Christians. Salvation. The recovery by creation and re-creation of the *imago Dei.* Writing is not a literary act but spiritual. And pastoring is not managing a religious business but a spiritual quest.

Prayer, intensity of spirit at attention before God, is at the heart of both writing and pastoring. In writing, I am working with words; in pastoring, I am working with people. Not mere words or mere people, but words and people as carriers of spirit/Spirit. The moment words are used prayerlessly and people are treated prayerlessly, something essential begins to leak out of life.

Be assured that from the first day we heard of you,
we haven't stopped praying for you, asking God
to give you wise minds and spirits attuned to his will,

and so acquire a thorough understanding of the
ways in which God works.

COLOSSIANS 1:9

SEPTEMBER 17

Moral Pollution

READ Jeremiah 3: 1–5, "You Have Polluted the Land"

Moral pollution works much the same way as environmental pollution. The waste product of careless living that is indifferent to consequences insidiously works itself into the soil of thought and streams of language and causes damage to generations yet unborn.

What kind of moral pollution is taking place today?

PRAYER: The danger, Lord, when I realize the extent of moral pollution in the land, is that I become overwhelmed and paralyzed into inaction. Protect me from despair and show me what I can say and do today that will be signs of the new heaven and earth that you are making. *Amen.*

The person who plants selfishness, ignoring the needs of others—
ignoring God!—harvests a crop of weeds. All he'll have to show
for his life is weeds!

GALATIANS 6:8A

The Risen Christ

In every visit, every meeting I attend, every appointment I keep, I have been anticipated. The risen Christ got there ahead of me. The risen Christ is in that room already. What is he doing? What is he saying? What is going on?

In order to fix the implications of that text in my vocation, I have taken to quoting it before every visit or meeting: "He is risen, . . . he is going before you to 1020 Emmorton Road; there you will see him, as he told you." Later in the day it will be, "He is risen, . . . he is going before you to St. Joseph's Hospital; there you will see him, as he told you." When I arrive and enter the room I am not so much wondering what I am going to do or say that will be pastoral as I am alert and observant for what the risen Christ has been doing or saying that is making a gospel story out of this life. The theological category for this is prevenience, the priority of grace. We are always coming in on something that is already going on. Sometimes we clarify a word or feeling, sometimes we identify an overlooked relationship, sometimes we help recover an essential piece of memory—but always we are dealing with what the risen Christ has already set in motion, already brought into being.

The angel spoke to the women: "There is nothing
to fear here. I know you're looking for Jesus,
the One they nailed to the cross. He is not here.

He was raised, just as he said. Come and look
at the place where he was placed.
"Now, get on your way quickly and
tell his disciples, 'He is risen from the dead.
He is going on ahead of you to Galilee.
You will see him there.' That's the message."

MATTHEW 28:5–7

Made in the "Image" *of God*

We who are made in the *"image"* of God have, as a consequence, *imag*-ination. Imagination is the capacity to make connections between the visible and the invisible, between heaven and earth, between present and past, between present and future. For Christians, whose largest investment is in the invisible, the imagination is indispensable, for it is only by means of the imagination that we can see reality whole, in context.

By an act of faith, [Moses] turned his heel on
Egypt, indifferent to the king's blind rage.
He had his eye on the One no eye can see, and
kept right on going.

HEBREWS 11:27

Meeting All the Needs

The world of religion generates a huge market for meeting all the needs that didn't get met in the shopping mall. Pastors are conspicuous in this religious marketplace and are expected to come up with the products that give customer satisfaction. Since the needs seem legitimate enough, we easily slip into the routines of merchandising moral advice and religious comfort. Before long we find that we are program directors in a flourishing business. We spend our time figuring out ways to attractively display god-products. We become skilled at pleasing the customers. Before we realize what has happened, the mystery and love and majesty of God, to say nothing of the tender and delicate subtleties of souls, are obliterated by the noise and frenzy of the religious marketplace.

But then who is there who will say the name of *God* in such a way that the community can see him for who he is, our towering Lord and Savior, and not the packaged and priced version that meets our consumer needs? And who is there with the time to stand with men and women, adults and children in the places of confusion and blessing, darkness and light, hurt and healing long enough to discern the glory and salvation being worked out behind the scenes, under the surface. If we all get caught up in running the store, who will be the pastor?

So the Twelve called a meeting of the disciples. They said, "It wouldn't be right for us to abandon our responsibilities for preaching and

teaching the Word of God to help with the care of the poor. So,
friends, choose seven men from among you whom everyone trusts,
men full of the Holy spirit and good sense, and we'll assign them
this task. Meanwhile, we'll stick to our assigned tasks of prayer
and speaking God's Word."

ACTS 6:2–4

SEPTEMBER 21

My First Spiritual Director

My first spiritual director didn't know he was a spiritual director. He
had never so much as heard the term *spiritual director,* and neither
had I. But our mutual ignorance of terminology did not prevent the
work. We were both doing something for which we had no name. For
a summer of Tuesday and Thursday evenings we met, conversing
and praying in the prayer room in the church basement. We got on
well. He was not only the first but among the best of the spiritual directors I have had. Those meetings shaped one of the significant relationships in my life with lasting effects. It would be twenty more
years before I acquired a vocabulary that would adequately account
for what took place between us.

A good person's mouth is a clear fountain of wisdom;
a foul mouth is a stagnant swamp.

PROVERBS 10:31

one. It is playful, anticipating the pleasures of friendship. It is prayerful, convinced that all honest words can involve us somehow or other, if we read with our hearts as well as our heads, in an eternal conversation that got its start in the Word that "became flesh." Spiritual reading is at home with Homer as well as Hosea.

> *I ponder every morsel of wisdom from you,*
> *I attentively watch how you've done it.*
> *I relish everything you've told me of life,*
> *I won't forget a word of it.*

PSALM 119:15–16

SEPTEMBER 25

The Marrow-Nourishment

Spiritual reading, for most of us, requires either the recovery or acquisition of skills not in current repute: leisurely, repetitive, reflective reading. In this we are not reading primarily for information, but for companionship. Baron Friedrich von Hügel once said it was like sucking on a lozenge in contrast to gulping a meal. It is a way of reading that shapes the heart at the same time that it informs the intellect, sucking out the marrow-nourishment from the bone-words.

> *His mother held these things dearly, deep within herself. And Jesus matured, growing up in both body and spirit, blessed by both God and people.*

LUKE 2:51B–52

The Primary Book

For Christians the Bible is the primary book for spiritual reading. In the course of reading Scripture, it is only natural that we fall into conversation with friends who are also reading it. These leisurely, relaxed, ruminating conversations continue across continents and centuries and languages by means of books—and these books offer themselves for spiritual reading. After a few years of this, as with the scriptures themselves, most of our spiritual reading turns out to be rereading. C. S. Lewis once defined an unliterary person as "one who reads books once only."

The Jews [in Berea] received Paul's message with enthusiasm and met with him daily, examining the Scriptures to see if they supported what he said.

ACTS 17:11B

A Constant Creative Activity

But leisurely and repetitively doesn't mean slovenly or lazily. G. K. Chesterton said there was a great difference between the lively person wanting to read a book and the tired person wanting a book to read. Nicolas Berdyaev represents the lively spirit: "I never remain passive in the process of reading: while I read I am engaged in a constant creative activity, which leads me to remember not so much the actual matter of the book as the thoughts evoked in my mind by it, directly or indirectly" [*Dream and Reality*].

The necessity for alert and ready responsiveness to the Spirit is on display in a diary entry by Julian Green for October 6, 1941: "The story of the manna gathered and set aside by the Hebrews is deeply significant. It so happened that the manna rotted when it was kept. And perhaps that means that all spiritual reading which is not consumed—by prayer and by works—ends by causing a sort of rotting inside us. You die with a head full of fine sayings and a perfectly empty heart."

> *Running up alongside, Philip heard the eunuch reading Isaiah and asked, "Do you understand what you're reading?"*
>
> *He answered, "How can I without some help?" and invited him into the chariot with him.*

ACTS 8:30–31

SEPTEMBER 28

Books by Dead Christians

I have a friend who became a Christian as a young adult, and then was ripped off and exploited by unscrupulous, predatory religious leaders. Disillusioned he wandered off into the world of alcohol and drugs and spent the next twenty years trying to get his spirituality from chemicals. One day in the mountains of Mexico, on a hunt for drugs, he met some drug dealers who had recently become Christians. They talked to him about Jesus, prayed for him, and he reentered the Christian way. Back home in Canada, he knew he needed support in his new life, but because of his earlier experience with religious leaders, was wary. One day he went into a bookstore and asked the manager, "Do you have any books by dead Christians? I don't trust anybody living." He was given a book by A. W. Tozer, and for the next year read nothing but Tozer—a "dead Christian." From there he cautiously worked himself back into the company of living Christians, in which he is now a most exuberant participant.

He rolled up the scroll [of Isaiah], handed it back to the assistant, and sat down. Every eye in the place was on him, intent. Then he started in, "You've just heard Scripture make history. It came true just now in this place."

LUKE 4:20–21

SEPTEMBER 29

Praying with Moses

It is impossible to exaggerate the life-shaping, character-forming power of the words written in the first five books of the Bible. For three thousand years they have served as the foundational text for Israel and Church. Millions of men and women have pored over these words, absorbing the meanings, reflecting on the implications, letting the rhythms and sounds of the sentences work into their souls.

And more often than not the reading has turned into praying. Praying, because in the process of being read these words become personal and seem to require a personal answer.

It is widely believed that God's Holy Spirit inspired the writing of Holy Scripture. It is also widely experienced that the reading of scripture is similarly inspired, the same Holy Spirit being present and active in the current reading as in the original writing. When that happens, when "reading the Bible" becomes "praying the Bible," the text moves from our heads into our hearts, where it gives shape and energy for living, not just ideas for thinking. Such reading/praying typically brings much delight. St. Ephrem of Edessa, a fifth-century Christian in Syria, described his experience on first opening Genesis and reading: "I read the opening of the book, and was full of joy, for its verses and lines spread out their arms to welcome me; the first [sentence] rushed out and kissed me, and led me on to the next. . . ."

God's Law is more real and lasting than the stars in the sky and the ground at your feet. Long after stars burn out and earth wears out, God's Law will be alive and working.

MATTHEW 5:18

SEPTEMBER 30

Intentional Meeting of Friends

I always encourage people who pray to invite others into the praying—in the intentional meeting of friends, in groups gathered for listening and study, in telephoning and letter writing. The early Christians seem to have been most convivial, delighting in one another's company, finding prayer to be as natural in their meetings with one another as conversation and food.

> *When our time was up, they escorted us out of the city to the docks. Everyone came along—men, women, children. They made a farewell party of the occasion! We all kneeled together on the beach and prayed. Then, after another round of saying goodbye, we climbed on board the ship while they drifted back to their homes.*

ACTS 21:5–6

October

The Secret

Jeremiah did not resolve to stick it out for twenty-three years, no matter what; he got up every morning with the sun. The day was God's day, not the people's. He didn't get up to face rejection, he got up to meet with God. He didn't rise to put up with another round of mockery, he rose to be with his Lord. That is the secret of his persevering pilgrimage—not thinking with dread about the long road ahead but greeting the present moment, every present moment, with obedient delight, with expectant hope: "My heart is ready!"

> *I'm ready, God, so ready,*
> > *ready from head to toe.*
> *Ready to sing,*
> > *ready to raise a God-song,*
> *"Wake, soul! Wake, lute!*
> > *Wake up, you sleepyhead sun!"*

PSALM 108:1–2

A Maintenance Psalm

The following five days are based on Psalm 131.

Psalm 131 is a maintenance psalm. It is functional to the person of faith as pruning is functional to the gardener: it gets rid of that which looks good to those who don't know any better and reduces the distance between our hearts and their roots in God.

The two things that Psalm 131 prunes away are unruly ambition and infantile dependency, what we might call getting too big for our breeches and refusing to cut the apron strings. Both of these tendencies can easily be supposed to be virtues, especially by those who are not conversant with Christian ways. If we are not careful, we will be encouraging the very things that will ruin us. We are in special and constant need of correction. We need pruning. Jesus said, "Every branch of mine that bears no fruit, he takes away, and every branch that does bear fruit he prunes, that it may bear more fruit" (John 15:2). More than once our Lord the Spirit has used Psalm 131 to do this important work among his people. As we gain a familiarity with an understanding of the psalm, he will be able to use it that way with us "that we may bear more fruit."

> *[Jesus said,] "I am the Real Vine and my Father is the Farmer. He cuts off every branch of me that doesn't bear grapes. And every branch that is grape-bearing he prunes back so it will bear even more. You are already pruned back by the message I have spoken."*

JOHN 15:1–2

Recognizing Pride as a Sin

It is difficult to recognize pride as a sin when it is held up on every side as a virtue, urged as profitable, and rewarded as an achievement. What is described in Scripture as the basic sin, the sin of taking things into our own hands, being our own god, grabbing what is there while you can get it, is now described as basic wisdom: improve yourself by whatever means you are able; get ahead regardless of the price; take care of me first. For a limited time it works. But at the end the devil has his due. There is damnation.

> *Don't push your way to the front; don't sweet-talk your way to the top. Put yourself aside, and help others get ahead. Don't be obsessed with getting your own advantage. Forget yourselves long enough to lend a helping hand.*

PHILIPPIANS 2:3–4

Aspiration Is Creative Energy

It is additionally difficult to recognize unruly ambition as a sin because it has a kind of superficial relationship to the virtue of aspiration—an impatience with mediocrity, and a dissatisfaction with all things created until we are at home with the Creator, the hopeful striving for the best God has for us—the kind of thing Paul expressed: "I press on toward the goal for the prize of the upward call of God in Christ Jesus" (Phil. 3:14). But if we take the energies that make for aspiration and remove God from the picture, replacing him with our own crudely sketched self-portrait, we end up with ugly arrogance. Ambition is aspiration gone crazy. Aspiration is the channeled, creative energy that moves us to growth in Christ, shaping goals in the Spirit. Ambition takes these same energies for growth and development and uses them to make something tawdry and cheap, sweatily knocking together a Babel when we could be vacationing in Eden.

> *By no means do I count myself an expert in all of this, but I've got my eye on the goal, where God is beckoning us onward—to Jesus. I'm off and running, and I'm not turning back.*

PHILIPPIANS 3:13–14

OCTOBER 5

Lives Lived Well

Our lives are only lived well when they are lived in terms of their creation, with God loving and we being loved, with God making and we being made, with God revealing and we understanding, with God commanding and we responding. Being a Christian means accepting the terms of creation, accepting God as our maker and redeemer, and growing day by day into an increasingly glorious creature in Christ, developing joy, experiencing love, maturing in peace. By the grace of Christ we experience the marvel of being made in the image of God. If we reject this way the only alternative is to attempt the hopelessly fourth-rate, embarrassingly awkward imitation of God made in the image of man.

We follow this sequence in Scripture: The First Adam received life, the Last Adam is a life-giving Spirit. Physical life comes first, then spiritual—a firm base shaped from the earth, a final completion coming out of heaven.

1 CORINTHIANS 15:45

OCTOBER 6

Willingly Trustful in Him

Many who have traveled this way of faith have described the transition from an infantile faith that grabs at God out of desperation to a mature faith that responds to God out of love . . . "as content as a child that has been weaned." Often our conscious Christian lives do begin at points of desperation, and God, of course, does not refuse to meet our needs. There are heavenly comforts that break through our despair and persuade us that "all will be well and all manner of things will be well." The early stages of Christian belief are not infrequently marked with miraculous signs and exhilarations of spirit. But as discipleship continues the sensible comforts gradually disappear. For

God does not want us neurotically dependent upon him but willingly trustful in him. And so he weans us. The period of infancy will not be sentimentally extended beyond what is necessary. The time of weaning is very often noisy and marked with misunderstandings: "I no longer feel like I did when I was first a Christian. Does that mean I am no longer a Christian? Has God abandoned me? Have I done something terribly wrong?"

The answer is, "Neither: God hasn't abandoned you, and you haven't done anything wrong. You are being weaned. The apron strings have been cut. You are free to come to God or not come to him. You are, in a sense, on your own with an open invitation to listen and receive and enjoy our Lord."

The last line of the psalm addresses this quality of newly acquired freedom: "O Israel, hope in the Lord from this time forth and for evermore." Choose to be with him; elect his presence; aspire to his ways; respond to his love.

The child [John] grew up, healthy and spirited. He lived out in the desert until the day he made his prophetic debut in Israel.

LUKE 1:80

OCTOBER 7

A Mirror

People look into mirrors to see how they look; they look into the Psalms to find out who they are. A mirror is an excellent way to learn about our appearance; the Psalms are the biblical way to discover ourselves. With a mirror we detect a new wrinkle here, an old wart there. We use a mirror when shaving or applying make-up to improve, if we can, the face we present to the world. With the Psalms we bring into awareness an ancient sorrow, release a latent joy. We use the Psalms to present ourselves before God as honestly and thoroughly as we are able. A mirror shows us the shape of our nose and the curve of our chin, things we otherwise know only through the reports of others. The Psalms show us the shape of our souls and the curve of our sin, realities deep within us, hidden and obscured, for which we need focus and names.

> *Investigate my life, O God,*
> *find out everything about me;*
> *Cross-examine and test me,*
> *get a clear picture of what I'm about . . .*

PSALM 139:23

OCTOBER 8

Poetry and Prayer

The Psalms are poetry and the Psalms are prayer. These two features, the poetry and the prayer, need to be kept in mind always. If either is forgotten the Psalms will not only be misunderstood but misused.

GOD, my shepherd!
I don't need a thing.
You have bedded me down in lush meadows,
you find me quiet pools to drink from.

PSALM 23:1

OCTOBER 9

Exposed and Sharpened

Poetry is language used with intensity. It is not, as so many suppose, decorative speech. Poets tell us what our eyes, blurred with too much gawking, and our ears, dulled with too much chatter, miss around and within us. Poets use words to drag us into the depths of reality itself, not by reporting on how life is, but by pushing-pulling us into the middle of it. Poetry gets at the heart of existence. Far from being cosmetic language, it is intestinal. It is root language. Poetry doesn't so much tell us something we never knew as bring into recognition what was latent or forgotten or overlooked. The Psalms are almost entirely this kind of language. Knowing this, we will not be looking primarily for ideas about God in the Psalms or for direction in moral conduct. We will expect, rather, to find exposed and sharpened what it means to be human beings before God.

Prayer is language used in relation to God. It gives utterance to what we sense or want or respond to before God. God speaks to us; our answers are our prayers. The answers are not always articulate. Silence, sighs, groaning—these also constitute responses. But always

God is involved, whether in darkness or light, whether in faith or despair. This is hard to get used to. Our habit is to talk *about* God, not *to* him. We love discussing God. But the Psalms resist such discussions. They are provided not to teach us about God but to train us in responding to him. We don't learn the Psalms until we are praying them.

> *I call to you, God, because I'm sure of an answer.*
>> *So—answer! bend your ear! listen sharp!*
> *Paint grace-graffiti on the fences;*
>> *take in your frightened children who*
> *Are running from the neighborhood bullies*
>> *straight to you.*

PSALM 17:6–7

OCTOBER 10

"Help!"

Psalm 3 is the first prayer in the Psalter. Psalms 1 and 2 prepared us for prayer; Psalm 3 prays. Prayer begins in a realization that we cannot help ourselves, so we must reach out to God. "Help!" is the basic prayer. We are in trouble, deep trouble. If God cannot get us out, we are lost; if God can get us out, we are saved. If we don't know that we need help, prayer will always be peripheral to our lives, a matter of mood and good manners. But the moment we know we are in trouble, prayer is a life-or-death matter.

Up, GOD! My God, help me!

PSALM 3:7A

OCTOBER 11

An Orienting Act

Prayer is an orienting act. We begin to discover *who* we are when we realize *where* we are. Disorientation is a terrible experience. If we cannot locate our place, we are in confusion and anxiety. We are also in danger, for we are apt to act inappropriately. If we are among enemies and don't know it, we may lose our life. If we are among friends and don't know it, we may miss good relationships. If we are alongside a cliff and don't know it, we may lose our footing. While praying Psalm 8, we find out where we are and some important aspects of who we are.

> *Why do you bother with us?*
> *Why take a second look our way?*
>
> *Yet we've so narrowly missed being gods,*
> *bright with Eden's dawn light.*
> *You put us in charge of your handcrafted world,*
> *repeated to us your Genesis-charge . . .*

PSALM 8:4–6

Praying Our Sin

Alongside the basic fact that God made us good (Psalm 8) is the equally basic fact that we have gone wrong. We pray our sins to get to the truth about ourselves and to find out how God treats sinners. Our experience of sin does not consist in doing some bad things but in *being* bad. It is a fundamental condition of our existence, not a temporary lapse into error. Praying our sin isn't resolving not to sin anymore; it is discovering what God has resolved to do with us as sinners.

> *Scrub away my guilt,*
> > *soak out my sins in your laundry.*
> *I know how bad I've been;*
> > *my sins are staring me down.*

PSALM 51:2–3

Praying Our Fear

The world is a fearsome place. If we manage with the help of parents, teachers and friends to survive the dangers of infancy and childhood, we find ourselves launched in an adult world that is ringed with terror—accident, assault, disease, violence, conflicts. Prayer brings fear into focus and faces it. But prayer does more than bravely face fear, it affirms God's presence in it.

> *Even when the way goes through*
>> *Death Valley,*
> *I'm not afraid*
>> *when you walk at my side.*

PSALM 23:4A

OCTOBER 14

Praying Our Hate

We want to be at our best before God. Prayer, we think, means presenting ourselves before God so that he will be pleased with us. We put on our "Sunday best" in our prayers. But when we pray the prayers of God's people, the Psalms, we find that will not do. We must pray who we actually are, not who we think we should be. Here (Psalm 137) is a prayer that brings out not the best but the worst in us: vile, venomous, vicious hate. Can God handle our hate?

> *And you, Babylonians—ravagers!*
>> *A reward to whoever gets back at you*
>> *for all you've done to us;*

Yes, a reward to the one who grabs your babies
and smashes their heads on the rocks!

PSALM 137:8–9

OCTOBER 15

Growing as a Healthy Christian

It is both natural and appropriate to be excited about a person's conversion. It is the most significant event in life—to be born anew, to be a new creature in Christ. But that significance and the excitement accompanying it do not excuse ignorance and indifference to the complex process of growth into which every Christian is launched via this new birth. Because growth involves so much—so much detail, so much time, so much discipline and patience—it is common to dismiss it and turn our attention to something we can get a quick handle on: the conversion event. Evangelism crowds spirituality off the agenda. But having babies is not a vocation; parenting is. It is easier, of course, to have babies. But a church that refuses or neglects the long, intricate, hard work of guiding its newborn creatures into adulthood is being negligent of most of what is in Scripture.

You've had a taste of God. Now, like infants at the breast, drink
deep of God's pure kindness. Then you'll grow up mature and
whole in God.

1 PETER 2:2

Growth and Growing

The Bible is full of references to growth and growing. Luke, for example, describes both Jesus and John as growing. John "grew and became strong in spirit" (1:80), and Jesus "grew in wisdom and stature, and in favor with God and men" (2:52). The word *grew* is the last word on both John and Jesus before their public ministries are narrated. Both the greatest of the prophets and the unique Messiah grew into the fullness of their ministries.

The apostle Paul used growth words frequently as he urged people to enter into the full implications of their life in the Spirit. When we become mature in the faith, he said, "we will no longer be infants, . . . (but) we will in all things grow up into him who is the Head, that is, Christ" (Ephesians 4:14,15). "Your faith is growing more and more" is his commendation to the church at Thessalonica (2 Thessalonians 1:3).

Peter urged believers to "grow in the grace and knowledge of our Lord and Savior Jesus Christ" (2 Peter 3:18). Comparing them to newborn babies, he said, "crave pure spiritual milk, so that by it you may grow up in your salvation" (1 Peter 2:2).

Growth is the basic metaphor in several parables that involve us in participation in the kingdom. The most dramatically placed growth image is at the center of the Gospel of John (12:24). Jesus said that unless a seed falls into the ground and dies, it does not grow, but if it dies, it grows. Growth is a major concern of John's Gospel—maturing into everything that God does in Christ, gathering all the parts of our lives and all the details of Jesus' life into a single whole.

John arranges his Gospel into two almost equal parts: this growth image in 12:24 is the hinge that holds the two halves together.

> *[Jesus said,] "Listen carefully: Unless a grain of wheat is buried in the ground, dead to the world, it is never any more than a grain of wheat. But if it is buried, it sprouts and reproduces itself many times over. In the same way, anyone who holds on to life just as it is destroys that life. But if you let it go, reckless in your love, you'll have it forever, real and eternal."*

JOHN 12:24–25

OCTOBER 17

Growth Is Not Painless

It is in the nature of what God is doing in us that we grow. But this "naturalness" does not mean that growth is painless. Growth calls into action new parts of our minds, our emotions, our bodies. What we experience at these times often feels like pain. We are not used to stretching ourselves in these ways. But the pain should not surprise us—our muscles ache when we take up any new activity. Athletes expect to get sore muscles when they begin training. A commitment to Christ and obedience to his commands stretch us beyond ourselves, and that hurts. But this is a very different pain from that inflicted by torture or punishment. Growth pain is the kind we don't regret; it leads to health and not disease or neurosis.

*I have a lot more to say about this, but it is hard to get
it across to you since you've picked up this bad
habit of not listening. By this time you ought to be
teachers yourselves, yet here I find you need someone
to sit down with you and go over the basics on God
again, starting from square one—baby's milk,
when you should have been on solid food long ago!*

HEBREWS 5:11–12

OCTOBER 18

Introspection

Introspection is ill-advised here. The spiritual masters in our faith consistently discourage introspection. Growth takes place in quietness, in hidden ways, in silence and solitude. The process is not accessible to observation. Constantly taking our spiritual temperature is bad for our health. When we are introspective about our growth, what we are actually doing is examining our feelings—and feelings are notorious liars, especially in matters of faith.

Attentiveness to spiritual growth that does not become introspectively neurotic is only accomplished by participation in a worshiping community. Healthy spiritual growth requires the presence of the other—the brother, the sister, the pastor, the teacher. A private, proudly isolated life cannot grow. The two or three who gather together in Christ's name keep each other sane.

Real religion, the kind that passes muster before God the Father, is this: Reach out to the homeless and loveless in their plight, and guard against corruption from the godless world.

JAMES 1:27

Public Worship

God gives us various means to grow: prayer and Scripture, silence and solitude, suffering and service. But the huge foundational means is public worship. Spiritual growth cannot take place in isolation. It is not a private thing between the Christian and God. In worship, we come before God who loves us in the presence of the others whom he also loves. In worship, more than at any other time, we set ourselves in deliberate openness to the action of God and the need of the neighbor, both of which require us to grow up to the fullness of the stature of Christ, who is both God and man for us. Regular, faithful worship is as essential to the growing Christian as food and shelter to the growing child. Worship is the light and air in which spiritual growth takes place.

They followed a daily discipline of worship in the Temple followed by meals at home, every meal a celebration, exuberant and joyful, as they praised God.

ACTS 2:46–47A

Blessed Are Those Who Are Persecuted

Unfriendly waters do a friendly
Thing; curses, cataract hurled
Stones, make the rough places
Smooth; a rushing whitewater stream
Of blasphemies hate-launched,
Then caught by the sun, sprays rainbow
Arcs across the Youghiogeny.
Savaged by the river's impersonal
Attack the land is deepened to bedrock.
Wise passivities are earned
In quiet, craggy, occasional pools
That chasten the wild waters to stillness,
And hold them under hemlock green
For birds and deer to bathe and drink
In peace—persecution's gift:
The hard-won, blessed letting be.

*[Jesus said,] "You're blessed when
your commitment to God provokes
persecution. The persecution drives
you even deeper into God's kingdom."*

MATTHEW 5:10

Vocational Holiness

In the following selection, you can substitute "homemakers,"
"shopkeepers," "teachers," "laborers," and so on for "pastors."

My first real find in Dostoyevsky was Prince Myshkin, "The Idiot." I
was looking for something that I later learned to name "vocational
holiness," and the Prince enlarged my imagination to grasp what it
might be.

How do I make a difference? The world is a mess: people are living in spiritual impoverishment, moral squalor, and material confusion. Some massive overhaul is indicated. Somebody has to *do* something. *I* have to do something. Where do I start?

What does it mean to represent the Kingdom of God in a culture
devoted to the Kingdom of Self? How do delicate, vulnerable, fragile
words survive in competition with money and guns and bulldozers?
How do pastors, who don't make anything happen, maintain a robust identity in a society that pays its top dollar to country singers,
drug lords, oil barons? All around me I saw men and women, pastors, hammering together a vocational identity from models given to
them from the "principalities and powers." The models were all
strong on power (making things happen) and image (appearing important). But none of them seemed congruent with the calling I
sensed forming within myself. But what actually did this unformu-
lated aspiration look like vocationally? Dostoyevsky's contribution to
my quest was Prince Myshkin.

Prince Myshkin strikes everyone who meets him as simple and naive. He gives the impression that he doesn't know how the world works. People assume that he has no experience in the complexities of society. He is innocent of the "real world." An idiot. . . .

The vocational question for anyone disgusted with society and wanting to do something about it for the better centers on means— *how* do I go about it? Is it to be guns or grace? Dostoyevsky created a series of characters, fools for Christ, who choose grace. Prince Myshkin is my favorite.

[Jesus said,] "This is a large work I've called you into, but don't be overwhelmed by it. It's best to start small. Give a cool cup of water to someone who is thirsty, for instance. The smallest act of giving or receiving makes you a true apprentice. You won't lose out on a thing."

MATTHEW 10:42

OCTOBER 22

Nero Wolfe, the Fat Detective

The following is a reflection on Rex Stout's Fer-De-Lance.

Nero Wolfe, the fat detective featured in the numerous Rex Stout murder mysteries, is not a clergyman, but for thirty years I have amused myself and some of my friends by reading him as a parable of the Christian contemplative presence in the world. The popular imagination, dulled by contemporaneity, sees nothing in the Nero

Wolfe stories but detection. But Stout has written a body of work every bit as theologically perspicuous as Swift with the result that he hits the best seller lists as a clever and resourceful detective novelist. To his financial benefit, of course, but still, for a serious writer to be misunderstood so completely must be humiliating no matter what the bank balance. But once the theological intent is suggested, the barest sleuthing quickly discerns Nero Wolfe as a type of the church's presence in the world. The most evident thing about him, his body, provides an analog to the church. His vast bulk is evidence of his "weight," recalling the etymology of the biblical "glory." More than anything else he is there, visibly. He must be reckoned with. He is corpulent or nothing. And the church is the body of Christ. Along with an insistence on bodily presence there is a corresponding observation that there is nothing attractive about that body. His body is subject to calumny and jokes. His genius is in his mind and his style. He does not fawn before customers, nor seek "contacts" (a word, incidentally, that he would never use. He once was found ripping apart a dictionary, page by page, and burning it because it legitimized "contact" as a transitive verb). Wolfe will not leave his house on business, that is, accommodate himself to the world's needs. He is a center around which the action revolves, a center of will and meditation, not a center of power or activity. He provides a paradigm for Christian spirituality which, while reticent and reserved, is there in vast presence when needed. He has no need for advertising techniques or public relations programs. He is there and needed because there is something wrong in the world (murder and other criminal extremes). He models a contemplative life which is not here to be loved, not designed to inspire affection. It is massive, central, important—a genius, in fact. But you don't have to like it. In all this there is an implied criticism of a church which has succumbed to public relations agents who have mounted Christian pulpits to make the church attractive, to personalize her, to sentimentalize her. Wolfe, as Christian ministry, levels a rebuke against that kind of thing. It follows that there is disdain for defensive explanations—a Barthian avoidance of "apologetics" to a world which seeks assurance of its reliability and effectiveness. To that kind of inquiry he says: "I can give you my word, but I know what it's worth and you don't." The spiritual life is cheapened when it tries to defend itself or make itself acceptable in terms the world can understand.

> *The church, you see, is not peripheral to the world; the world is peripheral to the church. The church is Christ's body, in which he speaks and acts, by which he fills everything with his presence.*

EPHESIANS 1:22–23

OCTOBER 23

Measuring Our Faith

I think it's wise to completely eliminate talk about how much faith we have, or how we need more faith. All too often when we say these things we aren't talking about faith at all but a feeling we have. When we define faith as a feeling—of belief, or of piety—what we're actually measuring is not faith but an emotion. Faith is not a feeling. It is simply an act of assent, of openness, and often doesn't feel like much at all. Faith has to do with what God is doing, not with what we are feeling.

When I start measuring my faith, I'm doing it from my point of view—and I'm always looking at the wrong things. If instead I try simply to be attentive to what God is doing, I become more and more aware of what he's doing—and that's a lot. Jesus said that God gives the Spirit without measure (John 3:34). He doesn't dole it out. There's immensity here, extravagance—but I never get that picture if I'm measuring things from my side.

[John said,] "And don't think he rations out the Spirit in bits and pieces. The Father loves the Son extravagantly. He turned everything over to him so he could give it away—a lavish distribution of gifts. That is why whoever accepts and trusts the Son gets in on everything."

JOHN 3:34B-35

OCTOBER 24

Wishing and Hoping

It is essential to distinguish between hoping and wishing. They are not the same thing.

Wishing is something all of us do. It projects what we want or think we need into the future. Just because we wish for something good or holy we think it qualifies as hope. It does not. Wishing extends our egos into the future; hope desires what God is going to do—and we don't yet know what that is.

Wishing grows out of our egos; hope grows out of our faith. Hope is oriented toward what God is doing; wishing is oriented toward what we are doing. Wishing has to do with what I want in things or people or God; hope has to do with what God wants in me and the world of things and people beyond me.

Wishing is our will projected into the future, and hope is God's will coming out of the future. Picture it in your mind: wishing is a line that comes out of me, with an arrow pointing into the future. Hoping is a line that comes out of God from the future, with an arrow pointing toward me.

Hope means being surprised, because we don't know what is best for us or how our lives are going to be completed. To cultivate hope is to suppress wishing—to refuse to fantasize about what we want, but live in anticipation of what God is going to do next.

> . . . *alert for whatever God will do next. In alert expectancy*
> *such as this, we're never left feeling shortchanged. Quite*
> *the contrary—we can't round up enough containers to hold*
> *everything God generously pours into our lives through*
> *the Holy Spirit.*

ROMANS 5:4B–5

OCTOBER 25

Expectant and Alive

Hope affects the Christian life by making us expectant and alive. People with minimal hope live in drudgery and boredom because they think they know what's going to happen next. They've made their assessment of God, the people around them, and themselves, and they know what's coming.

People who hope never know what's coming next. They expect it is going to be good, because God is good. Even when disasters occur, people of hope look for how God will use evil for good.

A person with hope is alive to God. Hope is powerful. It is stimulating. It keeps us on tiptoe, looking for the unexpected.

> . . . *waiting does not diminish us, any more than waiting diminishes a pregnant mother. We are enlarged in the waiting. We, of course, don't see what is enlarging us. But the longer we wait, the larger we become, and the more joyful our expectancy.*

ROMANS 8:24–25

OCTOBER 26

When Discipline Feels Dull and Dead

Believers must be aware that most of the time discipline feels dull and dead. We're impatient if we have to wait a long time for something, especially in America. If we don't find instant zest in a discipline, we make a negative snap judgment about it. But often what we describe as deadness, dullness, or boredom is simply our own slow waking up. We just have to live through that. Simple desire for more in our Christian lives is sufficient evidence that the life is there. Be patient and wait. It's the Spirit's work. We simply put ourselves in the way of the Spirit so he can work in us.

Meanwhile, the moment we get tired in the waiting,
God's Spirit is right alongside helping us along. If we
don't know how or what to pray, it doesn't matter.
He does our praying in and for us, making prayer out
of our wordless sighs, our aching groans.

ROMANS 8:26

OCTOBER 27

Learn to Listen to the Word

We are mistaken when we look at the Bible as a spiritual toolbox. We can't take things out of the Bible and make them work for us. The whole process of the spiritual life is to come before the God who is alive, who becomes present to us in his Word, and who by means of that Word creates and redeems. We don't use Scripture; God uses Scripture to work his will in us.

[Jesus said,] "You have your heads in your Bibles
constantly because you think you'll find eternal life
there. But you miss the forest for the trees. These
Scriptures are all about me! *And here I am, standing*
right before you, and you aren't willing to receive
from me the life you say you want."

JOHN 5:39–40

God's Word Written

It is a great blessing to have God's Word written so that we can read it at any time, but that the Word is written also involves us in difficulties not attended to often enough. These difficulties are at the very center of the spiritual life. The difficulties radiate out of a position of ownership—supposing that we own the Word, rather than letting the Word possess us. The simple act of buying a Bible has subtle side effects we need to counter. It is easy to suppose that since we bought it, we own it, and therefore can use it the way we wish.

This danger was not as acute when most Christians were illiterate, for they never read Scripture; they heard it. The words of the Bible were first spoken and listened to. Most of it was in oral form before it was written down. Even the Epistles, which originated as writings, were read aloud and listened to in the churches to which they were written.

Hearing a word is different from reading a word. When we hear, we are poised for response; something is happening. A listener doesn't take a word or a phrase, then walk off and analyze it—that would be to miss the message. A speaking person presents a whole message to us, and we respond as whole persons. But the moment the message is written down, we can stop listening if we are so minded.

[Jesus said,] ". . . don't you ever read the Bible? How God at the bush said to Moses, 'I am—not was—the God of Abraham, the God

of Isaac, and the God of Jacob'? The living God is God of the living, not the dead. You're way, way off base."

MARK 12:26B–27

OCTOBER 29

Being and Doing

"Don't look for shortcuts to God. The market is flooded with sure-fire, easygoing formulas for a successful life that can be practiced in your spare time. Don't fall for that stuff, even though crowds of people do. The way to life—to God!—is vigorous and requires total attention.

"Be wary of false preachers who smile a lot, dripping with practiced sincerity. Chances are they are out to rip you off some way or other. Don't be impressed with charisma; look for character. Who preachers *are* is the main thing, not what they say. A genuine leader will never exploit your emotions or your pocketbook. These diseased trees with their bad apples are going to be chopped down and burned.

"Knowing the correct password—saying 'Master, Master,' for instance—isn't going to get you anywhere with me. What is required is serious obedience—*doing* what my Father wills. I can see it now—at the Final Judgment thousands strutting up to me and saying, 'Master, we preached the Message, we bashed the demons, our God-sponsored projects had everyone talking.' And do you know what I am going to say? 'You missed the boat. All you did was use me to make yourselves important. You don't impress me one bit. You're out of here.' "

MATTHEW 7:13–23

Foundational Words

"These words I speak to you are not incidental additions to your life, homeowner improvements to your standard of living. They are foundational words, words to build a life on. If you work these words into your life, you are like a smart carpenter who built his house on solid rock. Rain poured down, the river flooded, a tornado hit—but nothing moved that house. It was fixed to the rock.

"But if you just use my words in Bible studies and don't work them into your life, you are like a stupid carpenter who built his house on the sandy beach. When a storm rolled in and the waves came up, it collapsed like a house of cards."

When Jesus concluded his address, the crowd burst into applause. They had never heard teaching like this. It was apparent that he was living everything he was saying—quite a contrast to their religion teachers! This was the best teaching they had ever heard.

MATTHEW 7:24–29

Blessed Are the Pure in Heart

Austere country, this, scrubbed
By spring's ravaging avalanche.
Talus slope and Appekunny
Mudstone make a meadow where
High-country beargrass gathers light
From lichen, rock, and icy tarn,
Changing sun's lethal rays
To food for grizzlies, drink for bees—
Heart-pure creatures living blessed
Under the shining of God's face.
Yet, like us the far-fallen,
Neither can they look on the face
And live. Every blossom's a breast
Holding eventual sight for all blind and
Groping newborn: we touch our way
Through these splendors to the glory.

[Jesus said,] "You're blessed when you get your inside world—your mind and heart—put right. Then you can see God in the outside world."

MATTHEW 5:8

November

Praying Before Scripture

Our whole educational system trains us to read Scripture in the wrong way. It teaches us to read it for information, to get a doctrine out of it, to make an argument from it. All the time the Spirit is speaking to us, drawing us into a relationship of love and faith. But we are busy grabbing verses and running off into our studies to try to figure them out. That is rude. We wouldn't tolerate this behavior with our children, but we positively encourage it in our churches. We need to do much less studying of Scripture and more praying before Scripture. Rather than analyzing the Word, we need to let it speak to us.

> *[Jesus said,] "Study this story of the farmer planting seed. When anyone hears news of the kingdom and doesn't take it in, it just remains on the surface, and so the Evil One comes along and plucks it right out of that person's heart. This is the seed the farmer scatters on the road."*

MATTHEW 13:18

In the Story

One of the great tasks of the Christian life is to open our ears before Scripture. The central way is through worship. Worship is fundamentally an act of listening and answering to the Word of God. The sanctuary, the basic gathering place for Christians, is not a study hall or a lecture room.

Another way believers can develop listening ears is by noticing that the Bible comes to us as a story. It does not come to us systematized into doctrine, or arranged as moral instruction. It is a story; and the story form is as important as the truth the story tells. This narrative style is intended to shape the way we read, for our spiritual life will not prosper if we are not drawn into the action of God through history, a story that has a beginning, an end, and a plot. Listening to Scripture in the form of story we learn that we are also in the story, traveling toward God, being drawn toward him. We develop a sense of journeying and discipleship. If we fail to develop this "story sense" we inevitably start "applying" the Bible—taking charge of a verse or doctrine or moral with which we intend to fix some fragment of ourselves. This is an excellent recipe for creating good Pharisees (who were great readers of Scripture, but notoriously poor listeners to God).

> *[Jesus said,] "The seed cast in the gravel—this is the person who hears and instantly responds with enthusiasm. But there is no soil of character, and so when the emotions wear off and some difficulty arrives, there is nothing to show for it."*

MATTHEW 13:20–21

Scripture in Its Double Context

It is also important to listen to Scripture in its double context: the context out of which it was spoken and listened to in Israel and Christ, and the context of our listening lives. God uses the same sentence to speak different things to different people. This is because we are at different stages of growth. We know how this works in families: a father tells a story and the two-year-old hears one dimension, the fifteen-year-old another, the wife still another. They all hear the same story; they all listen accurately; they all respond differently, but also appropriately. Since our contexts change daily, we keep listening to Scripture daily.

Our ancestors did this better than we do. They came before Scripture in a listening/responding way rather than in an academic/manipulative way. Becoming familiar with their reverent listening stance before Scripture helps us see the poverty of our students-getting-ready-for-an-exam approach. We are never exempt from the temptation to "use" and "apply" Scripture rather than submit to it and let God call forth things in us we didn't know were there. We have to be continually on guard. Our approach must be reading/listening to Scripture, letting the Word use us rather than using the Word for our well-intentioned but still self-defined purposes.

> *[Jesus said,] "The seed cast in the weeds is the person who hears the kingdom news, but weeds of worry and illusions about getting more and wanting everything under the sun strangle what was heard, and nothing comes of it."*

MATTHEW 13:22

Praying Our Tears (Psalm 6)

Tears are a biological gift of God. They are a physical means for expressing emotional and spiritual experience. But it is hard to know what to do with them. If we indulge our tears, we cultivate self-pity. If we suppress our tears, we lose touch with our feelings. But if we *pray* our tears we enter into sadnesses that integrate our sorrows with our Lord's sorrows and discover both the source of and the relief from our sadness.

> *You've kept track of my every toss and turn*
> *through the sleepless nights,*
> *Each tear entered in your ledger,*
> *each ache written in your book.*

PSALM 56:8

Praying Our Doubt (Psalm 73)

Doubt is not a sin. It is an essential element in belief. Doubt is honesty. Things are not as they appear. We see contradictions between what we believe and what we experience. What is going on here? Did God give us a bum steer? Why aren't things turning out the way we were taught to expect? No mature faith avoids or denies doubt. Doubt forces faith to bedrock.

> *The woman said, "Sir, you don't even have a bucket to draw with, and this well is deep. So how are you going to get this 'living water'? Are you a better man than our ancestor Jacob, who dug this well and drank from it, he and his sons and livestock, and passed it down to us?"*

JOHN 4:11–12

NOVEMBER 6

Praying Our Death (Psalm 90)

Death is not a popular subject. We live in a society characterized by the denial of death. This is unusual. Most people who have lived on this earth have given a great deal of attention to death. Preparing for a good death has been, in every century except our own, an accepted goal in life. Psalm 90 has been part of that preparation for millions of Christians.

> *We live for seventy years or so*
> *(with luck we might make it to eighty),*
> *And what do we have to show for it? Trouble.*
> *Toil and trouble and a marker in the graveyard....*
> *Oh! teach us to live well!*
> *Teach us to live wisely and well!*

PSALM 90:10, 12

Praying Our Praise (Psalm 150)

All prayer finally, in one way or another, becomes praise. Psalm 150 is deliberately placed as the concluding prayer of the church's book of prayers. No matter how much we suffer, no matter our doubts—everything finds its way into praise, the final consummating prayer. This is not to say that other prayers are inferior to praise, only that all prayer, pursued far enough, becomes praise.

> *Let every living, breathing creature praise GOD!*
> *Hallelujah!*

PSALM 150:6

Angels and Animals

Angels and animals. They make a nice combination, extending our awareness in the twin dimensions of spirit and sense. Animal stories, pets, photography, and observation extend our participation more deeply into the sensual beauty and vitality that is all around us, so much of which we are unaware. Angel stories, letters, books, and glimpses extend our participation more deeply into the spiritual beauty and vitality that is all around us, so much of which we are unaware. It is significant that in St. John's Revelation, our most prominent biblical integration of the sensual and spiritual, animals and angels flank the human representatives of Israel and the church in giving praise to God (Rev. 4–5). We humans need help from both sides in order to participate in the largeness of God's creation and salvation.

> *I heard a company of Angels around the Throne, the Animals, and the Elders—ten thousand times ten thousand their number, thousand after thousand after thousand in full song . . .*

REVELATION 5:11

NOVEMBER 9

Message-Bringers

Angels have never lacked for notice. Angel stories that run the gamut from serious to silly abound in folk religion. And learned angel speculation has occupied some of the best minds in Christendom, most notably Pseudo-Dionysius and Thomas Aquinas. But it is the novelists and poets who have shown the most immediate and natural affinity for angels. It is easy to see why, for writers and angels are alike concerned with bringing transcendence to our attention. Writers and angels are message-bringers, bringing the message that there is more here than meets the eye.

> *In the sixth month of Elizabeth's pregnancy,*
> *God sent the angel Gabriel to the Galilean village*

of Nazareth to a virgin engaged to be married
to a man descended from David.

LUKE 1:26

NOVEMBER 10

Elusiveness

Writers and angels share another quality—a penchant for elusiveness, for staying out of the way. Our best writers hide themselves in their work. And angels are for the most part invisible and inaudible, neither noticed nor heard. For transcendence cannot be forced upon us. It doesn't yell, doesn't announce its presence with a bullhorn, doesn't advertise itself on roadside billboards. There is nothing bullying about transcendence.

What it requires is noticing. Witnesses to transcendence don't create transcendence. The transcendence is already here, or there. But in our hurry to get someplace else, we miss it. There is always more here than meets the eye. We miss a lot. We need friends who will grab our shirttails, turn us around, and show us what we just now missed in our hurry to get across the street on our way to the bank. We need friends who will tap us on the shoulder, interrupting our non-stop commentary on the talk of the town so that we can hear the truth. We need witnesses to transcendence. Writers. Angels. We stop, we look, we listen.

[Jesus said,] "Father, put your glory on display."
A voice came out of the sky: "I have glorified it, and I'll glorify it
again."

The listening crowd said, "Thunder!"
Others said, "An angel spoke to him!"

JOHN 12:28–29

NOVEMBER 11

A Pedestrian Way

Christians read. For Christians, reading is a fundamental and assumed skill. If a person who cannot read becomes a Christian, we go to work and teach him, or her. And the reason, of course, is that God has revealed himself in Jesus, the Word made Flesh. We have 66 witnesses to this revelation; they have written their witness with ink on paper. The writings of these witnesses have been collected together and bound in a book of holy writings, Holy Scripture: the Bible. This is our primary, our authorized (and therefore authoritative) access to the revelation of God in Jesus. When Christians want to know who God is and how he works, what it means to be created in his image, saved by his Son and filled with his Spirit, we read scripture.

This Christian reading is a core activity and not an add-on. There are other ways some people prefer to go about this, but we say No to them and hold to this one. We say No, for instance, to working ourselves up into visionary states of ecstasy in order to get in touch with God. We say No to undertaking Herculean tasks of moral heroism in order to discover the divine potentialities within us. We say No to going off to a mountain cave and emptying ourselves of all thought and feeling and desire so that there is nothing left in us to separate us from immediate access to Reality. We Christians are sometimes impressed by these spiritual pyrotechnics, and on occasion even ooh and aah over them, but our wiser guides do not encourage us to go in for them ourselves. In contrast to the glamorous spiritualities, ours is a pedestrian way, literally pedestrian: putting one foot in front of the other we follow Jesus. In order to know who he is and where he's going and how to walk in his steps, we reach for a book, *the* book, and read it.

> *. . . a story of the wonderful harvest of Scripture and history that took place among us, using reports handed down by the original eyewitnesses who served this Word with their very lives.*

LUKE 1:1–2

NOVEMBER 12

Let the Reader Beware

Historically Christians have been as concerned in *how* we read as in *that* we read the Bible. The Christian community as a whole has never assumed that it is sufficient to place a Bible in a person's hands with the command, "Read it." That is quite as foolish as putting a set of car keys in an adolescent's hands, giving him a Honda and saying, "Drive it." And just as dangerous. The danger is that in having our hands on a piece of technology, we impose our ignorant or destructive will upon it.

Print is technology. We have God's word in our hands, *our hands*. We can now handle it. It is easy enough to imagine that we are in control of it, that we can manage it, that we can use it and apply it.

There is more to the Honda than the technology of mechanics. And there is more to the Bible than the technology of print. Surrounding the machine technology of the Honda there is a world of gravity and inertia, values and velocity, surfaces and obstructions, Chevrolets and Fords, traffic regulations and the police, other drivers, snow and ice and rain. Oh, there is far more to car than its gear shift and steering wheel. There is far more to driving a car than turning a key in the ignition and stepping on the accelerator. Those who don't know that are soon dead or maimed.

And those who don't know the *world* of the Bible are likewise dangerous to themselves and others. And so as we hand out Bibles and urge people to read them, we also say, Caveat Lector—let the reader beware.

*[Jesus said,] "The seed cast on good
earth is the person who hears and
takes in the News, and then produces
a harvest beyond his wildest dreams."*

MATTHEW 13:23

NOVEMBER 13

Spiritual Reading

Just having print on page and knowing how to distinguish nouns from verbs is not enough. Reading the Bible, if you do not do it rightly, can get you into a lot of trouble. You might own your own

Bible but you don't own the Word of God to do with what you want—God is sovereign. Your Morocco leather Bible might be a thing that you paid fifty dollars for, but the Word of God is personal, living and active—God is love. If in our Bible reading we do not submit to the sovereignty and respond to the love, we become arrogant in our knowing and impersonal in our behavior.

The wisdom, counsel, and skills that have developed around this concern through the centuries coalesce under the Latin heading, *Lectio Divina,* often translated as "spiritual reading," by which we are taught to read the Bible with humility and intimacy.

The word "spiritual" in the phrase doesn't refer to reading *about* spiritual things, but to the *way* in which a book is read. Primarily it has to do with the way we read Holy Scripture, listening to the Spirit, alert to intimations of God, but the skill can be extended to nearly anything written, including letters, poems, novels, even cookbooks.

The concern of *Lectio Divina* is quite simple, really—at least simple to grasp. It means reading personally, not impersonally, reading for a message that affects who we are and are becoming, the way we live our lives, and not merely for information that we can use to raise our standard of living.

. . . Paul talked to them all day, from morning to evening, explaining everything involved in the kingdom of God, and trying to persuade them all about Jesus by pointing out what Moses and the prophets had written about him.

Some were persuaded by what he said, but others refused to believe a word of it.

ACTS 28:23B–24

Running and Reading

The unique quality of spiritual reading in contrast to other kinds of reading, struck me full in the face about 20 years ago. I had taken up running again. I had run in college and seminary and enjoyed it immensely, but when I left school, I left running. It never occurred to me that running was something that an adult might do just for the fun of it. Besides, I was a pastor now and wasn't sure how my parishioners would take seeing their pastor running thinly clad along the roads of our community. But I was noticing other people, doctors and lawyers and executives whom I knew, running in unexpected places without apparent loss of dignity, men and women my age and older, and realized that I could probably get away with it too. I went out and bought running shoes—Adidas they were—and discovered the revolution in footwear that had taken place since my student days. I began having fun, enjoying again the smooth rhythms of long distance running, the quietness, the solitude, the augmented senses, the muscular freedom. Soon I was competing in 10K races every month or so, and then a marathon once a year. Running progressed from being a physical act to a comprehensive ritual—a mental/emotional/spiritual world which I inhabited. By this time I was subscribing to three running magazines, getting books from the library on runners and running. I never tired of reading about running—food, stretching, training methods, resting heart rate, endorphins, carbohydrate loading, electrolyte replacements—if it was about running, I read it. How much is there to say about running? None of it, with few exceptions, was written very well. But it didn't matter that I had read nearly the same thing twenty times before; it didn't matter if the prose was patched together with clichés; I was a runner and anything written about running was personal to me. Then I pulled a muscle and couldn't run for six weeks. It took me about two weeks to notice that since my injury I hadn't picked up a running book or opened a running magazine. I didn't *decide* not to read them. They were still all over the house. But I wasn't reading them. Not once during the period I was injured and not running did I read anything about running. I wasn't reading because I wasn't running. The moment I began running again, I started reading again.

That is when I caught the significance of the modifier "spiritual" in spiritual reading. It meant participatory reading. It meant that I read every word on the page as an extension or deepening or correction or affirmation of something that *I* was doing.

> *[Jesus said,]* "... *if you just use my words in Bible studies and don't work them into your life, you are like a stupid carpenter who built his house on the sandy beach. When a storm rolled in and the waves came up, it collapsed like a house of cards."*

MATTHEW 7:26–27

NOVEMBER 15

Lectio, Meditatio, Oratio, Contemplatio

There is a certain logical order to the four aspects of spiritual reading designated *lectio, meditatio, oratio, contemplatio.* But they rarely progress in orderly sequence. So even though reading is a linear act, spiritual reading is not: any one of the elements may be at the fore at any one time. These elements are not stages in which we advance one to the next; but moments that continuously recur and are repeated in random order. It is a mistake to try to impose sequentiality here. What we are after is *noticing*—seeing the interplay of elements, how one thing calls forth another, and then recedes to give place to another—the elements thrown together in a kind of playful folk dance, rather than marching in precise formation.

> *I set your instructions to music*
> *and sing them as I walk this pilgrim way.*
> *I meditate on your name all night, GOD,*
> *treasuring your revelation, O GOD.*

PSALM 119:54–55

NOVEMBER 16

Getting the Words Right

It isn't long before we're using the Bible more as a Rorschach test than a religious text, reading more into the ink than we read out of it. It isn't long before we're using the word "spiritual" primarily to refer to ourselves, and only incidentally to include God.

When that happens, as it so often does, one of our Christian brothers or sisters, collars us and insists, "Read. Read only what is here, but also everything that is here." *Lectio.* Our usual word for this careful, disciplined reading is "exegesis." We have a word to listen to, to read. It is God's word, and so we had better get it right. Exegesis is the care we give to getting the words right.

> [*Jesus said,*] *"Trivialize even the smallest item in God's Law and you will only have trivialized yourself. But take it seriously, show the way for others, and you will find honor in the kingdom."*

MATTHEW 5:19

NOVEMBER 17

Lovers Savor the Words

Exegesis is the farthest thing from pedantry; exegesis is an act of love. It is loving the one enough who speaks the words to want to get the words right. It is respecting the words enough to use every means we have to get the words right. Exegesis is loving God enough to stop and listen carefully to what he says. God has provided us with these scriptures that present us with his Word. Loving God means loving both what God speaks to us and the way God speaks to us. It follows that we bring the leisure and attentiveness of lovers to this text—cherishing every comma and semicolon, relishing the oddness of this preposition, delighting in the surprising placement of this noun. Lovers don't take a quick look, get a "message" or a "meaning" and then run off and gossip with their friends about how they feel. Lovers savor the words, relishing every nuance of what is said and written.

Paul went to their meeting place, as he usually did when he came to a town, and for three Sabbaths running he preached to them from the Scriptures. He opened up the texts so they understood what they'd been reading all their lives . . .

ACTS 17:2–3A

NOVEMBER 18

Quite Other

Face it, reality as God reveals it to us by his Word in Jesus, is strange and unexpected and disappointing. This is not the kind of world we would have created if we had been given the assignment; this is not the kind of salvation we would have arranged if we had been on the committee; this is not the system of rewards and punishments we would have legislated if we had had the vote. I love the audacious quip of Teresa of Avila when she was energetically engaged in reforming the Carmelite monasteries, traveling all over Spain by oxcart on bad roads, and one day was thrown from the cart into a muddy stream. She shook her fist at God, "God, if this is the way you treat your friends, no wonder you don't have many."

No, the Reality that God reveals to us in his Word is very different, quite other—Other!—than anything we could ever have dreamed or thought up. And thank goodness. For if we keep at this long enough, prayer by prayer, we find ourselves living in a reality that is far, far larger, far lovelier, far better. But it takes considerable getting used to. Prayer is the process of getting used to it—going from the small to the large, from control to mystery, from self to soul—to God. And God doesn't only reveal it to us by his Word so that we can know about it; he wants us engaged in it, participating in it.

So Caveat Lector: let the reader beware. Don't just understand it; don't just admire it; don't just think it's a wonderful thing; *oratio— pray* what you read, work yourself into active participation in what God reveals in the Word. God invites, yes, commands us to bring our words to this Word. He doesn't expect us to take this new reality lying down. We better *not* take it lying down, for this word of God intends to get us on our feet, walking, running, singing.

> *I grasp and cling to whatever you tell me;*
> *GOD, don't let me down!*
> *I'll run the course you lay out for me*
> *if you'll just show me how.*

PSALM 119:31–32

NOVEMBER 19

David, a Lay Person

It is highly significant and not sufficiently remarked that this David story, the story that provides more plot and detail, more characters and landscape than any other in scripture to show us how to live entirely before and in response to God, features an ordinary person. David was, in our dismissive and condescending terminology, "just" a lay person. His father omitted to present him to Samuel—it probably didn't even occur to him. To his brothers he was a nonentity. Worse, as we learn from examining his genealogy family tree, he had bad blood in his family tree, hated and despised Moabite blood.

The choice of David, the runt and the shepherd, to be the anointed, to be a sign and representative of God's working presence in human life and history, is surely intended to convey a sense of inclusion to all ordinary men and women, the plain folk, the undistinguished in the eyes of their neighbors, those lacking social status and peer recognition. Which is to say, the overwhelming majority of all who have lived on this old planet earth. Election into God's purposes is not by popular vote. Election into God's purposes is not based on proven ability or potential promise. . . .

So it is of considerable moment to realize that the centerfold account in scripture of a human being living by faith comes in the shape of a lay person. David was not ordained to the priesthood. He was not called, as we say, "to the ministry." He was "just" a lay person, *haqqaton*. But there is not a hint in the narrative that his status is evidence of inadequacy. This is humanity burgeoning and vital, bold and extravagant, skillful and inventive in love and prayer and work.

Passing along the beach of Lake Galilee, he saw Simon and his brother Andrew net-fishing. Fishing was their regular work. Jesus said to them, "Come with me. I'll make a new kind of fisherman out of you. I'll show you how to catch men and women instead of perch and bass." They didn't ask questions. They dropped their nets and followed.

MARK 1:16–18

Anointing

Work is our Spirit-anointed participation in God's work. When Jesus stood up in the Nazareth synagogue to announce that he was going to work and how he was going to go about it, he said, "The Spirit of the Lord is upon me because he has *anointed* me . . ." (Luke 4:18).

In our biblical texts anointing means being given a job by God. It means employment. We are, in effect, told that there is a job to be done and that we are assigned to do it, and that we *can* do it. Anointing connects our work with God's work. Anointing is the sacramental connection linking God's work with our work. God is a worker, a maker. God does things. He *is*, of course; but he also *acts*. And it is in his acts that we know who he is.

> *[Jesus said,] ". . . I, on my way to the Father, am giving you the same work to do that I've been doing."*

JOHN 14:12B

Kingwork

God-anointed, David entered the world of work. He worked as a shepherd before he was anointed, work that provided background and metaphor for so much of the Gospel. But now David's work was clearly seen as God-assigned, God-defined. All David's work now was kingwork.

I want to use the word *kingwork* to represent all true work. I am using this word in order to call attention to the essential dignity of work as such, that our work is of a kind with God's work. All real work, genuine work, is subsumed under kingwork. I am using the word here to distinguish true work from false work, spurious work, "work" that destroys or deceives. Just because energy is employed for a purpose does not qualify an action as *work*.

Work derives from and represents the sovereign God who expresses his sovereignty as a worker: kingwork. Sovereigns work to bring order out of chaos; guard and fight for the sanctity of things and people; deliver victims from injustice and misfortune and wretchedness; grant pardon to the condemned and damned; heal sickness; by their very presence bring dignity and honor to people and land. God's sovereignty is not abstract—it is a *working* sovereignty and is expressed in work. All of our work is intended as an extension of and participation in that sovereignty.

". . . What do we do then to get in on God's works?"
Jesus said, "Throw your lot in with the One that God has sent. That kind of a commitment gets you in on God's works."

JOHN 6:28–29

NOVEMBER 22

"What Do You Do?"

Why do we always want to know early on in our acquaintance with someone what their work is? "What do you do?" is virtually always among the repertoire of getting-acquainted questions. And the reason is this: occupation, career, job can do two things—usually both at the same time: work can reveal something essential about us—express our values, articulate our morals, act out our convictions of what it means to be a human being, created in the image of God. Or work can conceal our real identity. It can be used as a front to advertise something that we want people to see in us or believe about us, but which in fact we have never bothered to become within ourselves. For most of us, the two vocational things are mixed: revealing/ expressing, and concealing/diverting. As we get to know someone we want to know if their job is a role to hide in or behind, or if it is an honest expression of character.

> *The diligent find freedom in their work;*
> *the lazy are oppressed by work.*

PROVERBS 12:24

At the Heart of All Work

David's first job as king was making music, attempting to re-establish the divine order in Saul's disordered mind and emotions. Establishing order in the midst of chaos is basic to kingwork. Music is probably our most elemental experience of this essential work. Music, bringing rhythm and harmony and tunefulness into being, is at the heart of all work. Kingworkers, whatever their jobs, whistle while they work.

322   LIVING THE MESSAGE

Accompanied by dulcimer and harp,
  the full-bodied music of strings.

You made me so happy, GOD.
  I saw your work and I shouted for joy.

PSALM 92:3–4

Authenticity

David refuses King Saul's armor to fight the giant Goliath.

This is a common experience in the Valley of Elah when an amateur ventures into a field dominated by professionals. All around us people who care about us are suddenly there helping—piling armor on us, dressing us up in equipment that is going to qualify us for the task (even though it didn't seem to be doing them much good). We get advice. We get instruction. We are sent off to a training workshop. We find ourselves with an armload of books. These people are truly concerned about us and we are touched by their concern, in awe of their knowledge and experience. We listen to them and do what they tell us. And then we find that we can hardly move.

It wasn't easy to do what David did that day. David loved King Saul. He admired King Saul. He served King Saul. King Saul was splendid and powerful. King Saul loved him and was doing his best to help him. But despite all that, David removed the helmet, unbelted the sword and took off the armor. It couldn't have been easy to do that, walking away from all that proffered expertise. But to have gone to meet Goliath wearing Saul's armor would have been a disaster. It always is. David needed what was authentic to him.

What strikes me so forcibly in this picture is that David was both modest enough and bold enough to reject the suggestion that he do his work inauthentically (by using Saul's armor); and he was both modest and bold enough to use only that which he had been trained to use in his years as shepherd (his sling and some stones). And he killed the giant.

Be prepared. You're up against far more than you
can handle on your own. Take all the help you can
get, every weapon God has issued, so that when it's
all over but the shouting you'll still be on your feet.

EPHESIANS 6:13

NOVEMBER 25

Kneeled at the Brook

David left Saul's armor behind and walked out into the Valley of Elah clean and spare, traveling light, delivered from an immense clutter, and kneeled at the brook.

David at that moment, kneeling at the brook, frames something that is absolutely essential for each of us. Are we going to live this life from our knees imaginatively and personally? Or are we going to live it conventionally and second-hand? Are we going to live out of our

God-created, Spirit-anointed, Jesus-saved being? Or are we going toady and defer to eunuch professionals? Are we going to be shaped by our fears of Goliath or by God? Are we going to live by our admiration of Saul or by God?

> *Jesus, having prayed this prayer, left with*
> *his disciples and crossed over the brook*
> *Kidron at a place where there was a garden.*
> *He and his disciples entered it.*

JOHN 18:1

NOVEMBER 26

In Touch with Reality

The only person fully in touch with reality that day was David. The only fully human person in the Valley of Elah that day was David. Reality is made up mostly of what we can't see. Humanness is mostly a matter of what never gets reported in the newspapers. Only a prayer-saturated imagination accounts for what made holy history that day in the Valley of Elah—the striking immersion in God-reality, the robust exhibition of David-humanity.

> *"My kingdom," said Jesus, "doesn't consist of what*
> *you see around you."*

JOHN 18:36A

Laments

Seventy percent of the Psalms are laments. These laments either originate in or are derivative from the praying life of David. David faced loss, disappointment, death. He neither avoided, denied or soft-pedaled any of it. He faced everything and he prayed everything. The craggy majesty and towering dignity of David's life are a product of David's laments.

The contrast with our contemporary culture is appalling. We have a style of print and media journalism that reports disaster endlessly and scrupulously: crime and war, famine and flood, political malfeasance and societal scandal. The one virtually foolproof way for getting noticed in our culture is to do something bad—the worse the act, the higher the profile. In the wake of whatever has gone wrong or whatever wrong is done, commentators gossip, reporters interview, editors pontificate, Pharisees moralize, and then psychological analyses are conducted, political reforms initiated, academic studies funded. *And there is not one line of lament.*

There is no lament because truth is not taken seriously, love is not taken seriously. Human life does not matter as *life*, God-given, Christ-redeemed, Spirit-blessed life. It counts only as "news." There is no dignity to any of it. It is trivialized.

> *When the city came into view, he [Jesus]*
> *wept over it. "If you had only recognized this*
> *day, and everything that was good for you!*

But now it's too late. . . . All this because you
didn't recognize and welcome God's personal visit."

LUKE 19:41–42, 44B

NOVEMBER 28

Being in a Story

A failure to lament is a failure to connect. If we refuse to learn Davidic lamentation, our lives fragment into episodes and anecdotes, a succession of jerky starts and gossipy cul-de-sacs. But we're in a *story,* in which everything eventually comes together, a narrative in which all the puzzling parts finally fit and years later we exclaim, "Oh, so that's what that meant!" But being in a story means that we must not attempt to get ahead of the story—skip the hard parts, erase the painful parts, detour the disappointments. Lament, making the most of our loss without getting bogged down in it, is a primary way of staying *in* the story. *God* is telling this story, remember. It is a large, capacious story. He does not look kindly on our editorial deletions. But he delights in our poetry.

A huge crowd of people followed [Jesus], along with women weeping
and carrying on. At one point Jesus turned to the women and said,
"Daughters of Jerusalem, don't cry for me. Cry for yourselves and for
your children."

LUKE 23:27–28

A Pastor's Perspective

I confess to feeling a little awkward addressing the topic on which I have been asked to speak, "Spiritual Formation: A Pastor's Perspective." Such a topic is hard to talk about without falsifying the data just by talking about it. It is something like those experiments in physics, of which you have undoubtedly read, in which they have the laboratories completely free from contamination and then discover that the very presence of the experimenter distorts the data.

> *I don't want anyone imagining me as anything other than the fool you'd encounter if you saw me on the street or heard me talk.*

2 CORINTHIANS 12:6

NOVEMBER 30

Something Like a Mechanic

I am something like a mechanic who has been in the garage underneath cars all day, grime under my fingernails, bib overalls greasy, and the boss suddenly calls me and says, "Come out here. I want you to talk to these people." So he throws me in the shower, cleans me up, puts a suit and tie on me and stands me up before the listener. What am I going to talk about? Talk about what you do under cars, I am told. But what specific cars do you want me to talk about—Hondas or Cadillacs? Similarly, spiritual formation is not something we can do in generalities, it is always specific. If somebody from my congregation ever shows up in a place like this where I am speaking 500 miles from home I always feel doubly awkward; I feel at any moment they might stand up and say, "That is not right. That is not what he does. The facts might be right, but the context changes everything. You are getting it all wrong."

Spiritual formation, spirituality, is always local, intensely local. You cannot bring outside principles and impose them on the situation. Spirituality must grow out of the soil and weather conditions of the place, the parish, the pastor. This insistence on locale is what makes it difficult to talk accurately about spirituality and spiritual formation in a place like this because I am not in my parish. This is not my soil. This is not my weather. So things that I might say have a chance of being misunderstood.

Not only is spiritual formation local, but it always deals with particulars. If I am the mechanic tuning up the engine, it is a specific set of points I have to deal with, actual valves. It is not just a generic combustion engine, or electronics in general. Spiritual formation is never "in general," but always "in specific."

And by the way, get a room ready for me. Because of your prayers, I fully expect to be your guest again.

PHILEMON 22

December

Intensely Creative Work

. . . Spiritual formation is the most intensely creative work that the pastor does. When you are being creative, you are not copying, you are not transposing something that works someplace else and making it work here. When you are being creative, most of what you do is wrong. The creative people I know throw away 90% of what they produce. If you have ever tried to write a poem, you know that you do it wrong most of the time, and you work and work and work, throwing lines away, filling your wastebasket . . . until finally you have got it. Most of what creative people do is wrong.

Pastors do not like to hear that. We want to be efficient. But if we are being creative, we are working in this unformed chaos much of the time. We work the soil of the parish, working organically within the conditions, trusting the Spirit, trying to be an assistance to the Spirit and not a hindrance.

I'm not saying that I have all this together, that I have it made. But I am well on my way, reaching out for Christ, who has so wondrously

reached out for me. Friends, don't get me wrong: By no means do I
count myself an expert in all of this but I've got my eye on the goal . . .

PHILIPPIANS 3:12–13A

DECEMBER 2

In a Mess

Those first verses of Genesis are paradigmatic for pastoral work, especially in the area of spiritual formation. The wonderful phrase "formless and void," is a mess—and then in that mess, that chaos, the Spirit of God begins working and slowly creation and covenant begin to arise out of it: light, form, vegetation, animals, humans, love, virtue, hope, Christ. I once told a group of seminarians that the thing I like most about being a pastor is the mess. I do not mean I like messes as such, but I like that sense of being in a mess, held there by hope, knowing how God's creativity works, slowly, slowly, slowly, but always with surprises. Creation, creative work, never ends up the way we thought it would. It is always a surprise. "Creative" is by definition something new, and if we knew what the result was we might be a craftsman or assembly line worker or a manager of some kind but we would not be creative.

> *We don't yet see things clearly. We're squinting in a fog, peering*
> *through a mist. But it won't be long before the weather clears and the*
> *sun shines bright! We'll see it all then, see it all as clearly as God sees*
> *us, knowing him directly just as he knows us!*

1 CORINTHIANS 13:12

The Kingfisher

About a month ago we were just home from vacation and refreshed, ready to go again. The telephone rang. It was about 10:00 at night and on the other end of the line was a woman to whom I have been pastor for 26 years. When I entered this parish, she was 12 years old. Now she is 38. I confirmed her, married her, went through her divorce with her, went through a couple of deaths, depression, attempted suicide, ordained her into the leadership of the church, stood by as she left the church one year, opened the door as she came back the next year, prayed with her, listened to her. This night listening to her on the telephone I thought, "I have been her pastor for 26 years and she is not any better." After I hung up my wife said, "Who was that?" I said, "That was Regina. We are not very good at this, are we?" And Jan said, "Remember the kingfisher?"

And I remembered the kingfisher. We had been sitting at the shoreline of a lake in Montana and watching the kingfisher fish. The kingfisher is the "king" fisher, the best fisher, the bird that knows how to fish. This kingfisher was sitting on a dead limb out over the lake, preparing to fish. It is fun to watch a kingfisher fish. This kingfisher plummeted to the water and missed his fish 27 times. The kingfisher missed and missed and missed—and then, on the 28th try, he got one, a little three inch fish. Jan said, "Remember the kingfisher?" I said, "I remember—and it has only been 26 years."

That is the context for spiritual formation. If you are in a hurry, you probably should not do it, because it is messy and lengthy and marked by much failure—burrowing into the soil of your place, your people, your congregation, your own life, sticking with it creatively, waiting for creation and covenant to form.

There has never been the slightest doubt in my mind that the God who started this great work in you would keep at it and bring it to a flourishing finish on the very day Christ Jesus appears.

PHILIPPIANS 1:6

DECEMBER 4

Seeking for Intimacy

This world is no friend to grace. Seeking for intimacy at any level—with God or with persons—is not a venture that gets the support of many people. Intimacy is not good for business. It is inefficient, it lacks "glamour." If love of God can be reduced to a ritualized hour of worship, if love of another can be reduced to an act of sexual intercourse, then routines are simple and the world can be run efficiently. But if we will not settle for the reduction of love to lust and of faith to ritual, and run through the streets asking for more, we will most certainly disturb the peace and be told to behave ourselves and go back to the homes and churches where we belong. If we refuse to join the cult of exhibitionists who do a soul striptease on cue, or the "flashers" who expose their psychic nudity as a diversion from long-term covenantal intimacy, we are dismissed as hopeless puritans. Intimacy is no easy achievement. There is pain—longing, disappointment, and hurt. But if the costs are considerable, the rewards are magnificent, for in relationship with another and with the God who loves us we complete the humanity for which we were created. We stutter and stumble, wander and digress, delay and procrastinate; but we do learn to love even as we are loved, steadily and eternally, in Jesus Christ.

> *The longer this waiting goes on, the deeper the ache. I so want to be there to deliver God's gift in person and watch you grow stronger right before my eyes! But don't think I'm not expecting to get something out of this, too! You have as much to give me as I do to you.*

ROMANS 1:11–12

DECEMBER 5

Pure Silver Words

Quick, GOD, I need your helping hand!
The last decent person just went down,
All the friends I depended on gone.
Everyone talks in lie language;
Lies slide off their oily lips.
They doubletalk with forked tongues.

Slice their lips off their faces! Pull
The braggart tongues from their mouths!
I'm tired of hearing, "We can talk anyone into anything!
Our lips manage the world."

Into the hovels of the poor,
Into the dark streets where the homeless groan, God speaks:
"I've had enough; I'm on my way
To heal the ache in the heart of the wretched."

God's words are pure words,
Pure silver words refined seven times
In the fires of his word-kiln,
Pure on earth as well as in heaven.
GOD, keep us safe from their lies,
From the wicked who stalk us with lies,
From the wicked who collect honors
For their wonderful lies.

PSALM 12

DECEMBER 6

We Need a Theologian

Beginners at prayer—children, new converts—find it easy. The capacity and impulse to pray both are embedded deep within us. We are made, after all, by God, for God. Why wouldn't we pray? It is our native tongue, our first language. We find ourselves in terrible trouble and cry out for help to God. We discover ourselves immensely blessed and cry out our thanks to God. "Help!" and "Thanks!" are our basic prayers. Monosyllables. Simple.

God speaks to us, calls to us, has mercy on us, loves us, descends among us, enters us. And we answer, respond, accept, receive, praise. In a word, we pray. It's that simple. What more is there?

But prayer doesn't stay simple. We spend years slogging through a wilderness of testing and begin to question the childlike simplicities with which we started out. We find ourselves immersed in a cynical generation that corrodes our early innocence with scorn and doubt. Along the way we pick up notions of prayer magic and begin working on slight of hand rituals and verbal incantations that will make life easier. It isn't long before those early simplicities are all tangled up in knots of questions, doubts, and superstitions.

It happens to all of us. Everyone who prays ends up in some difficulty or other. We need help. We need a theologian. For those of us who pray and who mean to continue to pray, a theologian is our indispensable and best friend.

> *[Jesus said,] "Here's what I want you to do: Find a quiet, secluded place so you won't be tempted to role-play before God. Just be there as simply and honestly as you can manage. The focus will shift from you to God and you will begin to sense his grace."*

MATTHEW 6:6

DECEMBER 7

We Cannot Be Trusted in Prayer

The reason that we who pray need a theologian at our side is that most of the difficulties of prayer are of our own making, the making of well-meaning friends, or the lies of the devil who always seems to be looking after our best self-interests. We get more interested in ourselves than in God. We get absorbed in what is or is not happening in us. We get bewildered by the huge discrepancies between our feelings and our intentions; we get unsettled by moralistic accusations that call into question our worthiness to even engage in prayer; we get attracted by advertisements of secrets that will give us access to a privileged, spiritual elite.

But prayer has primarily to do with God, not us. It includes us, certainly—everything about us down to the last detail. But God is primary. And the theologian's task is to train our thinking, our imagination, our understanding to begin with God, not ourselves. This is not always reassuring, for we want someone to pay attention to us. But it is more important to pay attention to God. Prayer, which began simply enough by paying attention to God, can only recover that simplicity by re-attending to God. Prayer is the most personal thing that any of us do, the most human act in which we can engage. We are more ourselves, our true, image-of-God selves, when we pray than at any other time. This is the glory of prayer, but it is also the trouble with prayer, for these selves of ours have a way of getting more interested in themselves than in God.

[Jesus said,] "The world is full of so-called prayer warriors who are prayer-ignorant. They're full of formulas and programs and advice, peddling techniques for getting what you want from God. Don't fall for that nonsense. This is your Father you are dealing with, and he knows better than you what you need."

MATTHEW 6:7–8

LIVING THE MESSAGE   337

Prayerbooks and Hymnbooks

The next thirteen entries are Take and Read, *from an annotated reading list of books containing twenty categories.*

I was reared in a tradition that scorned written and read prayers. Book prayers. Dead prayers. Reading a prayer would have been like meeting an old friend on the street, quickly leafing through a book to find an appropriate greeting suitable for the meeting and then reading, "Hello, old friend; it is good to see you again. How have you been? Remember me to your family. Well, I must be on my way now. Good-bye." And then closing the book and going on down the street without once looking my friend in the eye. Ludicrous. The very nature of prayer required that it be spontaneous and from the heart.

But along the way, I began to come across books of prayers that gave me words to pray when I didn't seem to have any of my own. I found that books of prayers sometimes primed the pump of prayer when I didn't feel like praying. And I found that left to myself, I often prayed in a circle, too wrapped up in myself, too much confined to my immediate circumstances and feelings, and that a prayerbook was just the thing to get out of the brambles and underbrush of my ego, back out in the open country of the Kingdom, under the open skies of God.

In the process of discovering, to my surprise, alive and praying friends in these books, I realized that all along the prayers that had most influenced me were *written* (in the Bible), and that the lively and spirited singing we did in church was, for the most part, praying from a book, the hymnbook. My world of prayer expanded.

All you saints! Sing your hearts out to GOD!
  Thank him to his face!
He gets angry once in a while, but across
  a lifetime there is only love.
The nights of crying your eyes out
  give way to days of laughter.

PSALM 30:4–5

DECEMBER 9

North American Spirituality

Each culture carries with it spiritual assets and liabilities. Cultures of other languages, centuries, and histories offer up unique insights into spirituality, but they also display blind spots. The Platonism of Augustine's age, for instance, provided a large intellectual framework that helped communicate the faith to the pagan mind, and at the same time blunted, for the unwary, the sharp particularities of the cross and all its attendant materialism. Similar "double-entry bookkeeping" can be done on the Aristotelianism of the Middle Ages, on post-Reformation Calvinism, and on Enlightenment romanticism. Each age requires discernment to embrace its gospel-generated energies and truths and to avoid repeating its culture-conditioned errors. North American spirituality has its own flavor, requiring a trained palate to discern the best from the worst.

There at the Jordan River those who came to confess their sins were baptized into a changed life.

LIVING THE MESSAGE   339

When John realized that a lot of Pharisees and Sadducees were showing up for a baptismal experience because it was becoming the popular thing to do, he exploded, "Brood of snakes! . . ."

MATTHEW 3:6–7A

DECEMBER 10

Karl Barth, The Epistle to the Romans *(1933)*

Barth wrote this commentary while pastor of a small congregation in the Swiss village of Safenwil. I read it when I was pastor of a small congregation in Maryland. I was trying to learn how to be a pastor in a territory bordered on one side by a believing (or semi-believing) congregation, on the other side by an indifferent (and occasionally scornful) world, and on the third side by the biblical text that I had promised to faithfully preach and teach. I was most at ease with the biblical text. When I had it all to myself, it was almost simple. But when I realized that as a pastor I would never again have it all to myself, that I was now exposed on the two other fronts of church and world, I knew that I was in over my head and needed help. The textual front required intelligence and attention, but I was used to that and enjoyed it. The congregational front was a surprise. These people were my friends and allies, but they were constantly interpreting my interpretations through filters of self-interest. I found that the Scriptures that I was preaching and teaching were being rewritten, unconsciously but constantly, in the minds of my parishioners to give sanction to behaviors and values that, more often than not it seemed to me, were in the service of the American way (in which indulgent consumerism was conspicuous) rather than the way of the cross (where sacrificial love was prominent). The large Sinai and fresh Galilee proclamations that I made on Sundays were coming back to me on weekdays in the reporting that people unconsciously provide in their confidences and small talk as stale bromides and puny moralisms. I had, it seemed, a vigorous cottage industry in miniaturization thriving in my congregation. Meanwhile, on the third front, the indifference of the world to what I was grandly calling the Kingdom of God put into question the validity of the whole enterprise. If I could be ignored so blithely and totally, could I be doing anything of significance? Barth helped me on every front in his commentary on Romans. He dove into the text, into these living waters, with abandon. He is such an exuberant exegete! It hardly mattered, I sometimes felt, whether he was right or wrong on a specific point; he was so patiently passionate with the text that it was at least safe from pedantry, a terrible fate. On the second front, the congregational, I found him page after page disentangling gospel spirituality from cultural religion, commending the former and rejecting the latter. All the subtle seductions to "another gospel" that I was noticing around me Barth had also but more discerningly noticed. How much well-meaning religious nonsense he saved me from! As for the world, Barth was immensely knowledgeable but quietly unintimidated. He knew politics and labor and prisons; but he believed in prayer and Scripture and the cross of Christ. Every re-reading of Barth's Romans makes me less timid on the world front. Nobody in this century has done this better for me than Karl Barth.

This resurrection life you received from God is not a timid, grave-tending life. It's adventurously expectant, greeting God with a childlike, "What's next, Papa?" God's Spirit touches our spirits and confirms who we really are. We know who he is, and we know who we are: Father and children.

ROMANS 8:15–16

DECEMBER 11

Mysteries

When my children were young, I was full of devout idealism regarding ways in which we as a family would replicate the church as we gathered around the dinner table. Especially on Sundays. When we returned home after a morning of worship and sat down to Sunday dinner, I would attempt to initiate and direct a discussion that would bring the prayer and praise from the sanctuary into the eating and drinking at our dining room table. I would ask what they thought of the second hymn, or how they liked the introduction to the sermon. Did they notice the novel twist the assisting elder had given to pronouncing Melchizedek in the Scripture reading? No real conversation ever developed. One Sunday in a moment of inspired desperation I took another tack. I said, "After the pastoral prayer, Mr. Green, head bowed, never straightened up. Those around him thought he was still praying. After the benediction when he still hadn't moved, he was discovered dead. Murdered. How was it done, and what was the motive?" Conversation developed. *Real* conversation. What it lacked in devoutness it made up for in liveliness. We searched the Scripture readings for clues, sifted the hymns for evidence, examined the possibilities of sin behind the congregational facade of Presbyterian rectitude. Each week there would be another victim.

> *The children around your table*
> *as fresh and promising as young olive shoots.*

PSALM 128:3B

DECEMBER 12

The Escapist Pleasures

Our cottage industry in murder mysteries didn't last long—a few weeks as I recall. But it was enough to introduce me to the escapist pleasures of detective fiction. I soon found that it is a pleasure much indulged in by scholars, pastors and theologians. Gabriel Marcel always insisted that we have to choose whether we will treat life as a problem to be solved or as a mystery to be entered. Why then do so many of the men and women who choose to enter the mystery slip aside from time to time to read mysteries that aren't mysteries at all, but problems that always get solved by the last page? I think one reason may be that right and wrong, so often obscured in the ambiguities of everyday living, are cleanly delineated in the murder mystery. The story gives us moral and intellectual breathing room when we are about to be suffocated in the hot air and heavy panting of relativism and subjectivism.

[*Jesus said,*] *"We're not keeping secrets,*
we're telling them. We're not hiding things;
we're bringing everything *out into the open."*

LUKE 8:17

Commentaries

I read commentaries the way some people read novels, from beginning to end, skipping nothing. I admit that they are weak in plot and character development, but their devout attention to words and syntax keeps me turning the pages. Plot and character—the plot of salvation, the character of Messiah—are everywhere implicit in a commentary and persistently assert their presence even when unmentioned through scores, even hundreds, of pages. The power of these ancient nouns and verbs century after century to call forth intelligent discourse from learned men and women continues to be a staggering wonder to me.

[Apollos] was particularly effective in public
debate with the Jews as he brought out proof

after convincing proof from the Scriptures
that Jesus was in fact God's Messiah.

ACTS 18:28

Conversation with Friends

Among those for whom Scripture is a passion, reading commentaries has always seemed to me analogous to the gathering of football
fans in the local bar, replaying in endless detail the game they have
just watched, arguing (maybe even fighting) over observations and
opinion, and lacing the discourse with gossip about the players. The
level of knowledge evident in these boozy colloquies is impressive.
These fans have watched the game for years; the players are household names to them; they know the fine print in the rule book and
pick up every nuance on the field. And they care immensely about
what happens in the game. Their seemingly endless commentary is
evidence of how much they care. Like them, what I relish in commentary is not bare information but conversation with knowledgeable and experienced friends, probing, observing, questioning the
biblical text. Absorbed by this plot that stretches grandly from Genesis to Revelation, captured by the messianic presence that in death
and resurrection saves us one and all, there is much to notice, much
to talk over.

I'm chewing on the morsel of a proverb;
I'll let you in on the sweet old truths,
Stories we heard from our fathers,
counsel we learned at our mother's knee.

PSALM 78:2–3

DECEMBER 15

A Holy Place

The following is a reflection on Norman Maclean's
A River Runs Through It and Other Stories.

I know a man who used to buy this book in lots of ten or twenty and give it away, as he put, to "those who are worthy of reading it." He gave me a copy. It soon became a family book as my wife and children and I would read it aloud to each other. One reason that we liked it so much was that it gave dignity and a sense of holiness to *our* place, a place that was home to us. The story Maclean writes takes place a hundred miles from where I grew up in Montana and where our family returned each summer for holiday. We already knew it was a holy place, but the book confirmed and deepened our reverence. The book functioned as a shrine, calling attention to *this* place: *this* is holy ground—worship God *here*.

. . . Judas, his betrayer, also knew the place because Jesus and his disciples went there often.

JOHN 18:2

Oregano and Crabgrass

Hagiography, writing about holy men and women, is a notoriously failed genre. It gets high marks in boredom and dishonesty, and not much else. I very much doubt whether Fox's *Book of Martyrs,* the staple hagiography of my childhood, did much to further holy living in me or my friends. Mostly, as I remember, it replaced fear of God with the fear of Catholics. And Butler's *Lives of the Saints,* a work of unquestionable usefulness, is as often used, by scholars at least, to debunk sanctity as to confirm it.

All of us have impulses from time to time to live a holy life—life lived as it should be, life true and good and beautiful, life lived for and in and by means of our Creator, Redeemer, and Sanctifier. And then someone telephones with an invitation to the hockey game, or we notice that the salad needs oregano, or the crabgrass in the lawn suddenly becomes a pressing priority. We are distracted by the mundane and forfeit, for yet another time, the holy. Or so we assume.

And then we find ourselves in the company of a writer or writers who penetrate the surface pieties and show us what the holy life is really like, that it is the hockey game and the oregano and the crabgrass that provide the raw material for holiness. Holiness is not being nice. A holy life isn't a matter of men and women being polite with God, but of humans who accept and enter into God's work of shaping salvation out of the unlikely materials of our sin and ignorance, our ambition and waywardness—also our loves and aspirations and nobilities, but never by smoothing over our rough edges. Holiness is not polish.

As obedient children, let yourselves be pulled
into a way of life shaped by God's life, a
life energetic and blazing with holiness. God
said, "I am holy; you be holy."

1 PETER 1:14–16

The Business of Holy Living

All Christians, in some way or another, are about the business of holy living, whether we have acquired a suitable vocabulary for it or not. But it is difficult to know exactly what it consists of. We hardly know what to look for anymore. For the last hundred years and more, those who have set themselves up as our authorities in how to live have been taking us on thrilling roller-coaster prospects of either social utopianism or psychological fulfillment—or both. And we are worse. The only things that have improved, if that is the word for it, are our capacities to move faster and spend more.

There are husbands who, indifferent as they are to
any words about God, will be captivated by your life
of holy beauty. . . . Cultivate inner beauty, the gentle,
gracious kind that God delights in. The holy women
of old were beautiful before God that way . . .

1 PETER 3:1B, 4–5

Our Wiser Ancestors

Herman Melville once wrote to a friend, "I love all men who *dive*." Most of us do. But where do we find them? Not in the men and women who attract attention. The trivial and evil feed the appetite for gossip in a journalistic culture. Neither goodness nor righteousness make headlines. Anything which cannot be programmed for mass production, particularly moral excellence, is discarded. Maturity, since it cannot be mastered in a semester course, is no longer a personal goal.

Our ancestors were wiser. They looked around for saints, looked for the men and women whose lives were courageously conversant with God, and let them be their teachers in how to live as human beings, which is to say, how to live holy lives. Our secularized world, surfeited on celebrities and victims, has lost the capacity to see God working in ordinary and often unlikely people, that is, to recognize saints. The word itself has been so drained of meaning that it is more likely to be heard as disclaimer—"I'm no saint"—than as an honorific. Leon Bloy puts us on the way to recovering appreciation and insight in his blunt and bold sentence, "The only sadness, not to be a saint" (Tristesse—de pas etre Saint).

I'm about to die, my life an offering on God's altar. This is the only race worth running. I've run hard right to the finish, believed all the way. All that's left now is the shouting—God's applause!

2 TIMOTHY 4:6–8A

Elie Wiesel, Souls on Fire *(1972)*

Incarcerated as a young person in the Auschwitz death camp, Wiesel was one of the few to come out of it alive. That early experience of being surrounded by evil and immersed in death was turned somehow into an adult vocation as a writer exulting in holiness and celebrating life. In addition to writing novels, Wiesel does this by telling the stories of the Baal Shem Tov and his successors. The Baal Shem, an obscure Jew who lived in eighteenth-century Eastern Europe, ignited a revival of spirituality that spread wildly from community to community with a sense of playful wonder, readiness for miracle, and holy aliveness among poor, persecuted, and marginalized Jews. Hasidism, it was called, an exuberant explosion of stories and songs. Elie Wiesel tells the stories. This is the first of several similar books giving witness to the alive mysteries of holy lives.

> *[Jesus said,] "Let me lay it out for you as plainly as I can: No one in history surpasses John the Baptizer, but in the kingdom he prepared you for, the lowliest person is ahead of him."*

LUKE 7:28

Sin and the Devil

The most popular contemporary spiritualities pretty much ignore sin and the devil. The prevailing assumption seems to be that men and women are basically innocent and good, and all that is needed is training and encouragement to "become our best selves," and "blossom where we're planted." "Selfism" is fobbed off as spirituality. Sappy aphorisms from Khalil Gibran substitute for the tempered steel imperatives of Jesus.

But we Christians are well warned not to be fooled by superficial appearances of holiness, especially at those times when we think we catch glimpses of them in the mirror. We need rigorous and detailed schooling in the nuances of temptation, the ways of the devil, and our seemingly endless capacity for deceiving ourselves and being deceived.

Keep a cool head. Stay alert. The Devil is poised to pounce, and would like nothing better than to catch you napping. Keep your guard up.

1 PETER 5:8–9A

DECEMBER 21

The World of Words

Is it not significant that the biblical prophets and psalmists were all poets? . . . In reading poets, I find congenial allies in the world of words. In writing poems, I find myself practicing my pastoral craft in a biblical way.

[Jesus said,] "And don't say anything you don't mean. This counsel is embedded deep in our traditions. You only make things worse when you lay down a smoke screen of pious talk."

MATTHEW 5:33

The Greeting (Christmas 1986)

The following six days are selected Christmas poems written
for annual Christmas greetings.

Hail, O favored one,
the Lord is with you! (Luke 1:28)

My mail carrier, driving his stubby white
Truck, trimmed in blue and red, wingless
But wheeled, commissioned by the civil service
Daily delivers the Gospel every Advent.

This Gabriel, uniformed in gabardine,
Unsmiling descendent of his dazzling original,
Under the burden of greetings is stoical
But prompt: annunciations at ten each morning.

One or two or three a day at first;
By the second week momentum's up,
My mail box is stuffed, each card stamped

With the glory at a cost of only twenty-five cents
(Bringing the news that God is here with us)
First class, personally hand addressed.

"Good morning!
You're beautiful with God's beauty,

Beautiful inside and out!
God be with you."

LUKE 1:28

DECEMBER 23

The Tree (Christmas 1975)

There shall come forth a shoot from the stump of Jesse,
and a branch shall grow out of his roots. (Isaiah 11:1)

Jesse's roots, composted with carcasses
Of dove and lamb, parchments of ox and goat,
Centuries of dried up prayers and bloody
Sacrifice, now bear me gospel fruit.

David's branch, fed on kosher soil,
Blossoms a messianic flower, and then
Ripens into a kingdom crop, conserving
The fragrance and warmth of spring for winter use.

Holy Spirit, shake our family tree;
Release your ripened fruit to our outstretched arms.

I'd like to see my children sink their teeth
Into promised land pomegranates

And Canaan grapes, bushel gifts of God,
While I skip a grace rope to a Christ tune.

The Holy Spirit will come upon you,
the power of the Highest hover over you;
Therefore, the child you bring to birth
will be called Holy, the Son of God.

LUKE 1:35

The Dream (Christmas 1974)

. . . an angel of the Lord appeared to him in a dream. (Matthew 1:20)

Amiably conversant with virtue and evil,
The righteousness of Joseph and wickedness
Of Herod, I'm ever and always a stranger to grace.
I need this annual angel visitation

—sudden dive by dream to reality—
To know the virgin conceives and God is with us.
The dream powers its way through winter weather
And gives me vision to see the Jesus gift.

Light from the dream lasts a year. Impervious
To equinox and solstice it makes twelve months

Of daylight by which I see the crèche where my
Redeemer lives. Archetypes of praise take shape

Deep in my spirit. As autumn wanes I count
The days 'til I will have the dream again.

Then Joseph woke up. He did exactly what God's angel commanded
in the dream: He married Mary. But he did not consummate the
marriage until she had the baby. He named the baby Jesus.

MATTHEW 1:24–25

DECEMBER 25

The Pain (Christmas 1978)

. . . and a sword will pierce through your own soul
also, that thoughts out of many hearts may be revealed. (Luke 2:35)

The bawling of babies, always in a way
Inappropriate—why should the loved and innocent
Greet existence with wails?—is proof that not all
Is well. Dreams and deliveries never quite mesh.

Deep hungers go unsatisfied, deep hurts
Unhealed. The natural and gay are torn
By ugly grimace and curse. A wound appears
In the place of ecstasy. Birth is bloody.

All pain's a prelude: to symphony, to sweetness.
"The pearl began as a pain in the oyster's stomach."

Dogwood, recycled from cradle to cross, enters
The market again as a yoke for easing burdens.

Each sword-opened side is the matrix for God
To come to me again through travail for joy.

> *"This child marks both the failure and*
> *the recovery of many in Israel,*
> *A figure misunderstood and contradicted—*
> *the pain of a sword-thrust through you—*
> *But the rejection will force honesty,*
> *as God reveals who they really are."*

LUKE 2:34B–35

DECEMBER 26

The Gift (Christmas 1976)

> *For to us a child is born,*
> *to us a son is given . . .*
> *and his name will be called*
> *"Wonderful Counselor, Mighty God,*
> *Everlasting Father, Prince of Peace." (Isaiah 9:6)*

Half-sick with excitement and under garish lights
I do it again, year after year after year.
I can't wait to plunder the boxes, then show
And tell my friends: Look what I got!

I rip the tissues from every gift but find
That all the labels have lied. Stones.
And my heart a stone. "Dead in trespasses
And sin." The lights go out. Later my eyes,

Accustomed to the dark, see wrapped
In Christ-foil and ribboned in Spirit-colors

The multi-named messiah, love labels
On a faith shape, every name a promise

And every promise a present, made and named
All in the same breath. I accept.

A Savior has just been born in David's town,
a Savior who is Messiah and Master. This is
what you are to look for: a baby wrapped in a
blanket and lying in a manger.

LUKE 2:11–12

DECEMBER 27

The Offering (Christmas 1983)

May the kings of Tarshish and of isles render him tribute,
*   may the kings of Sheba and Seba bring gifts!*
Long may he live,
*   may gold of Sheba be given to him! (Psalm 72:10, 15)*

Brought up in a world where there's no free lunch
And trained to use presents for barter, I'm spending
The rest of my life receiving this gift with no
Strings attached, but not doing too well.

　Three bathrobed wise men with six or seven
　Inches of jeans and sneakers showing, kneel,
　Offering gifts that symbolize the gifts
　That none of us is ready yet to give.

A few of us stay behind, blow out the candles,
Sweep up the straw and put the crèche in storage.

　We open the door into the world's night
　And find we've played ourselves into a better

Performance. We leave with our left-over change changed
At the offertory into kingdom gold.

　Overcome, they kneeled and worshiped him. Then they opened their
　luggage and presented gifts: gold, frankincense, myrrh.

MATTHEW 2:11B

DECEMBER 28

Heaven

Heaven, in gospels and the Apocalypse (and throughout scripture) is
the metaphor that tells us that there is far more here than meets the

eye. Beyond and through what we see there is that which we cannot see, and which is, wondrously, not "out there" but right here before us and among us: *God*—his rule, his love, his judgment, his salvation, his mercy, his grace, his healing, his wisdom.

Calling the word *heaven* a metaphor does not make it less real; it simply recognizes that it is a reality inaccessible at this point to any of our five senses. . . .

Then I looked, and, oh!—a door open into Heaven. The trumpet-voice, the first voice of the vision, called out, "Ascend and enter. I'll show you what happens next."

REVELATION 4:1

DECEMBER 29

The Heavens and the Earth

"The heavens and the earth" means, simply, everything. "Heavens," literally, is skies—the great dome of lights that is over us and beyond us, the dazzling theater in which we watch the fine-tuned choreography of constellations and the wildly beautiful raging of storms. We know these heavens through our senses—we see the stars and hear the thunder—but we cannot handle or shape or control them. "Earth," literally is that which is beneath and around us, that which we are in touch with, can handle, shape, and, up to a point, control. It is the sure ground under our feet, the yellow asphodels we pick, the fields we plow, plant, and harvest. It is more extensively physical than we are able to follow with our five senses. Even with the help of devices that greatly extend our sensory perceptions—telescope, microscope, radar, sonar, radio, television, and instrument-laden space capsules—we have not yet come anywhere close to a complete accounting for and cataloguing of the seemingly endless combinations of electron and proton that stretch from Betelgeuse in Orion to Birmingham jail in Alabama. The two words *heaven* and *earth*, together tie us to a material creation that, as far as our senses report it to us, never ends.

> ... *may GOD of Zion bless you—*
> *GOD who made heaven and earth!*

PSALM 134:3

DECEMBER 30

Materiality

We are immersed in materiality from start to finish. At the Genesis beginning we are immersed in materiality; at the Revelation ending we are reimmersed in materiality. Between these boundaries nothing takes place apart from geology and history, geography and weather, incarnation and sacrament. Our existence is framed in matter. Nothing in the gospel is presented apart from the physical, nor can it be understood or received apart from the physical. That is not to say that there is nothing but matter, for that would deny most of what living by faith asserts. But it does mean that nothing can be experienced apart from matter. The great invisibles, God and the soul, are incomprehensible apart from the great visibles, heaven and earth.

Things unseen are only apprehended by means of things seen. The gospel is the enemy of all forms of gnosticism. The gospel does not begin with matter and then gradually get refined into spirit. The revelation of God does not begin with a material universe and a flesh and blood Jesus and then, working itself up through the grades, finally graduate into ether and angels and ideas.

The City shimmered like a precious gem, light-filled, pulsing light. She had a wall majestic and high with twelve gates.

REVELATION 21:11–12A

DECEMBER 31

The Completion of What Is

Heaven is also more, far more. But the "more" is the completion of what is, not an escape from it. It is the wholeness of what we now see in part, not the repudiation of it. The vision of heavens is thus thoroughly practical—it keeps us convinced of the reality of all the acts and words whose good sense is disputed by the age we live in. Heaven is not a purple passage tacked onto the end of the Apocalypse to give a flourish to the rhetoric, but an immersion in the realities of God's rule in our lives that has the effect of reviving our obedience, fortifying us for the long haul, and energizing a courageous witness. By using the stuff that is in our lives right now—

places and people, sights and sounds—the invisible and visible parts of our lives are connected in a fresh way. Heaven is an affirmation and confirmation that the beauties and sanctities of the visible creation—tree and rock, Jesus and Eucharist—are not illusions that trick us into what cynics think of as the naive, useless, and silly practices of love, hope and faith, but are realities that are in strict correspondence with what has been begun in us and will be complete in us. . . .

There is not so much as a hint of escapism in St. John's heaven. This is not a long (eternal) weekend away from the responsibilities of employment and citizenship, but the intensification and healing of them. Heaven is formed out of dirty streets and murderous alleys, adulterous bedrooms and corrupt courts, hypocritical synagogues and commercialized churches, thieving tax-collectors and traitorous disciples: a city, but now a holy city.

> *I heard a voice thunder from the Throne: "Look! Look! God has moved into the neighborhood, making his home with men and women! They're his people, he's their God . . . Look! I'm making everything new."*

REVELATION 21:3, 5A

BOOKS BY EUGENE H. PETERSON

Answering God. San Francisco: Harper & Row, 1989.

The Contemplative Pastor. Waco, TX: Word, 1989; Grand Rapids, MI: Wm. B. Eerdmans, 1993.

Earth and Altar. Downers Grove, IL: InterVarsity Press, 1985; *Where Your Treasure Is.* Grand Rapids, MI: Wm. B. Eerdmans, 1993.

Five Smooth Stones for Pastoral Work. Atlanta: John Knox Press, 1980; Grand Rapids, MI: Wm. B. Eerdmans, 1992.

Growing Up in Christ. Atlanta: John Knox Press, 1976; *Like Dew Your Youth.* Grand Rapids, MI: Wm B. Eerdmans, 1994.

Leap Over a Wall. Forthcoming. San Francisco: HarperCollins.

Like Dew Your Youth. Grand Rapids, MI: Wm. B. Eerdmans, 1994. Previously published as *Growing Up in Christ.* See above.

A Long Obedience in the Same Direction. Downers Grove, IL: InterVarsity Press, 1980.

The Message: New Testament with Psalms and Proverbs. Colorado Springs: NavPress, 1993.

Praying with Jesus. San Francisco: HarperCollins, 1993.

Praying with Moses. San Francisco: HarperCollins, 1994.

Praying with Paul. San Francisco: HarperCollins, 1995.

Praying with the Early Christians. San Francisco: HarperCollins, 1994.

Praying with the Prophets. San Francisco: HarperCollins, 1995.

Praying with the Psalms. San Francisco: HarperCollins, 1993. Previously published as *A Year with the Psalms.* See below.

Proverbs: The Message. Colorado Springs: NavPress, 1995.

Psalms: The Message. Colorado Springs: NavPress, 1994.

Psalms: Prayers of the Heart. Downers Grove, IL: InterVarsity Press, 1987.

Reversed Thunder. San Francisco: Harper & Row, 1988.

Run with the Horses. Downers Grove, IL: InterVarsity Press, 1983.

Subversive Spirituality. Vancouver, B.C.: A Regent College Reprint, 1994.

Take and Read. Grand Rapids, MI: Wm. B. Eerdmans, 1996.

Traveling Light. Downers Grove, IL: InterVarsity Press, 1982; Helmers and Howard, 1988.

Under the Unpredictable Plant. Grand Rapids, MI: Wm. B. Eerdmans, 1992.

Where Your Treasure Is. Grand Rapids, MI: Wm. B. Eerdmans, 1993. Previously published as *Earth and Altar.* See page 363.

Working the Angles. Grand Rapids, MI: Wm. B. Eerdmans, 1987.

A Year with the Psalms. Waco, TX: Word, 1979; *Praying with the Psalms.* San Francisco: HarperCollins, 1993.

JOURNAL SOURCES

"Back to Square One: God Said (The Witness of Holy Scripture)," *Crux* 31, no. 1 (March 1995): 2–10.

Christianity Today (October 7, 1977): 23.

Leadership Journal (Summer 1991): 87.

"Writers and Angels: Witnesses to Transcendence," *Theology Today* 51, no. 3 (October 1994): 394–404.

FOREWORDS TO OTHER BOOKS

Forsyth, P. T., *The Soul of Prayer.* Vancouver, B.C.: A Regent College Reprint, 1995, 3–5.

Terry, June Lewers, *When Teardrops Dance.* Grand Rapids, MI: Fleming H. Revell, 1994, 9–11.

OTHER BOOKS (CONTRIBUTIONS)

Neff, LaVonne et al., eds., *Practical Christianity.* Wheaton, IL: Tyndale House Publishers, Inc., 1987, 52–54, 202, 210, 310, 403–04.

"Spiritual Formation: A Pastor's Perspective," in Garth M. Rosell, ed., *The Vision Continues, Centennial Papers of Gordon-Conwell Theological Seminary.* South Hampton, MA, 1992, 28–41.

PUBLIC LECTURE

Regent College, Vancouver, B.C., Canada, "Caveat Lector," July 31, 1995.

SOURCES BY BOOK

Answering God (AG), March 12–16, June 1–2, 5–15

The Contemplative Pastor (CP), January 10–11, July 16–28, October 20,
    October 31, December 21–27

Earth and Altar/Where Your Treasure Is (WT), January 26–February 7,
    February 13, February 15–17

Five Smooth Stones for Pastoral Work (FS), March 11, May 2–12,
    December 4

Growing Up in Christ/Like Dew Your Youth (LD), February 12, April 28–30,
    May 24, June 19–26, July 15

Leap Over a Wall (LW), November 19–28

A Long Obedience in the Same Direction (LO), January 12–25, February
    19–23, September 15, October 2–6

The Message: New Testament with Psalms and Proverbs (NT), January 1, Jan-
    uary 6, February 18, March 10, April 9, May 1, May 23, June 17–18,
    June 27, July 31, August 5, September 10, October 29–30

Praying with the Early Christians (EC), August 14, August 24,
    September 30

Praying with Jesus (PJ), March 31–April 1

Praying with Moses (PM), August 2, August 6, September 29

Praying with the Prophets (PWP), September 17

Proverbs: The Message (PR), May 13, September 14

Psalms: The Message (PS), February 8, March 17, August 23, December 5

Psalms: Prayers of the Heart (PH), February 11, October 7–14,
  November 4–7
Reversed Thunder (RT), February 24–March 9, March 30, April 5–8,
  August 25–30, December 28–31
Run with the Horses (RH), April 15–27, July 29–30, August 3–4, October 1
Subversive Spirituality (SS), January 2–5, January 8–9, August 31–
  September 9
Take and Read (TR), September 23–28, October 22, December 8–20
Traveling Light (TL), June 28–July 14, August 1, August 15–22
Under the Unpredictable Plant (UP), January 7, February 9, May 14–22,
  May 25–31, August 7–11, September 16, September 18–22,
  October 21
Working the Angles (WA), March 18–28, April 2–4
A Year with the Psalms/Praying with the Psalms (PP), March 29, June 3–4,
  June 16

OTHER SOURCES

"Back to Square One: God Said (The Witness of Holy Scripture)," *Crux*
  (CR), April 10–14
"Caveat Lector" (CL), November 11–18
Christianity Today (CT), February 14
Forsyth, P. T., *The Soul of Prayer* (SP), September 11–13, December 6–7
Leadership Journal (LJ), February 10
Neff, LaVonne et al., eds., *Practical Christianity* (PC), October 15–19,
  October 23–28, November 1–3
"Spiritual Formation: A Pastor's Perspective," in Garth M. Rosell, ed., *The
  Vision Continues* (VC), November 29–December 3
Terry, June Lewers, *When Teardrops Dance* (TD), August 12–13
"Writers and Angels: Witnesses to Transcendence," *Theology Today* (TT),
  November 8–10

SOURCES BY DAY

INDEX BY TITLE

PERMISSIONS

Grateful acknowledgment is made to the following for permission to reprint material:

From *Practical Christianity*. Compiled and edited by LaVonne Neff, Ron Beers, Bruce Barton, Linda Taylor, Dave Veerman and Jim Galvin. Copyright © 1987 by Youth for Christ/USA. Used by permission of Tyndale House Publishers, Inc. All rights reserved.

From *Run with the Horses* by Eugene H. Peterson. Copyright © 1983 by InterVarsity Christian Fellowship of the USA. Used by permission of InterVarsity Press, P.O. Box 1400, Downers Grove, IL 60515.

From *A Long Obedience in the Same Direction* by Eugene H. Peterson. Copyright © 1980 by InterVarsity Christian Fellowship of the USA. Used by permission of InterVarsity Press, P.O. Box 1400, Downers Grove, IL 60515.

From *Psalms: Prayers of the Heart (LBS)* by Eugene H. Peterson. Copyright © 1987 by Eugene H. Peterson. Used by permission of InterVarsity Press, P.O. Box 1400, Downers Grove, IL 60515.

The poem "Let Not Man Put Asunder" first appeared in *Christianity Today,* October 7, 1977.

The excerpt for February 10 first appeared in the *Leadership Journal,* Summer 1991, in the article "Stumbling Across the Supernatural."

From the foreword to *When Teardrops Dance* by June Lewers Terry. Fleming H. Revell, a division of Baker Book House Co., Grand Rapids, MI, 1994.

From *Working the Angles: The Shape of Pastoral Integrity* by Eugene H. Peterson, Wm. B. Eerdmans Publishing Co. Copyright © 1987 by Eugene Peterson. Used by permission of the publisher.

From *Take and Read: Spiritual Reading: An Annotated List* by Eugene H. Peterson, Wm. B. Eerdmans Publishing Co. Copyright © 1996 by Eugene H. Peterson. Used by permission of the publisher.

From *Five Smooth Stones for Pastoral Work* by Eugene H. Peterson, Wm. B. Eerdmans Publishing Co. Copyright © 1980 by Eugene H. Peterson. Used by permission of the publisher.

From *The Contemplative Pastor: Returning to the Art of Spiritual Direction* by Eugene H. Peterson, Wm. B. Eerdmans Publishing Co. Copyright © 1993 by Eugene H. Peterson. Used by permission of the publisher.

From *Under the Unpredictable Plant: An Exploration in Vocational Holiness* by Eugene H. Peterson, Wm. B. Eerdmans Publishing Co. Copyright © 1992 by Eugene H. Peterson. Used by permission of the publisher.

From *Like Dew Your Youth: Growing Up With Your Teenager* by Eugene H. Peterson, Wm. B. Eerdmans Publishing Co. Copyright © 1976, 1987, 1994 by Eugene H. Peterson. Used by permission of the publisher.

From *Where Your Treasure Is: Psalms that Summon You from Self to Community* by Eugene H. Peterson, Wm. B. Eerdmans Publishing Co. Copyright © 1985 by Eugene H. Peterson. Used by permission of the publisher.

From *Subversive Spirituality*, 1994 by Eugene H. Peterson. Used by permission Regent College, Vancouver, B.C.

From *Traveling Light* by Eugene H. Peterson, 1988. Used by permission Helmers & Howard, Colorado Springs, CO.

Article "Writers and Angels" reprinted from *Theology Today*, Princeton, NJ. Used by permission.